Endangered Wildlife and Plants of the World

Volume 5
FRA–IGU

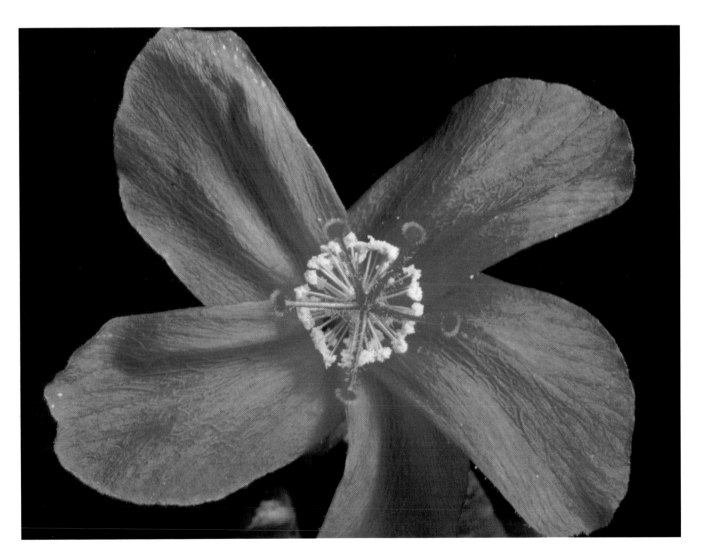

Marshall Cavendish
New York • London • Toronto • Sydney

Marshall Cavendish Corporation
99 White Plains Road
Tarrytown, NY 10591-9001

Created by Brown Partworks Ltd.
Project Editor: Anne Hildyard
Associate Editors: Paul Thompson, Amy Prior
Managing Editor: Tim Cooke
Design: Whitelight
Picture Research: Helen Simm
Index Editor: Kay Ollerenshaw
Production Editor: Matt Weyland
Illustrations: Barbara Emmons, Jackie Harland, Tracy Williamson

Library of Congress Cataloging-in-Publication Data

Endangered wildlife and plants of the world
p.cm.
Includes bibliographical references (p.).
ISBN 0-7614-7194-4 (set)
ISBN 0-7614-7199-5 (vol. 5)
1. Endangered species--Encyclopedias. I. Marshall Cavendish Corporation.

QH75.E68 2001
333.95'22'03--dc21
99-086194

Printed in Malaysia
Bound in the United States of America
07 06 05 04 03 02 01 00 7 6 5 4 3 2 1

39365432

TABLE OF CONTENTS/VOLUME 5

ESA and IUCN

In this set of endangered animals and plants, each species, where appropriate, is given an ESA status and an IUCN status. The sources consulted to determine the status of each species are the Endangered Species List maintained by the U.S. Fish and Wildlife Service and the Red Lists compiled by IUCN–The World Conservation Union, which is a worldwide organization based in Switzerland.

ENDANGERED SPECIES ACT

The Endangered Species Act (ESA) was initially passed by the U.S. Congress in 1973, and reauthorized in 1988. The aim of the ESA is to rescue species that are in danger of extinction due to human action and to conserve the species and their ecosystems. Endangered plants and animals are listed by the U.S. Fish and Wildlife Service (USFWS), which is part of the Department of Interior. Once a species is listed, the USFWS is required to develop recovery plans, and ensure that the threatened species is not further harmed by any actions of the U.S. government or U.S. citizens. The act specifically forbids the buying, selling, transporting, importing, or exporting of any listed species. It also bans the taking of any listed species in the U.S. and its territories, on both private and public lands. Violators can face heavy fines or imprisonment. However, the ESA requires that the protection of the species is balanced with economic factors.

The ESA recognizes two categories of risk for species:

Endangered: A species that is in danger of extinction throughout all or a significant part of its range.

Threatened: A species that is likely to become endangered in the foreseeable future.

RECOVERY

Recovery takes place when the decline of the endangered or threatened species is halted or reversed, and the circumstances that caused the threat have been removed. The ultimate aim is the recovery of the species to the point where it no longer requires protection under the act.

Recovery can take a long time. Because the decline of the species may have occurred over centuries, the loss cannot be reversed overnight. There are many factors involved: the number of individuals of the species that remain in the wild, how long it takes the species to mature and reproduce, how much habitat is remaining, and whether the reasons for the decline are clear cut and understood. Recovery plans employ a wide range of strategies that involve the following: reintroduction of species into formerly occupied habitat, land aquisition and management, captive breeding, habitat protection, research, population counts, public education projects, and assistance for private landowners.

SUCCESS STORIES

Despite the difficulties, recovery programs do work, and the joint efforts of the USFWS, other federal and state agencies, tribal governments, and private landowners have not been in vain. Only seven species, less than 1 percent of all the species listed between 1968 and 1993, are now known to be extinct. The other 99 percent of listed species have not been lost to extinction, and this confirms the success of the act.

There are some good examples of successful recovery plans. In 1999, the peregrine falcon, the bald eagle, and the Aleutian goose were removed from the endangered species list. The falcon's numbers have risen dramatically. In 1970, there were only 39 pairs of falcons in the United States. By 1999, the number had risen to 1,650 pairs. The credit for the recovery goes to the late Rachel

Carson, who highlighted the dangers of DDT, and also to the Endangered Species Act, which enabled the federal government to breed falcons in captivity, and took steps to protect their habitat.

Young bald eagles were also successfully translocated into habitat that they formerly occupied, and the Aleutian Canada goose has improved due to restoration of its habitat and reintroduction into former habitat.

IUCN–THE WORLD CONSERVATION UNION

The IUCN (International Union for Conservation of Nature) was established in 1947. It is an alliance of governments, governmental agencies, and nongovernmental agencies. The aim of the IUCN is to help and encourage nations to conserve wildlife and natural resources. Organizations such as the Species Survival Commission is one of several IUCN commissions that assesses the conservation status of species and subspecies globally. Taxa that are threatened with extinction are noted and steps are taken for their conservation by programs designed to save, restore, and manage species and their habitats. The Survival Commission is committed to providing objective information on the status of globally threatened species, and produces two publications: the *IUCN Red List of Threatened Animals*, and the *IUCN Red List of Threatened Plants*. They are compiled from scientific data and provide the status of threatened species, depending on their existence in the wild and threats that undermine that existence. The lists for plants and animals differ slightly.

The categories from the *IUCN Red List of Threatened Animals* used in *Endangered Wildlife and Plants of the World* are as follows:

Extinct: A species is extinct when there is no reasonable doubt that the last individual has died.

Extinct in the wild: A species that is known only to survive in captivity, well outside its natural range.

Critically endangered: A species that is facing an extremely high risk of extinction in the wild in the immediate future.

Endangered: A species that is facing a very high risk of extinction in the wild in the near future.

Vulnerable: A species that is facing a high risk of extinction in the wild in the medium-term future.

Lower risk: A species that does not satisfy the criteria for designation as critically endangered, endangered, or vulnerable. Species included in the lower risk category can be separated into three subcategories:

Conservation dependent: A species that is part of a conservation program. Without the program, the species would qualify for one of the threatened categories within five years.

Near threatened: A species that does not qualify for conservation dependent, but is close to qualifying as vulnerable.

Least concern: A species that does not qualify for conservation dependent or near threatened.

Data deficient: A species on which there is inadequate information to make an asssessment of risk of extinction. Because there is a possibility that future research will show that the species is threatened, more information is required.

The categories from the *IUCN Red List of Threatened Plants*, used in *Endangered Wildlife and Plants of the World*, are as follows:

Extinct: A species that has not definitely been located in the wild during the last 50 years.

Endangered: A species whose survival is unlikely if the factors that threaten it continue. Included are species whose numbers have been reduced to a critical level, or whose habitats have been so drastically reduced that they are deemed to be in immediate danger of extinction. Also included in this category are species that may be extinct but have definitely been seen in the wild in the past 50 years.

Vulnerable: A species that is thought likely to move into the endangered category in the near future if the factors that threaten it remain.

Rare: A species with small world populations that are not at present endangered or vulnerable, but are at risk. These species are usually in restriced areas or are thinly spread over a larger range.

FRANCOLINS

Class: Aves
Order: Galliformes
Family: Phasianidae
Subfamily: Phasianinae
Tribe: Perdicini

Francolins mix the traits of both pheasants and quails to form their own unique group. Like pheasants, they grow a single spur on each foot. The spur is not a claw or nail associated with a toe, but a distinct structure used by males who fight for territory for breeding.

Pheasants sport long and often elegant tails, which they display when courting females. Francolins do not sport fancy tails, but have short tails more like that of the quail. They have the short, rounded, and cupped wings common to both quails and pheasants. Such wings give the birds explosive power, so they can shoot off the ground and attain full flight speed quickly. Being terrestrial birds, or birds that primarily inhabit a ground environment, they need this skill. The same dense vegetation that hides them from their enemies also hides their enemies from them, hence the need to take off fast should an enemy approach.

People have probably hunted francolins for food for thousands of years. Most francolins can easily withstand the hunting pressure because, for the most part, humans are just one more predator that the species has learned to avoid. What the francolins cannot withstand are the simultaneous pressures of hunting and habitat loss. Several francolins are declining in number, and at least two of the 41 species are in trouble.

Djibouti Francolin

(Francolinus ochropectus)

ESA: Endangered

IUCN: Critically endangered

Length: 12 in. (30.5 cm)
Weight: 33½ oz. (940 g)
Clutch size: Unknown, but 4–10 eggs in related species
Incubation: Unknown
Diet: Seeds and fruits
Habitat: Juniper woodlands
Range: Goda Mountains in the Republic of Djibouti

IN A TINY FRAGMENT of a once expansive woodland, a medium-sized bird struggles to survive. Each day the sun rises, the bird's hopes for survival fade a little more. One can almost count the days until the Djibouti francolin slips into extinction.

The bird is named for a country, the Republic of Djibouti. Once a European colony known as French Somaliland, this tiny country is the size of Massachusetts. Djibouti forms the western shore of the strait between the Red Sea and the Gulf of Aden. The Goda Massif—a small plateau—rises from the otherwise flat landscape. The land is hot, arid, and stony, with only dry land vegetation and trees that can withstand the harsh conditions.

The primary vegetation of the Goda highlands was once a mixed woodland of juniper (*Juniperus procera*), boxwood (*Buxus hildebrandtii*), wild olive (*Olea chrysophylla*), and a woody shrub (*Clutia abyssinica*). Two millennia ago, the woodland probably sprawled across a million acres (400,000 hectares). By 1990 this area scarcely covered 3.5 square miles (9 square kilometers). Some of this loss may be due to natural climatic changes, but people have caused the greater loss.

Nearly a half million people live in Djibouti. Many of them are refugees from the tribal, ethnic, and political wars that plague the African continent. Djibouti has no valuable natural resources on which to base an industrial economy. The agricultural potential of its land is marginal. The many rural people of Djibouti are poor and hungry, and they maintain livestock as best they can by grazing them in the hills. Too many people with too many cattle, sheep, goats, burros, and camels have destroyed the juniper woodland's capacity to renew itself. The heavy grazing and constant trampling by livestock are hard enough on this land, but people have also cut the trees and burned the woodlands to open up more space where grass can grow to feed livestock.

The tiny remaining woodland is called the Forêt du Day, and lies entirely within Day National Park. Despite its park status, the Djibouti government had development plans for the area in the late 1980s that would have destroyed the last remnant of native woodland and doomed the last of the Djibouti francolins.

A shy bird, the Djibouti francolin remains hidden in dense undergrowth of boxwood and *Clutia* during the day. It also roosts in the trees, most of which grow between 16 and 26 feet (5 to 8 meters) tall. The francolin

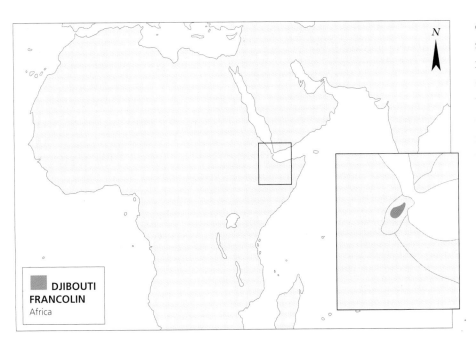

DJIBOUTI
FRANCOLIN
Africa

created by transporting other species to places where they did not belong. Either action, however, may be more desirable than the alternative: premature and certain extinction. One human misfortune has benefited the francolin. Regional wars have disrupted trade agreements and the granting of international loans that would have kept habitat-destroying development work on schedule. However a steep decline in the population of the bird is predicted as the result of human strife and civil conflict.

has been seen roosting as high as 13 feet (4 meters). At the twilight hours of dawn and dusk, the francolin actively searches for seeds and small fruits such as figs (*Ficus*). It also readily takes termites and probably other insects as well. Almost nothing else is known of the Djibouti francolin, except that it is not the only species in this situation.

At least 17 francolin species inhabit various parts of eastern and northeastern Africa. Many of them occupy very small habitats that are leftovers from an earlier time when the landscape looked very different to the way it does now. Other francolins are less specialized and more able to adapt to other plant communities. The Djibouti francolin has been found in second growth, but it is not known whether it can or will reproduce in such habitat.

The francolin is pale overall, but darker above than below. Its neck and body feathers are gold or straw-colored in the center, bordered with a thin dark brown line and edged in white. The chin and throat are whitish, and its

crown is a yellowish tan. It has a black forehead, lore, and eye stripe, which gives its face a dark, masked appearance.

A doubtful future

Ornithologists have variously estimated the Djibouti francolin's population from the hundreds to an optimistic 5,000 in the mid-1980s. With only two-tenths of one percent of its original habitat still available, the species cannot be found in great numbers and in 1985 a more realistic estimate was 1,500 individuals.

The International Council for Bird Preservation (ICBP) has become actively involved with the Djibouti government to try to save the Djibouti francolin. Proposals have included capturing birds for a captive-breeding program and for moving them to other woodlands. Both proposals have drawbacks. First, even if Djibouti francolins are raised in captivity, the species needs habitat in order to live in the wild. Second, moving the Djibouti francolin to other woodlands threatens to repeat the mistakes

Swamp Francolin
(Francolinus gularis)

IUCN: Vulnerable

Length: 15 in. (38 cm)
Weight: 18 oz. (510 g)
Clutch size: 3-5 eggs
Incubation: Unknown
Diet: Seeds, insects, small crustaceans
Habitat: Swamps
Range: Northern India, southern Nepal

UNLIKE OTHER francolins, the swamp francolin shuns prairies and woodlands. Rather than being a bird that lives on dry land, it haunts the dense reeds and elephant grass (*Typha elephantina*) of swamps in northern India and southern Nepal.

All male francolins are aggressive, but swamp francolins are especially fierce. They have a reputation for being high-spirited birds, quick to fight among themselves. Such spirit does not go

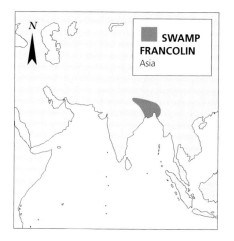

unnoticed by humans. Many people enjoy watching contests of stamina and will by pitting animal against animal. Bullfights, dog fights, and cock fights are just a few examples. People even bet on the outcome of such fights between animals. This bird's personality, combined with the sharp spurs on its feet, make swamp francolins popular fighters. Local people know where to find francolin nests and how to raise them for this purpose.

The swamp francolin has a uniformly dark upper body finely barred with tan, buff, and brown; its underparts are patterned with white, black, and brown, giving it a white-striped look from lower throat to undertail. The outer tail feathers and undertail are a rich chestnut color.

The swamp francolin flies well after a noisy take-off, but it spends most of its time on the ground. A strong runner, it escapes swiftly when threatened. Unlike other francolins, it even wades in shallow water. When water gets too deep, it walks up and over the available aquatic

The swamp francolins' high spirits and quickness to fight among themselves have been exploited by humans, who bet on the outcome of violent contests between the birds.

plants. At nesting time the female builds a small mound of vegetation on shore or a much larger mass over water, among reeds or in elephant grass.

Beyond these few details, ornithologists know very little about the swamp francolin other than it is disappearing. The bird originally inhabited a large area of swamps and other wetlands. Known as the *terai*, this complex covered vast acreages of river bottoms in southern Nepal and across northern India. But the *terai* could not withstand the collective hunger of nearly a billion people. As India's human population has grown, the country's need to produce food has forced people to grow crops in places where they never did before. The *terai* has been drained a little at a time to make space for various crops such as corn, wheat, and rice. As the *terai* has shrunk, the swamp francolin has lost habitat.

The swamp francolin does visit rice paddies, grasslands such as pastures, and freshly plowed fields. The bird usually wanders into these areas early in the morning, so it can feed on various seeds and insects. These lands cannot support the species in the same numbers as native swampland can. By the late 1990s no recent population estimates existed for the remaining swamp francolin population.

Because of continuing habitat destruction and pesticide run-offs, a plan to protect its habitat is imperative if this species is to continue to survive.

Kevin Cook

Freira

(Pterodroma madeira)

IUCN: Critically
endangered

Class: Aves
Order: Procellariiformes
Family: Procellariidae
Length: 14–18 in. (35.6–
45.7 cm)
Weight: Unknown
Clutch size: 1 egg
Incubation: Probably 51–54
days
Diet: Unknown, probably small
squids, crustaceans, and fish
Habitat: Lives at sea and comes
ashore only to breed
Range: Breeds on Madeira
Island and the North Atlantic
Ocean

Seabirds such as the freira are
sometimes difficult to classify, and their
migratory patterns are almost
impossible to trace. This bird is
considered pelagic—it lives at sea, and
comes ashore only to breed.

TUBE-NOSED BIRDS that nest in
the ground and come and go by
night attract little sympathy from
a human population accustomed
to eating them. The freira is such
a bird. It nests only on Madeira
Island in the North Atlantic and
has declined to less than 100
birds. In addition to being the
home of this rare bird, Madeira
grows grapes that are made into a
fine wine acclaimed by connoisseurs around the world. The wine
is a source of national pride,
while the unique bird facing
extinction goes virtually ignored.

The freira (pronounced fray-
EAR-uh) is one of the seabirds
known as "gadfly petrels." Gadfly
petrels are about the size of gulls.
They are related to the fulmars,
prions, and shearwaters. They
differ from the albatrosses
(*Diomedeidae*) in that their nostrils are united into a single tube

atop the beak, rather than having
separate nostrils on either side.
They differ from storm-petrels
(*Hydrobatidae*) in having a plate
that separates the nostrils inside
the tube. Storm-petrels are small
birds, some of them scarcely
larger than sparrows.

The exact relationship of
these gadfly petrels has long
caused ornithologists problems.
First, collecting seabirds can be
confusing. If they are collected at
sea, determining exactly where
they breed may be impossible. If
the petrels are collected on
islands during the breeding season, it may also be impossible to
ascertain their full range at sea.

Lack of information

Another problem is that variations in size and coloring may or
may not help to identify geographic boundaries.

In addition, declining, endangered, and vanished populations
create enormous gaps in the
information that is available. An
ornithologist can hardly justify
collecting specimens of a bird
with only 40 or 50 surviving individuals merely to clarify its

taxonomy. Yet understanding
relationships often determines
the correct strategy for saving a
species. People have limited
resources of time, money, and
enthusiasm to spend on saving
other species from extinction.
Those resources cannot justifiably be spent on birds that may
represent only a small, separate
group of individuals and not a
more common species.

North Atlantic gadfly petrels
are sometimes thought by
ornithologists to be a single,
complex species with many subspecies scattered about the
ocean. Other experts claim they
are all separate species with a
common origin. Another view
recognizes a few species, each
with subspecies. The freira is just
one bird in this muddled bunch
of seabirds that include the soft-
plumaged petrel (*Pterodroma
mollis*), the Cape Verde petrel
(*Pterodroma feae*), the cahow

(*Pterodroma cahow*), and the black-capped petrel (*Pterodroma hasitata*)—and possibly others.

Where is Madeira?

Madeira is one of two habitable islands in the Madeira Archipelago of Portugal. Situated north of the Canary Islands and southeast of the Azores, it was colonized by the Portuguese about 1418. Madeira is a rugged volcanic island with level lowlands that were converted to sugarcane fields. All the mountain slopes with usable soil were terraced for more agriculture. Oranges, bananas, avocados, and pears became standard crops. Grapes also flourished on the island. Madeira wine became highly prized, so vineyards replaced the sugarcane. Wine remains a vital export of Madeira.

The freira probably inhabited much of the island during and immediately after the last glacial period. Madeira would have been wetter and cooler then. As the global climate changed, the lower slopes of Madeira became warmer and drier, so the freira retreated up the mountain slopes, where conditions were moist and cool. The Cape Verde petrel has colonized the lower slopes. It is not known how the two petrels affect each other, if at all, or to what extent terracing and grape production have harmed the freira.

Estimates from the late 1980s indicated a breeding population of perhaps 20 pairs and recent population estimates indicate 20–30 pairs. A few non-breeding individuals and immature birds probably boost the population a little. Whereas the cahow across the Atlantic on Bermuda has become a source of national pride and a focus of international preservation efforts, the freira has gone largely unnoticed. In 1985 and 1986 the freira failed to nest at all. The few nesting burrows that were found and checked had been raided, probably by rats, an exotic predator of eggs and nestlings. Only three pairs were found nesting in 1987. Madeirans eat sea birds, and petrels are taken without a second thought. The appetite pressures of rats and humans seriously threaten a species with less than 100 surviving individuals. Introduced predators and habitat alteration still remain a problem in the late 1990s.

Perhaps if the relationships of gadfly petrels could be resolved and the freira universally accepted by ornithologists as a valid species, people could summon more enthusiasm for protecting and valuing this unique island treasure.

Kevin Cook

See also Cahow, Petrels.

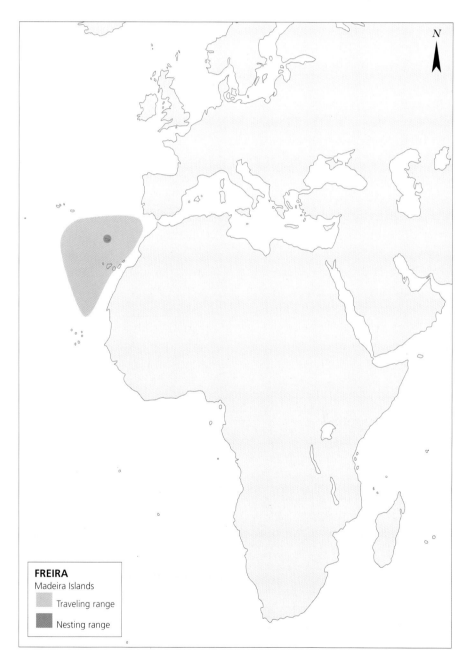

FREIRA
Madeira Islands
Traveling range
Nesting range

Christmas Frigatebird

(Fregata andrewsi)

ESA: Endangered

IUCN: Vulnerable

Class: Aves
Order: Pelecaniformes
Family: Fregatidae
Length: 37 in. (94 cm)
Weight: 2–3½ lb. (0.9–1.6 kg)
Clutch size: 1 egg
Incubation: 55–60 days
Diet: Squids, crustaceans, fish, turtles, birds
Habitat: Oceanic
Range: Breeds on Christmas Island in the eastern Indian Ocean; nonbreeding birds seen in coastal Africa, east into the Banda Sea, north to Thailand

ANY BIRD THAT CAN catch a flying fish in flight and snatch a squid as it leaps above the sea deserves some merit as being one of the best fliers among birds. Frigatebirds can do both of these things.

They are built for flight and they perform well.

Frigatebirds have hollow bones, a common trait among sea birds. But their bones are more hollow than most, and therefore are very light, making their skeletons only 5 percent of their total body weight. This is the lowest percentage skeletal weight of any bird. They also qualify as the lightest of any birds, with seven-foot (2.1-meter) wingspans. As a final adaptation for specialized flight, frigatebirds have three fused bones that are separate in other birds. The fused bones anchor the flight muscles, giving the frigatebirds the strength they need for their often remarkable aerobatic feats.

Webbed feet

A bird so exquisitely adapted to flight has little need to walk or swim. Accordingly, frigatebirds have extremely short legs and feet. All four toes are webbed together, a unique trait among members of the pelican order, but the webbing is not as complete on frigatebirds as on other seabirds. When not flying, frigatebirds perch in trees or on shrubs. Only rarely do they sit on water. They have been seen on the water, but becoming airborne from this position is difficult for them. Their flying power is not in their flapping but in their soaring and maneuvering ability.

The presence or absence of wind may have had a lot to do with the frigatebird's range. All five species inhabit tropical oceans, although some individuals wander regularly into temperate waters. On calm days they remain perched. When the wind returns, they resume their activities. Some researchers believe frigatebirds may even take short naps while on the wing.

Within their range, frigatebirds can be quite common. Their large size and their singular behavior always makes them conspicuous. The exception is the Christmas frigatebird, which,

During most of the year the bright red sac of the male frigatebird is concealed, but as breeding season nears, the inflated sac makes quite an impression.

although it closely resembles all the other species of frigatebirds, is far less common.

Mighty wingspan

A large bird, the Christmas frigatebird sails on wings that measure a little more than 7 feet (2 meters). It wears an overall black plumage, but unlike other frigatebirds, the male has a white belly. The female differs from the male in being slightly larger. Females have more white that extends onto the breast as well as covering the belly. The male has a large inflatable sac that protrudes from the chin, throat, and breast. All male frigatebirds of all five species have these sacs. As breeding season approaches, the males inflate the bright red sacs to attract females and to intimidate other males.

A single egg

Like other frigatebirds, the Christmas frigate lays only one egg per year. And like its kin, it spends two months incubating, then many more months tending the developing chick. It spends a few more months attending the fledgling that may return to the nest for weeks or months to be fed by the parents. Many young frigatebirds die—only a few ever reach adulthood. Evidence suggests that nearly six years pass before the frigatebird is mature enough to breed, and they only nest every other year. This means that their breeding potential is low, and declining populations recover very slowly.

The Christmas frigatebird takes its name from the only place where it is known to nest: Christmas Island, a territory of Australia. For decades people

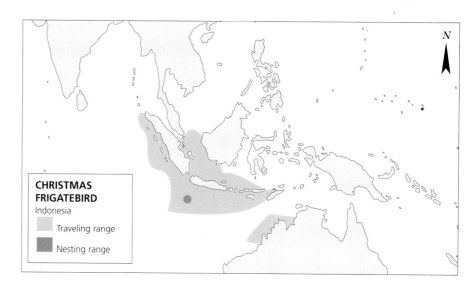

CHRISTMAS FRIGATEBIRD
Indonesia
Traveling range
Nesting range

have worked the island for guano. Guano, the accumulated droppings of birds, contains valuable concentrations of phosphates and nitrogen compounds. When processed, the guano yields high quality fertilizer. It has also been used historically to manufacture gunpowder. Recovering the guano requires cutting trees and clearing shrubs to get at the deposits. This has caused problems for the frigatebirds.

The Christmas frigatebird nests in only three colonies on the island. Its population probably did not exceed 1,600 pairs in the late 1980s and that number was approximately the same in the late 1990s. No one is sure whether this figure includes all Christmas frigatebirds or just those breeding in a given year. If the latter is true, the total population might exceed 5,000 birds.

Either way, the Christmas frigatebird is vulnerable. Guano mining continued through the 1980s, although some effort was made to extract the guano with less damage to the forests on Christmas Island. Two of the three colonies within the Christmas Island National Park are legally protected.

After the young frigatebirds fledge, they eventually gain their independence and begin wandering the Indian Ocean and its associated seas. They have been seen as far west as Madagascar and coastal Kenya, as far east as Timor in the Banda Sea, and as far north as Hong Kong. On these great wanderings, Christmas frigatebirds usually feed by catching flying fish and squids. When food is scarce, they resort to piracy. These birds will chase and harass other seabirds, even going so far as to grab them by the tails, yanking them upwards. In desperation to escape, the other birds either drop their own prey or disgorge food they have swallowed. When the sharp-eyed frigatebirds see the food drop, they swoop down to catch it before it hits the water. Hungry frigatebirds often chase each other after one has successfully intimidated another bird.

There are no plans to help bolster the Christmas frigatebird population by preserving habitat away from its breeding grounds, so it is essential to preserve Christmas Island and to maintain a healthy ocean.

Kevin Cook

FROGS

Class: Amphibia

Order: Anura

Frogs are any of a large group of tailless amphibians. There are almost 3,000 species around the world. Together with toads, frogs make up the order known as Anura and are referred to as anurans. This order is divided into 14 families.

In general, a toad is a dry-skinned amphibian that lives on land, while a frog is semiaquatic and moist-skinned.

Most frogs lay eggs, which hatch into tadpoles. The tadpole has a tail and is almost fully aquatic, possessing gills to breathe underwater. The tadpoles metamorphose, or change, into froglets and then into adult frogs. Most tadpoles feed on vegetation, while adult frogs feed on a variety of invertebrates, including insects, and mollusks. Sometimes they will even eat other amphibians.

Recent investigations suggest that there is a worldwide decline in the amphibian populations. Frogs, as well as other amphibians, possess a number of characteristics that make them vulnerable to environmental disturbances, such as global climate change, pollution, ultraviolet radiation, and habitat destruction. Because they exist both on land and in the water, sometimes migrating between the two, these animals are subject to the damaging effects that occur in both situations. Frogs have thin, permeable skin, that easily absorbs contaminated ions from the environment. Many species breathe through their skin, which must remain moist, so droughts or reduced water habitats are very threatening.

Conondale Gastric-brooding Frog

(Rheobatrachus silus)

ESA: Threatened

IUCN: Critically endangered

Size: Female, 2 in. (5 cm); Male, 1½ in. (4 cm)

Clutch size: Approximately 25

Diet: Invertebrates

Habitat: Rocky mountain streams and wet forests

Range: The Blackall and Conondale Ranges of southeastern Queensland, Australia

ALSO KNOWN AS THE platypus frog, this unusual amphibian was only discovered in 1973 and already there is concern that it may be dangerously close to extinction. It is brown or olive brown to almost black in color with faint spots on its back. A dark streak runs from the eye to the forearm, and there are darker crossbars on the limbs. The underside of the frog is white except on the limbs, which are bright orange. The digits on the hind legs are webbed, while those of the forearms are free. The species has a blunt snout, giving it a slightly pug-nosed appearance, and the upper jaw has two fan-like teeth. A broad tongue is attached to the floor of the mouth. The eyes are very prominent and directed upward.

The gastric-brooding frog is aquatic and nocturnal, hiding under rocks in fast-flowing creeks during the day. At night, it may sit on rocks or cling to them while partly submerging itself in the water. It is a shy animal, hiding on the bottom of the creek when disturbed. The species is rarely seen and population estimates are rather bleak. A field census in the late 1970s marked 34 frogs, and estimates suggested that the total population was as low as 78. Because the species was discovered such a short time ago, there are no past figures with

CONONDALE GASTRIC-BROODING FROG
Australia

which to compare current populations, but the markedly small numbers of the animal are alarming, particularly because it has been some time since the frog was last seen in the wild. Deforestation has occurred in its range, but the exact reason for the decline of the gastric-brooding frog is unknown.

The gastric-brooding frog is so named because of the remarkable way in which it gives birth to its young. Its reproductive habits are unique in the entire animal kingdom. The female frog swallows its fertilized eggs, then converts its stomach to a uterus. Finally, it gives birth to fully formed young through the mouth. The mother eats nothing while the babies are in her stomach. During the gestation period, the stomach stops producing acid, and crushing digestive motions cease. A few days after the birth of the last tadpole, the mother begins to eat normally again. There are usually about 25 babies in a single pregnancy, but the survival rate of the young is apparently low.

When the gastric-brooding frog was first discovered, scientists did not know about its unusual reproductive habits, but it was still of interest because it appeared to be the only member of its genus. Researchers were studying this frog closely to learn more about it when the "gastric brooding" was first observed. Scientists began to think that the frog's ability to stop secreting hydrochloric acid might be applied to medical science. In human beings, the acid causes ulcers when too much of it is secreted; researchers thought that perhaps they could learn something to inhibit the process by studying this frog.

Unfortunately, the scarcity of the animal, together with the difficulty of breeding amphibians in captivity, has made this frog very difficult to study.

Golden Coqui Frog

(Eleutherodactylus jasperi)

ESA: Threatened

IUCN: Data deficient

Size: ¾ in. (2 cm)
Clutch size: 3–5
Diet: Insects
Habitat: Mountains
Range: Puerto Rico, restricted to a small area south of Cayey

THE GOLDEN COQUI measures only ¾ inch (2 centimeters) in length. It is olive-gold to yellow-gold in color and it lives in the axils (the angle where a leaf or branch is attached to a plant) of bromeliads. These tropical plants, such as pineapples and spanish moss, do not need soil to grow. The golden coqui is found on dense clusters of bromeliads that grow upward from the ground, on rock edges, and even from trees. Water collects in the leaf axils, supplying a habitat for the tiny frog. During the day it feeds on insects that enter the axils, but at night the frog ventures out onto leaves. It retreats quickly when it is disturbed.

Females give birth between April and August. One month passes between fertilization and birth in captive golden coquis. Field observation has suggested that a female may produce two clutches per year. Fertilization occurs inside the body, and the female retains five to six developing embryos. Three to five tadpoles survive to become frogs.

There are only three known populations of the golden coqui in existence, all occurring in the mountaintops of the Cayey region of Puerto Rico. They exist at 2,295 to 2,790 feet (700 to 850 meters) in elevation. The only available population estimates for the golden coqui are from field studies conducted in 1973 and 1974. Researchers at that time believed that only 1,500 to 3,000 of the amphibians existed. Because there are no past population estimates, it is impossible to document the decline of the species. Perhaps the biggest single reason for the decline is loss of habitat. In addition, this frog is believed to have a particularly low reproductive rate, making it difficult to maintain populations. The animal also has a difficult time moving from one site to another, and if its home is lost, it cannot move easily to a new location.

The golden coqui was listed as threatened in the 1970s, but at the close of the 1990s there was insufficient data to make a risk assessment possible. It exists primarily on privately owned lands, which makes conservation of the

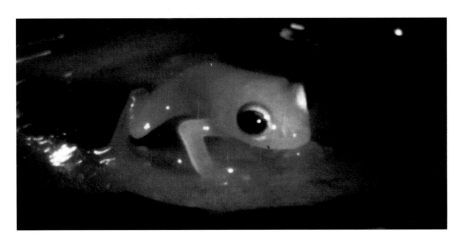

One threat to the survival of the golden coqui frog is the possibility of natural catastrophes like fires or hurricanes that could wipe out its tiny environment.

species more difficult. Fortunately, all native wildlife is protected by the Commonwealth of Puerto Rico.

The U.S. Fish and Wildlife Service has suggested a recovery plan to bring the population to a level where the golden coqui will no longer be considered endangered. The goals include establishing whether the three populations are stable or growing, and that a minimum of 1,000 individuals exist.

Hopefully, a population of this size would provide a large enough gene pool to ensure healthy offspring, and such a thriving population may even withstand a catastrophic event such as a fire or a hurricane.

Goliath Frog
(Conraua goliath)

ESA: Threatened

IUCN: Vulnerable

Size: Up to 12½ in. (32 cm) head and body length
Clutch size: Unknown
Diet: Insects, mollusks, crustaceans, small amphibians
Habitat: Large, swiftly flowing rivers, especially around waterfalls or rapids
Range: Confined to the rain forest belt of coastal Cameroon and Equatorial Guinea

THE GOLIATH FROG is the world's largest anuran. Its total length, including the hind leg and foot, can reach up to 32 inches (81 centimeters) and it can weigh as much as 7¼ pounds (3.3 kilo-grams). There have been unconfirmed reports of even larger individuals. Surprisingly, the frog has a rather small range. It is found only in Cameroon and Equatorial Guinea in an area only about 150 miles (240 kilometers) long and 60 miles (95 kilometers) wide. By contrast, the common bullfrog, which is about half the size of the goliath, occurs all across eastern North America from Quebec to Mexico. Within the goliath frog's small range, it is found only in the vicinity of large, swift-flowing rivers in dense rain forests. This habitat is being destroyed—mainly by human activities that include deforestation for agricultural purposes, building of dams, and establishing new villages.

Goliath frogs lay the majority of their eggs during the dry season, which occurs from June through August, but some may also be deposited in "the little dry season" of December and January. Metamorphosis of the tadpoles takes place 85 to 95 days later. Unlike the extraordinary size of the adults, goliath tadpoles are about the same size as other ranids. These offspring have special adaptations that allow them to exist in the swift flowing habitats of the adults despite their small size. Young frogs spend most of the day in the water with only the tops of their heads above the surface.

No accurate figures are available regarding the number of goliath frogs that still exist today. The animal was first formally described in 1906, and this original description was from a single specimen. Researchers have remarked on how difficult the species is to locate, approach,

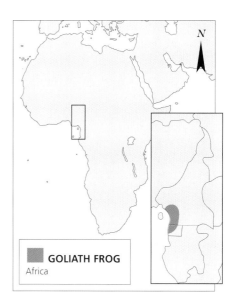

GOLIATH FROG
Africa

and capture, which suggests that the frog is not common. One collection sponsored by the Duisberger Zoo collected 21 animals, 15 of them young; a similar project in 1981 captured 41 individuals over a three-week period after intensive collection with the assistance of native hunters. Most researchers believe the frog is found in low concentrations throughout its range.

While this species has probably never been particularly abundant in nature, it is now faced with steadily decreasing numbers, largely because of its unusual size. Zoos around the world are interested in displaying "the biggest frog in the world," and consequently sponsor expeditions specifically to catch the goliath frog. Animal dealers in the United States, Germany, Holland, Italy, and Japan have begun importing the frogs to sell as pets. The animals are listed for sale at prices between $1,500 and $3,000. Cameroon alone allows 300 of the frogs to be exported abroad each year.

Unfortunately, whether the goliath frog is imported for display, profit, or scientific research,

Italian Agile Frog
(Rana latastei)

IUCN: Lower risk

Size: 3 in. (7.5 cm)
Clutch size: Unknown
Diet: Insects
Habitat: Slow-flowing brooks, ponds, and pools in meadows and deciduous forests
Range: Po Valley in Italy and adjacent region; southern Switzerland, northern Italy, and extreme northwestern Yugoslavia

it travels poorly, damages easily, and does not do well in captivity over the long term. Survival rates in importations have not been high, primarily because of the stress caused to the animal during shipping and the time it takes for the frog to adjust to captive conditions.

Media interest

Since 1990, the United States news media has paid a great deal of attention to the species, increasing the demand for the animal from private collectors. One U.S. dealer is reported to have imported 50 individuals. Most zoos in the United States and Canada are aware of the difficulty of maintaining the species in captivity; in 1991 only two U.S. zoos held the animals in their collections.

In addition to the threats of habitat destruction and trade exploitation, the native people of the forests consider the meat of the goliath frog a delicacy, and capturing the animal is cause for celebration. Native hunting does pose a threat, and effective protective measures are necessary. The frog is not protected by the

Convention on International Trade in Endangered Species (CITES), and there are no measures that restrict exploitation, trade, or habitat destruction.

Although the goliath is the largest frog in the world, the tadpoles and young frogs are comparable in size to other frogs. It is believed that it takes longer for the animal to reach sexual maturity, and that a mature animal removed from the wild will not be replaced quickly.

Because the mortality rate of goliath frogs in captivity is high, and zoos have been unable to run successful captive breeding programs, the wild populations are the only hope for this animal's continued survival.

Habitat management

To save the goliath frog, it has been proposed that the animal's habitat be managed and protected. In addition, it is believed that the goliath frog's status should be changed from vulnerable to endangered and that exportation should be made illegal. The unusual size of this frog has, in many ways, created its biggest threat.

THE ITALIAN AGILE FROG belongs to the genus *Rana*, which is Latin for frog. These amphibians are the most familiar of frogs and differ from others by their ossified sternum and tapered fingers. *Ranae* exist on all large land masses except Greenland.

The Italian agile frog is a small brown animal, typically red-brown on the upper side with a dark brown throat displaying a fine line in the center. There is a clear band on the upper jaw between the corner of the mouth and the eye.

The frog is found in floodplains with high water tables, near a small stream, river, or lake with moist deciduous forest, swampy ground, and lush vegetation. It does not appear to occur beyond 1,500 feet (458 meters) above sea level.

Individuals do not show a tendency to migrate, remaining

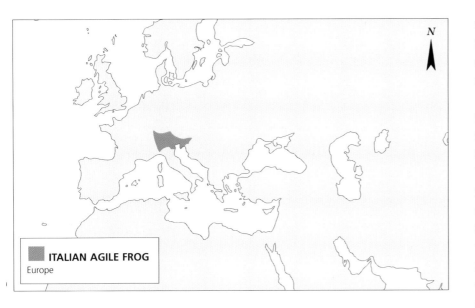

ITALIAN AGILE FROG
Europe

close to their spawning sites throughout their life. The breeding season peaks in March, when small clumps of eggs are deposited in the backwaters of streams or small ponds. Shallow, slow-flowing water appears to be the best location for these deposits, although they appear in still water as well. During the season, males remain several yards from one another and produce a weak mating call, which is normally sounded underwater, or with only the head above water.

In the spring, the breeding population of the agile frog is made up of small, one-year-old animals. The following autumn, several hundred young offspring can be found in the most suitable habitats. However, adults frogs are rare at this time, and by the next spring, the population has declined significantly. It is believed that the species suffers high mortality rates during winter hibernation. Adult mortality during the breeding season also seems to be high, and observation of mature individuals during spring and summer are rare. By autumn, the proportion of adults is again low. These observations

suggest that the population of the Italian agile frog changes constantly. A successful reproductive season may produce a large number of offspring, but the population increase is temporary.

Adults seem to behave differently throughout the year. In the spring, the forest floor is bare and humidity is low. At this time, only a few frogs are found away from breeding sites. As summer arrives, the forest grows thick with vegetation and the frog's activity increases greatly. After spawning, adult behavior and activity is influenced by ground water availability and weather conditions. For example, in years of light autumn rainfall, young adults tend to remain grouped

together in areas with lush vegetation near water sources such as ditches or river banks, and they emerge only at night.

There are about 35 populations of the Italian agile frog in the lowlands of northern Italy, Switzerland, and into northern Yugoslavia. The amphibian was first collected near Milan, but today that population is extinct. Several populations exist in protected reserves in Italy and Switzerland, but the reserves were not created for the Italian agile frog. These populations, however, are not well managed.

Two reserves have been proposed with the Italian agile frog's survival as the primary aim. The two sites are at Bosco della Fontana and Le Bine, in northern Italy. Bosco della Fontana has been protected as a Natural Forest Reserve since 1910, and since 1976 the capture of frogs has been forbidden. Part of the forest is closed to the public.

Bosco della Fontana represents one of the last primeval riverine forests that once covered most of the surrounding area. The land looks much as it would

The red-eyed tree frog (*Aqalychnis callidryas*) is aptly named. Frogs and other amphibians are vanishing in record numbers around the world.

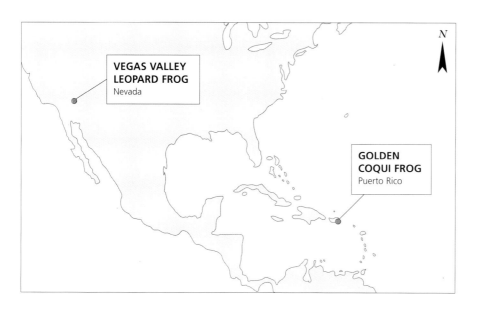

have centuries ago. A small river crosses the forest, and its clear waters serve as the frog's main spawning site. The waters are usually high, and the vegetation is lush, producing high humidity. For this reason, the Italian agile frog remains relatively abundant in Bosco della Fontana. Unfortunately, the water level is falling, as it has become a source for local agricultural and drinking water, and the size and number of breeding sites are decreasing, accounting for the decline in the Bosco della Fontana's frog population. One of the major goals in protecting this frog is to stop the "drying out" of its habitat by preventing the pumping of ground water from the forest. New ponds in secluded parts of the forest should be created. Ponds and ditches must be replenished with water in mid-February to ensure that they will be in good condition for the breeding season.

The Le Bine site has a high population of the Italian agile frog, probably because the conditions there are perfect for breeding. It is the largest existing population, and provides an ideal site for a reserve.

Another species of the same genus is in greater danger of extinction than the Italian agile frog. *Rana holtzi* is endemic to Turkey. Its entire world range is confined to two very small lakes. It is abundant in both sites, but is considered vulnerable to threats of habitat change, pollution, and the introduction of predatory fish. Turkey has been slow to protect its wildlife. The country is comparatively underdeveloped, however, and there is great potential for large-scale conservation efforts in a country that still boasts the most tremendous range of wildife resources.

Vegas Valley Leopard Frog
(Rana fisheri)

IUCN: Extinct

Size: 1¾–3 in. (4.5–7.5 cm)
Clutch size: Unknown
Diet: Invertebrates
Habitat: Spring basins or trickling streams in fields
Range: Las Vegas, Nevada

THE VEGAS VALLEY leopard frog was spotted with light stripes along the dorso-lateral folds; females tended to be more spotted than the males. The hind limbs were honey colored in both males and females. The female was an olive green with dark brownish olive spots. The groin and hind legs were deep olive to a pale olive gray. The throat was light green and pale brown. Males ranged from cedar green to dark greenish olive. The head was broad with a rounded snout. Older males may have been smooth, but younger males and females had more warts. The species probably bred in spring.

The Vegas Valley frog was last seen in 1942. The increased water demands of human populations since Las Vegas became a gambling resort in the 1930s destroyed the habitat of the frog. The introduction of bullfrogs, which prey on smaller amphibians, into remaining habitats, furthered the decline of the Vegas Valley frog. Trout eat eggs and tadpoles, causing further decline in potential numbers. The frog was probably easy to capture because it was not very alert.

Distinct species
For many years this frog was thought to be the same species as those found in Utah and Nevada, but in the late 1920s, scientists decided that the Vegas Valley frog was sharply isolated from related species in neighboring regions. Because the range of the frog was so limited, human activity caused great damage to the population. The frog was left with nowhere to go, and is now extinct.

Elizabeth Sirimarco

See also Toads.

Rapa Fruit-dove

(Ptilinopus huttoni)

IUCN: Vulnerable

Class: Aves
Order: Columbiformes
Family: Columbidae
Length: 12 in. (30.5 cm)
Weight: Unknown
Clutch size: Unknown
Incubation: Unknown
Diet: Unknown
Habitat: Montane tropical forest
Range: Rapa Island and Durango, Mexico

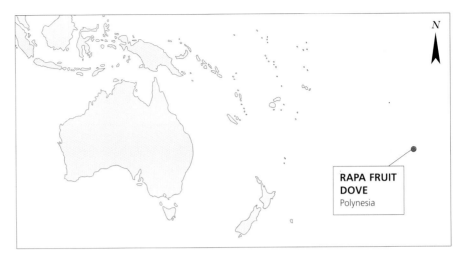

RAPA FRUIT DOVE
Polynesia

RAPA ISLAND IS PART of French Polynesia in the South Pacific. Covering 54 square miles (140 square kilometers), it is hilly and was once heavily forested. Fruit-doves inhabited Rapa Island long before people lived there. This dove is somewhat different from other fruit-doves.

The Rapa fruit-dove is one of 49 fruit-dove species in the genus *Ptilinopus*. Only the pigeon genus *Columba* is larger within this family. The term *dove* usually conjures up visions of either a snow-white bird or one having colors of tans and grays. The fruit-doves break this stereotype. Some of them wear plumage as gaudy as any parrot. The Rapa fruit-dove reaches 12 inches (30.5 centimeters).

Species in decline

The Rapa fruit-dove is declining. Estimates in the 1970s suggested perhaps 125 pairs, which would indicate a population slightly over 250 birds when allowing for nonbreeding individuals. There has been no serious decline in population since 1974, and the population was estimated to be 274 individuals in 1989–1990.

Islanders hunt the Rapa fruit-dove as food and have cleared many of the forests, which are its habitat. Other uncleared forests have been severely damaged by goats. Goats eat young trees and seedlings, as well as leaves and small twigs off saplings. Often goats kill all the young trees, which prevents forests from replacing themselves. Those animals that depend on forests or woodlands disappear. Without research, no one can say for certain how much of the fruit-dove's decline is due to goats and how much is due to human destruction of habitat. The forests of Rapa, however, have been drastically depleted. The hunting of birds was legally abolished in 1967, but enforcement is nonexistent. A similar prohibition needs to be enacted against tree cutting in order to save the last forest cover on the island.

Kevin Cook

Much remains to be learned about the fruit-dove, including reproductive habits, diet, type of nest construction, and other aspects of its natural history.

Gold-fronted Fulvetta

(Alcippe variegaticeps)

IUCN: Vulnerable

Class: Aves
Order: Passeriformes
Family: Muscicapidae
Subfamily: Timaliinae
Length: 4½ in. (11.4 cm)
Weight: Unknown
Clutch size: Unknown
Incubation: Unknown
Diet: Probably insects
Habitat: Undergrowth of montane broadleaf forests
Range: Southern Sichuan Province and Guangxi Province, China

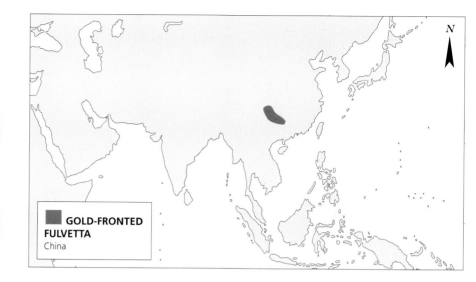

GOLD-FRONTED FULVETTA
China

THERE ARE SOME 18 SPECIES of the babbler group known as fulvettas. Ornithologists have regarded the babblers both as a distinct family and as a subfamily of a larger group called the Old World flycatchers. The relationships among these songbirds is not clear, and ornithologists do not always agree on how certain birds should be classified.

Gray to olive-gray above, it has a white chin with a yellow throat, a yellow stripe down the breast, and its belly is bordered by gray sides. The forehead is bright yellow, the crown is streaked black and white, and the nape is streaked rufous and buff. Its face is white around the eye with a black cheek patch.

Little is known about this bird other than that its population seems to be declining. However, as a fulvetta, some useful generalizations can be drawn based on the traits and behaviors of other fulvettas. As a group, fulvettas range from eastern India and Nepal through southern China and into Southeast Asia. At least one species exists on the islands of Borneo and Sumatra. They mostly inhabit montane forests and shrub lands of around 3,000 to 8,000 feet (915 to 2,439 meters) elevation.

The gold-fronted fulvetta is known only from southern China in the brushy undergrowth of broad-leaved forests between 1,968 and 6,580 feet (600 to 2,000 meters) elevation. Babblers eat insects and small fruits. Some species search for food beneath the leaf debris on forest floors, while others find their food in trees and shrubs. The small size of most fulvettas suggests that they eat insects and other small invertebrates.

Breeding habits among babblers are also diverse with clutch sizes varing from two to five eggs. Some groups build domed nests with entrance holes on the side, while other groups build cup-like nests. Depending on the species, nests may be built just above ground level, in shrubs, in forest undergrowth, or higher up in trees. These assumptions help

ornithologists refine their efforts when they go into the field to study little-known birds such as the gold-fronted fulvetta.

However, successful wildlife preservation really depends on knowing much more about the natural history of the species.

Declining numbers

The bird was known to be declining throughout the 1980s. Its previous status and historical distribution in China were not well documented, because the Chinese government did not encourage any ornithological research by outsiders. Observations of the gold-fronted fulvetta in the 1980s were almost entirely limited to southern Sichuan province, where there was severe forest cutting at that time. Ornithologists feared the bird would lose all remaining habitat in Sichuan in the early 1990s. One bird was found in the Dafengding Panda Reserve in south-central Sichuan. It is not known if a population of gold-fronted fulvettas lives in the panda reserve. To help this bird, we must determine its life needs and preserve its habitat.

Kevin Cook

See also Babblers.

GALAXIAS

Class: Actinopterygii

Order: Salmoniformes

Family: Galaxiidae

With a name that means "Milky Way" it might be assumed that the galaxiids are from another world, but the name "galaxias" concerns appearance. Milky skin tones under a blizzard of small colored spots and flecks inspired those who gave the name *galaxias* to these fishes.

While many of the threatened galaxiids are located in Australia (in particular in the exotic island state of Tasmania), their overall distribution includes New Zealand, Lord Howe Island in the Tasman Sea, South America, the Falkland Islands in the south Atlantic, and South Africa. These temperate areas of the Southern Hemisphere are ideal for a group of fishes that shuns more tropical and warm water environments.

Most galaxiids live their entire lives in freshwater, but some move from freshwater into salt water to spawn, a behavior called catadromy. Relatively few fish are capable of making this physiological jump from a freshwater to saltwater species, both as juveniles and as sexually mature adults.

Sometimes confused with small trout, these fishes lack scales and the fleshy adipose fin on the back that is distinctive to trout and other salmon-like fishes. Also, the galaxiids have a much smaller mouth. These fishes are voracious insect eaters and move nimbly when looking for food. Aquarium galaxiids can be trained to leap out of the water for food items such as chopped worms.

With a limited tolerance for salt water, their widespread distribution is hard to explain. Experts suggest a theory that the ancestors of the galaxiids lived in an Antarctic region that was once much larger and had many rivers. As this prehistoric continent broke up and parts of it became submerged under the oceans, patches of land like Tasmania, the Falkland Islands, and Lord Howe Island became the only remaining remnants, with their fish populations isolated by the newer oceans.

Of the approximately 45 galaxiids around the world the five threatened or endangered species, all native to Tasmania, live in isolated freshwater environments that restrict their movement and limit their range. Because of their small individual ranges, the loss of a single population is damaging to the species as a whole. Many experts agree that the problem of possible extinction of the Australian galaxiids is largely due to the introduction of the non-native brown trout (*Salmo trutta*). This fish is larger than the galaxias and is also a formidable predator.

Clarence Galaxias

(Galaxias johnstoni)

IUCN: Critically endangered

Length: 3½ in. (9 cm)

Reproduction: Egg layer

Habitat: Cool lakes and streams

Range: Central Tasmania

AT ONE TIME THE Clarence galaxias was plentiful throughout central Tasmania's Clarence River basin. Now it is restricted to a small and remote headwaters creek and two natural lakes. The brown trout (*Salmo trutta*), which occupies similar habitat, is partly responsible for this fish's decline. It is a notorious predator, is larger than the galaxias, and can make an easy meal of it. The non-native brown trout was introduced to Tasmania from Europe in 1864 as a game fish when concern for native fishes was not prevalent. The brown trout has been responsible for reductions in populations and extinction of other species in Tasmania and other regions of Australia. The brown trout was damaging to this galaxias because of their restricted range.

This small fish, while sometimes mistakenly identified as a kind of trout (Salmonidae), has a shape that is, in many respects, a combination of features of salmonids and esocids. In fact, this fish and other galaxiids were initially categorized as esocids.

The Clarence galaxias has a slender and tubular body with a blunt snout and a large mouth. The dorsal fin on the back and the anal fin are well behind the center of the body and have a fleshy base. The tail fin is broad and straight at the end. The other fins are small, rounded at the ends, and unpigmented. The fish has a dark greenish background color on the back and sides and a medium-brown belly. It has darker tigerlike vertical stripes, patches on the sides, and a patch on the gill covers. The skin displays gold-colored flecks.

The habits of this fish are not well known. There is little evidence to suggest that it migrates to the ocean to spawn. Insects and other small invertebrates are the likely food of this species.

The Inland Fisheries Commission of Tasmania wants to secure habitat for the galaxias that has not been invaded by predators such as the brown trout, and to prevent the introduction of any more non-native fishes into these areas.

Pedder Galaxias

(Galaxias pedderensis)

IUCN: Critically endangered

Length: 4⅓ in. (11 cm)
Reproduction: Egg layer
Habitat: Slow-flowing streams with boulders or vegetation
Range: Lake Pedder, Tasmania

SOUTHWESTERN TASMANIA and Lake Pedder, the site of a massive hydroelectric project, is home to the most endangered fish in Australia, the Pedder galaxias. When the Huon and Serpentine Rivers were dammed for the generation of electricity, Lake Pedder was much enlarged. Despite initial concerns that alteration of Lake Pedder would be harmful to native fishes, these species adjusted well to their changed environment. However, recently the population of Pedder galaxias has taken a nose dive and the species is now in more trouble than ever, with the result that the Pedder galaxias is now no longer found in the lake, only in a few

Many galaxiids have a torpedo-like appearance. Their name comes from the flecked appearance of their skin, which reminded scientists of stars.

streams that run into the lake. The enlargement of the lake due to the hydroelectric project enabled the introduction of the Brown Trout (*Salmo trutta*) and the Climbing galaxias (*Galaxias brevipinnis*). It is the interaction with these species that is believed to have resulted in the decline of the Pedder galaxias in the lake. Translocations to other areas have been attempted, but have not been a success.

The Pedder galaxias is a strikingly beautiful fish, with variable and alternating bold patches of brown and cream coloration on the back and sides, much like the patterns on a giraffe. The belly is a pale cream-color. These patterns extend somewhat onto the head, throat, and chin as well as onto the fleshy bases of the fins.

This fish spawns during late fall or winter within several of the streams that flow into Lake Pedder. This species is capable of upstream migration from the lake and can swim over obstacles and even small waterfalls. Other information on the life history and habits of the Pedder galaxias is incomplete, but a diet consisting of insects and other small river and lake-dwelling creatures is most likely.

The future of this fish is uncertain, but there may be hope. The construction of the dam at Lake Pedder and its neg-

ative effects on wildlife in general have sparked controversy and increased environmental awareness in Australia. This wave of concern for the environment may have a positive effect on the Pedder galaxias and other wildlife of Tasmania and Australia.

Saddled Galaxias

(Galaxias tanycephalus)

IUCN: Vulnerable

Length: 6 in. (15 cm)
Reproduction: Egg layer
Habitat: Shoreline rocks and boulders
Range: Arthur's Lake and Wood's Lake, Tasmania

THE SADDLED GALAXIAS lives in two high-altitude lakes above 4,000 feet (1,220 meters) in central Tasmania, in Arthur's Lake and Wood's Lake. The lack of additional sites is reason enough for concern about this fish's continued well-being. However, while evidence is not conclusive, the brown trout (*Salmo trutta*) may be partly responsible for threatening the survival of this fish within its home range. The saddled galaxias tends to grow larger than other galaxiids, but it

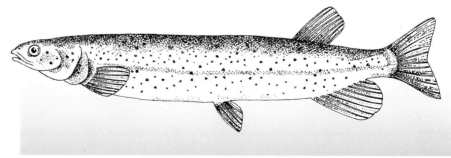

is still much smaller than the brown trout. Both occupy similar habitat. The brown trout, a notorious predator, can make an easy meal of a saddled galaxias.

The saddled galaxias is darker overall than other galaxiids, with gray-black to olive-green on the back and sides and an olive belly with silvery overtones; some purple is apparent on the sides of some specimens in bright light. The back is covered with a row of gray saddlelike blotches from the base of the head to the base of the tail. It has a slender and bullet-shaped body, with a sharper snout and large mouth. The dorsal fin and the anal fin are well behind the fish's center, much like the muskellunge (*Esox masquinongy*) and northern pike (*Esox lucius*) of North America. All fins except the tail fin are small relative to the body size, rounded at the ends, and contain olive or amber pigmentation, except for the fleshy base. The tail fin is broad, amber or olive colored, and mildly forked at the end. This is a common feature of strong swimmers.

Because of its relatively high-altitude home range and distance from the sea, it is assumed that this species does not migrate to salt water to spawn and stays within its home lakes and nearby streams to reproduce.

As with other galaxias, the future depends in part on the efforts of the Inland Fisheries Commission of Tasmania to balance the needs of native fishes against the desire of the public for a greater variety of sport fishes. Secure habitat must be provided to protect the saddled galaxias from non-native sport fishes. The best solution would

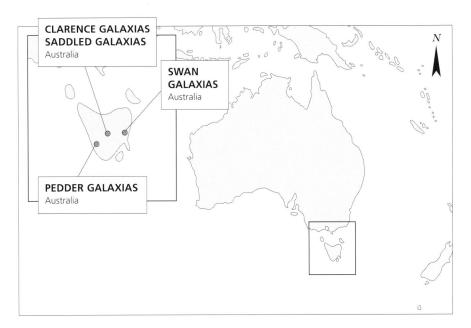

be eradication of brown trout from Tasmania. This approach would meet stiff opposition, and a compromise will be required.

Swan Galaxias

(Galaxias fontanus)

IUCN: Critically endangered

Length: 3½ in. (9 cm)
Reproduction: Egg layer
Habitat: Stream edges near cover or vegetation
Range: Upper Swan River, Tasmania, tributaries of the Macquarie River

DESPITE THE CLOSE proximity of the Swan River to the ocean, the Swan galaxias spends its time in the upper reaches of the river. It does not make a yearly migration to the sea to spawn because an impassable waterfall between its home and the ocean prevents the fish leaving. The waterfall acts as a physical barrier to downstream migration and expansion of its range, but also prevents the upstream movement of Tasmania's notorious predator, the non-native brown trout (*Salmo trutta*), which occupies all stream segments below the waterfall and has completely eliminated the Swan galaxias from those areas.

The Swan galaxias is similar in size and shape to the Clarence galaxias, although not as boldly patterned. It is blotchy and displays less spectacular coloration. The skin color of this scaleless fish is a dull green-olive on the back and sides and silvery olive on the belly. The sides and back show brown blotches and spots.

Efforts to save this endangered species have focused on securing the upper reaches of the Swan River by preventing the introduction of brown trout into these segments.

The introduction of this predator into the upper Swan River would most assuredly mean complete elimination of the Swan galaxias from its habitat. Forestry operations are also a threat to this fish's habitat.

William E. Manci

GAMBUSIA

Class: Actinopterygii

Order: Atheriniformes

Family: Poeciliidae

Of the approximately 20 species of the family Poeciliidae in North America, five are members of the genus *Gambusia* and are listed as threatened or endangered. In the United States they are commonly called gambusia; in Mexico they go by the name *guayacón*. Unfortunately, several of these fishes are rapidly disappearing and other gambusia such as the Clear Creek gambusia and the San Marcos gambusia recently have become extinct in the wild.

Like all fishes of the family Poeciliidae, gambusia are known for their ability to give birth to live young; the most familiar member of this family is the guppy (*Poecilia reticulata*), a aquarium fish that is fairly common.

Gambusia carry on a relatively specialized lifestyle compared to some other fishes outside their family. Aside from the reproductive characteristics they share with other poeciliids, gambusia are distinguished by their habitat preference for dense vegetation and a specific taste for adult and larval mosquitoes, a feature that has earned them the name of *mosquitofish* (*Gambusia affinis*), and has made these fish a valuable commodity in regions with mosquito problems. Despite the sometimes bad results caused by their domination of other native fishes, they are of help in the fight against malaria.

Live-bearing fishes like gambusia and other Poeciliidae do not lay eggs like most fishes. They hold the eggs within their body, and males fertilize them within the female. Male gambusia insert a sperm-filled sac (spermatophore) into the female, who is not required to utilise the sperm immediately—it may be carried for as long as 10 months.

As eggs mature and become ready for fertilization, the female may then release sperm from the sac to fertilize the eggs. After several weeks the eggs hatch and the young emerge from the mother's abdomen. This unusual process of reproduction is called ovovivipary, which literally means "live birth from eggs."

Other characteristic physical features of gambusia include an upturned mouth for catching insects at the surface, large scales on the body only (the head usually is unscaled), a dorsal fin that is positioned far back toward the tail, and a tail fin that is rounded instead of forked. The rounded tail is an adaptation that probably stems from their preference for still waters. None of the fins carry spines as protection from predators.

Big Bend Gambusia

(Gambusia gaigei)

ESA: Endangered

IUCN: Vulnerable

Length: 2 in. (5 cm)
Reproduction: Live bearer
Habitat: Shallow, spring-fed pools
Range: Big Bend National Park, Texas

THIS HIGHLY ENDANGERED fish is attempting a comeback after reaching the brink of extinction in 1956. In that year, only three individuals could be found at two spring sites in Brewster County, Texas, when two males and one female were located. In the years following the capture of the last three living specimens, introductions of offspring were made at other locations within Brewster County, but those introductions were unsuccessful. Today, the only remaining population of Big Bend gambusia within its original range is found in a protected, artificial pool and in nearby streams in Big Bend National Park; a second population has been established at Dexter National Fish Hatchery in New Mexico to replenish the Texas population, if necessary.

Threat of flooding

Even in the National Park, the proximity of the pool and spring to the Rio Grande River poses a seasonal threat of flooding that could carry away the remaining individuals or bring in competitors like the mosquitofish (*Gambusia affinis*). In addition, flood waters carrying sediments and other runoff materials could severely degrade water quality. Other threats to the Big Bend gambusia include diversion by the U.S. National Park Service of spring water that is needed by this fish to survive. The Park Service diverted the water to create an artificial oasis near the park's Rio Grande Village. The result has been a lower water table and lower spring flow rate.

The recovery plan for the Big Bend gambusia includes augmenting water flow from the spring during dry periods, restoring the spring outfall streams, eradicating mosquitofish from nearby springs and pools to prevent their migration, and introducing individuals from this highly endangered species to other appropriate sites. Another threat to the species is hybridization with introduced species. Hybridization leads to the eventual decline of a species.

While the favorite foods of the Big Bend gambusia are not specifically known, it is assumed that they have the same taste for mosquitoes and other small surface insects as other gambusia.

Upturned mouth

The Big Bend gambusia varies little in appearance from other gambusia. It is a yellowish color overall and sports dark bars under the eyes and chin. The sides of this fish display muted horizontal stripes, and the body is generously scaled. The big bend gambusia has a wide, upturned mouth with a projecting lower jaw, and teeth in both jaws for holding prey. The base of the inside of the throat contains comblike pharyngeal teeth to further crush and process food items. In most respects the male and female of the species are very similar. However, males possess a gonopodium, a modification and extension of the anal fin on the belly that is used to insert a sperm packet into the female during mating.

In the female the anal fin remains unmodified in its shorter, flat, and rounded shape. Additionally, during the breeding season the female has a prominent spotted genital pore (a visible target for the male's gonopodium), and the belly of the female becomes distended and bulbous during pregnancy.

Pecos Gambusia
(Gambusia nobilis)

| **ESA:** Endangered |
| **IUCN:** Vulnerable |

Length: 1½ in. (4 cm)
Reproduction: Live bearer
Habitat: Springs, sinkholes, and small, quiet tributaries
Range: Pecos River basin of New Mexico and Texas

THE PECOS GAMBUSIA is a fish under attack by competitors and invaders. Specifically, this insect-eater faces competition from a more aggressive gambusia, the mosquitofish (*Gambusia affinis*), and from the green sunfish (*Lepomis cyanellus*), a voracious predator. Given its small size and less belligerent demeanor, as well as a lower reproductive rate than the mosquitofish, the Pecos gambusia is no match for these other species that inhabit its range. Some cross-breeding between the Pecos gambusia and the mosquitofish has been observed, an occurrence that can be just as damaging to a species as predation or competition for food. Found only in the Pecos River basin of Texas and New Mexico, this species has increasingly fewer locations in which to live without disturbance. The Pecos gambusia is not only sensitive to

The small size and non-aggressive tendencies of the Pecos gambusia have played an important role in its threatened status. The fish is often under attack by competitors and invaders. The fish that compete for the Pecos gambusia's habitat and food sources are much larger.

the effects of other inhabitants of its range, but it is also intolerant of poor water quality. While other fish can survive comfortably in water of hardness above 5,000 parts per million (a condition that is fairly common in the Pecos River basin), this fish will quickly perish when exposed to these conditions.

Complicating the situation is a trend to lower water tables in this species' range. Many of the sinkholes and springs it formerly occupied have quit producing water and have dried up.

During the late 1970s the Pecos gambusia was transplanted to several sinkhole lakes in the Bitter Lake National Wildlife Refuge in southern New Mexico.

Some of these lakes contained mosquitofish as well as green sunfish. Predictably, the Pecos gambusia flourished only in lakes that did not hold these or other competitors.

The Pecos gambusia is not particularly spectacular in coloration and has an overall yellow-brown skin tone and yellow belly. The top of the head and area around the eye carry faint black patches, and the sides, dorsal fin on the back, and tail fin are sparsely spotted with black. The Pecos gambusia has a wide, upturned mouth with a projecting lower jaw and teeth in both jaws for holding prey. The base of the inside of the mouth contains comblike pharyngeal teeth to fur-

ther process food items. In most respects, the male and female of the species are very similar, but the male sex organ, the gonopodium, is clearly visible on the belly as a modification of the anal fin. In the female, the anal fin remains unmodified in its shorter, flat, and rounded shape. Additionally, during the breeding season the female has a prominent spotted genital pore (a visible target for the male's gonopodium) and the belly of the female becomes distended and bulbous during pregnancy.

Sexually mature Pecos gambusia engage in a specific pattern of courtship behavior before mating occurs. However, given the problem of cross-breeding between Pecos gambusia and mosquitofish, the courtship "dance" is not always specific enough to prevent mating with other species. When a successful mating does occur during the spring and summer months, about 40 young are born after an internal incubation period of several weeks. This number of young is significantly less than the 200 offspring that a female mosquitofish is capable of producing and may partially explain the Pecos gambusia's lack of competitive success.

The favorite foods of this species are mosquito larvae and adults and other water bugs such as the water boatman.

It is hoped, at least within the confines of the wildlife refuge, that the Pecos gambusia will be safe from any intentional or accidental introductions of competitors such as mosquitofish, and from damage to their habitat by people.

William E. Manci

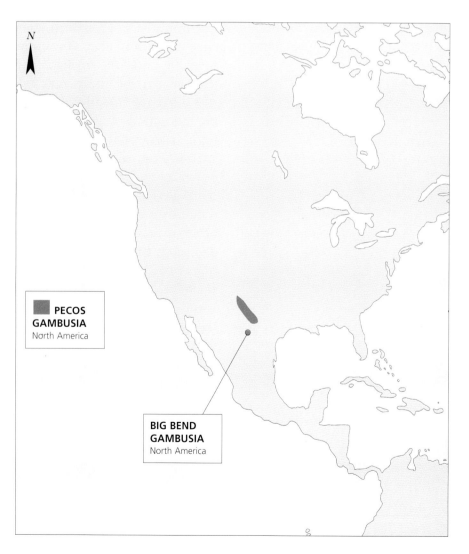

N

PECOS GAMBUSIA
North America

BIG BEND GAMBUSIA
North America

Gaur
(Bos frontalis)

IUCN: Vulnerable

Class: Mammalia
Order: Artiodactyla
Family: Bovidae
Subfamily: Bovinae
Tribe: Bovini
Weight: 1,540–2,200 lb.
(700–1,000 kg)
Shoulder height: 67–79 in.
(170–200 cm)
Diet: Grasses, leaves, shoots,
and twigs
Gestation period: 270 days
Longevity: 20 years
Habitat: Tropical and deciduous
forest
Range: India, Nepal, Bhutan,
Bangladesh, Southeast Asia,
southern China, Malay
Peninsula

THE GAUR IS THE LARGEST of the wild cattle. It is a relatively shy, retiring animal in the forest. It has a wide distribution from Sri Lanka to the Malay Peninsula. Within these areas it was once quite numerous. The main problem for the gaur is that its forest habitat is disappearing rapidly.

The gaur has been poached for its meat and hide and killed for raiding crops. In the more remote areas of its range the gaur persists in the wild, but most are found in protected game parks, and even there poaching still goes on.

Although known as the Indian bison, the gaur is not a bison; it is variously called the *fladang*, *seladange*, and *mitham*.

For all its size and bulk, the gaur has small hooves, but it has surprising strength and agility for so massive an animal. The gaur has been known to leap over six-foot (1.8-meter) barriers from a standing start.

The gaur has pale gray eyes that have been described as sinister looking—quite different from those of any other member of the cattle family.

The gaur has a purplish black hide with whitish stockings on all four legs and a light cast to the tail. The long curving horns have a greenish yellow look, with a buff patch in between.

This bovine is very shy in the wild. It is occasionally preyed upon by tigers, the young being the most likely target, but a tiger will generally avoid an adult gaur. The gaur browses and grazes on grasses and bamboo, twigs, and on the bark of trees.

Young bulls sometimes gather together, but old bulls are virtually solitary. Females, however, are quite social and are almost always found in groups. Unless wounded, the gaur in the wild is not dangerous to humans. If its status does not improve, the gaur's last frontier will be in protected reserves. Fortunately, there is a healthy self-sustaining captive population in Europe and North America.

Warren D. Thomas

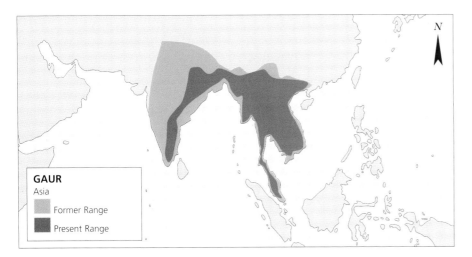

GAUR
Asia

Former Range

Present Range

GAZELLES

Class: Mammalia

Order: Artiodactyla

Family: Bovidae

Subfamily: Antelopinae

Tribe: Antelopini

Gazelles inhabit open grasslands and semidesert. They are extremely well adapted to harsh environments and tolerate extreme temperatures. Some of them can go for long periods of time without drinking water; some can even spend their entire lives without drinking water but they will drink it if it is available

Both the males and females are armed with horns, although the females' horns tend to be brittle, so it is not uncommon to see them broken off. The males are often territorial, but in some cases gazelles act like nomads.

Gazelles depend on excellent eyesight and a keen sense of smell to detect danger. Their hearing is not as acute as some other antelopes, but in the great open spaces where they live, eyesight is more important.

Many gazelles have something called preorbital glands, which emit secretions that they use to mark their territory. They also mark their territory with scratch marks, dung, and urine. In some areas where there is sparse rainfall, the reproductive cycle is actually attuned to the seasonal coming of the rain.

Because they have adapted to their environment, if they had no predators, they could become the most successful hoofed animals in Africa and the Middle East, with the risk of over-population and overgrazing. However, a wide variety of animals prey on gazelles, and baby gazelles are taken by almost any species that can carry them away. Even though females defend their offspring, a persistent jackal or hyena can easily take their young.

Arabian Sand Gazelle

(Gazella subgutturosa marica)

ESA: Endangered

IUCN: Vulnerable

Weight: 55–99 lb. (25–45 kg)

Shoulder height: 24–32 in. (60–80 cm)

Diet: Grass, leaves, and twigs

Gestation period: 165–180 days

Longevity: 10–12 years

Habitat: Semidesert and desert

Range: Middle East

THE ARABIAN SAND Gazelle, part of a larger group, which is known as the Persian or goitered gazelle, ranges throughout the Arabian peninsula into eastern Jordan, Kuwait, and Iraq.

This gazelle derives its scientific name from an enlarged Adam's apple, which gives the appearance of having a goiter.

The Arabian sand gazelle prefers a semidesert with occasional shrubs to a complete desert habitat. It is most active at twilight, feeding on any available vegetation. This gazelle lives in small herds, migrating during the winter when it can be found in larger numbers. The most common predator of this gazelle used to be the Arabian wolf, but this predator has been reduced to insignificant numbers. Today the biggest danger to the gazelle is poaching, which is performed with the help of modern motor vehicles. Overgrazing by domestic livestock has also ruined much of the sand gazelle's feeding habitat.

Cuvier's (Edmi) Gazelle

(Gazella cuvieri)

ESA: Endangered

IUCN: Endangered

Weight: 33–77 lb. (15–35 kg)

Shoulder height: 23½–31½ in. (60–80 cm)

Diet: Grass, leaves, and twigs

Gestation period: 165–180 days

Longevity: 10–12 years

Habitat: Dry forest and mountainous desert

Range: Algeria, Morocco, Tunisia

THIS SMALL GAZELLE was formerly found over much of northern Africa, but it is now restricted to small pockets. Cuvier's gazelle is the only true mountain-dwelling gazelle in Africa, where it is generally found in a variety of habitats, from open oak forests to stony desert.

The gazelle migrates in winter time, but within a limited range. This gazelle's decline has been primarily due to hunting by local people for its skin and meat. Cuvier's gazelle has succumbed to these hunting pressures and become more vulnerable.

Larger and heavier than the dorcas gazelle, the horns of the adult Cuvier's gazelle can reach up to 14 inches (35.5 centimeters) in length and are upright and parallel to each other. The color of the coat is dark fawn, and a dark brown lateral band is displayed.

There is a group of Cuvier's gazelles kept in captivity (approximately 100 in North America) that has been fairly successful. Some Cuvier's gazelles have been kept in Spain, others in private herds on the Arabian peninsula.

The Arabian sand gazelle ranges throughout the Arabian peninsula into eastern Jordan, Kuwait, and Iraq. Recent destruction of habitat in those areas, which have been stricken by war for years, has hurt native wildlife.

Captive management of these gazelles is fairly simple, and their reproduction rate is relatively high. The biggest problem is that few Cuvier's gazelles have been added to the captive population (80–100); therefore, the gene pool is narrow because it is not being infused with new genes to better increase the chances of producing healthy offspring. This can cause the captive group to deteriorate and decline in health over many generations.

Today there are estimated to be only about 1,000 Cuvier's gazelles remaining in the wild.

Dama Gazelle
(Gazella dama)

IUCN: Endangered

Weight: 88–187 lb. (40–85 kg)
Shoulder height: 33½–47 in. (85–120 cm)
Diet: Grass, leaves, and twigs
Gestation period: 165–180 days
Longevity: 10–12 years in captivity
Habitat: Semidesert and desert
Range: Sahara Desert

THE DAMA GAZELLE is a large gazelle, standing nearly 4 feet (1.2 meters) at the shoulder. Several subspecies of dama gazelle have been identified, primarily based on variation in color from nearly pure white to dark brown, depending upon their specific range. The taxonomy is further confused by the lack of specimens—many of the subspecies once described are now extinct.

The dama gazelle's present distribution is in fragmented populations throughout the Sahara region. Its habitat is primarily stony desert to semidesert areas with scrub brush. It lives either singularly or in small groups, and is active both at twilight and in the daytime.

Habitat destruction, hunting, and competition for food from domestic grazing livestock have reduced the numbers of dama gazelles in the wild to less than approximately 2,500.

In the rainy season—which is very limited—the dama gazelle migrates into the Sahara, returning to the brushy desert in the dry season. Like other gazelles, it is able to survive for long periods

of time without drinking water; however, it obtains enough moisture for its needs through its food. Even early morning dew offers water for its use.

One group of dama gazelles in captivity has done well. There is a strong self-sustaining population of one of the subspecies, *G. dama ruficollis*, that was taken from the nation of Chad. In recent years a small group of mhorr gazelles (*G. dama mhorr*) were captured and taken to Spain, then transplanted to several European and North American zoos. These gazelles are somewhat inbred because of

Captive populations of the Cuvier's gazelle are known to do well, but few new specimens have been added to breeding projects, resulting in a narrow gene pool. This lessens the chances of producing healthy offspring, which leads to decline of the species over generations. To create a healthy species, diversity is needed.

the limited number captured. Where all the other dama gazelles are basically white with some red on their neck, the mhorr gazelle is a very dark-colored animal with white underparts and a white patch on its neck.

The dama gazelle once lived in southwestern Morocco, where it became endangered. Its continued existence in the wild is now open to question.

Some 400 *G. dama ruficollis* were recorded in North American zoos and ranches; while less than 150 *G. dama mhorr* are in captivity. Unfortunately, not all the subspecies are represented in the captive state.

There is no reason to believe, however, that these subspecies would not fare just as successfully as their relatives have managed to do in a captive breeding program.

Dorcas Gazelle
(Gazella dorcas)

IUCN: Lower risk

Weight: 33–44 lb. (15–20 kg)
Shoulder height: 20–25½ in. (50–65 cm)
Diet: Grass, leaves, and twigs
Gestation period: 170–180 days
Longevity: 10–14 years
Habitat: Semidesert and desert
Range: Northern Africa

THE DORCAS GAZELLE is the most common gazelle of the Sahara and Middle East. Its population has been reduced to relatively small numbers because of competition from domestic animals and hunters. Once it was commonly hunted on horseback, but

The dama gazelle of Africa is one species that has done particularly well in captive breeding projects to produce a healthy population.

the introduction of motor vehicles and firearms led to greater problems. It is estimated that some 50,000 remain in the wild in isolated pockets within its once-broad range.

In its habits the dorcas gazelle is very much like the dama gazelle (*Gazella dama*), and it is found in similar habitats: stony desert or semidesert regions of grass and bush. When it rains, it migrates into the desert and returns in the dry season.

The dorcas gazelle has a short gestation period and the survivability of its young is good. There is also a captive population producing what are probably hybrids composed of subspecies found in Tunisia and Sudan. But the

future is poor. Without habitat preservation, hunting restrictions, and reduced competition from livestock, little can be done to improve the remaining numbers of dorcas.

One severe case is the Saudi gazelle (*Gazella saudiya*). Once considered a subspecies of *Gazella dorcas*, it is now classified as a separate species.

The Saudi gazelle is apparently extinct in the wild, and probably less than 50 individuals exist in captivity. There is some hope that they can be reintroduced into the wild.

Mountain Gazelle
(Gazella gazella)

ESA: Endangered

IUCN: Lower risk

Weight: 44–77 lb. (20–35 kg)
Shoulder height: 23½–31½ in. (60–80 cm)
Diet: Grass, leaves, and twigs
Gestation period: 165 days
Longevity: 10–12 years
Habitat Desert
Range: Middle East

THE MOUNTAIN GAZELLE once had a wide range that incorporated much of the Middle East and the Arabian peninsula but has now been reduced to small pockets in Saudi Arabia, Oman, and Yemen. There is a protected population in Israel of 9,000 to 10,000—the single largest group of mountain gazelle anywhere. Mountain gazelles are also found on some of the adjacent Farsan

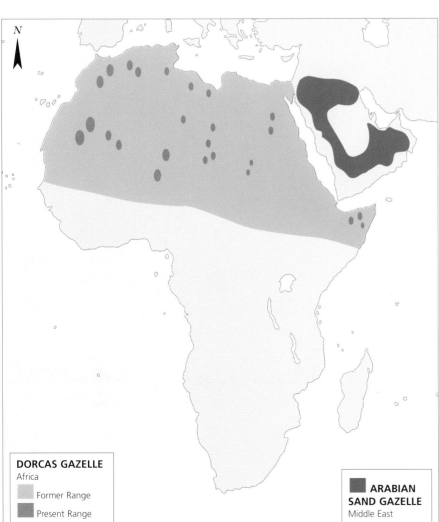

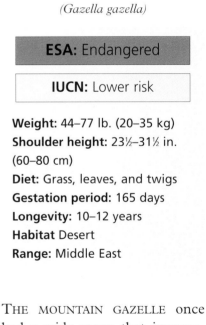

DORCAS GAZELLE
Africa

Former Range

Present Range

ARABIAN SAND GAZELLE
Middle East

Islands in the Red Sea. Most are found in groups of 50 to 500 individuals.

Conservation dependent

This gazelle is dependent on conservation for its survival, although there is no substantial captive population that will support the rebuilding of a wild population.

Although the gazelles are protected over part of their range, competition, destruction of habitat, and hunting continue to reduce their numbers. In the wild this species is endangered and is still on the decline.

Red-fronted Gazelle

(Gazella rufifrons)

IUCN: Vulnerable

Weight: 44–77 lb. (20–35 kg)
Shoulder height: 25½–35½ in. (65–90 cm)
Diet: Grass, leaves, and twigs
Gestation period: About 180 days
Longevity: 10–12 years
Habitat: Mixed woods and grassland to semidesert and desert
Range: Senegal to Ethiopia

THE RED-FRONTED GAZELLE has a typical gazelle body form and the characteristic pale fawn coloration, but it gets its name from a russet patch that can be seen on its forehead.

It is a small gazelle, once found from Senegal through Ethiopia but now gathered in small patches of its former range.

However, it can still be found in more substantial numbers in Chad. The western branch of the red-fronted gazelle, however, is now drastically reduced to small isolated groups.

All red-fronted gazelles are threatened by a variety of factors. Hunting pressure and destruction of their habitat by the overgrazing of domestic animals are common problems.

Adding to their woes are catastrophic droughts that have affected this region for many years. Even though the red-fronted gazelles are adjusted to living in extremely dry areas, the drought has taken its toll because humans have had to take their domestic animals farther to forage, thus encroaching on the gazelle's grazing land. This change has been disastrous for the population of gazelles.

There is a tiny captive population of red-fronted gazelles existing primarily in private collections on the Arabian peninsula, but this group is not yet large enough to act as a secure reservoir to back up the wild population.

The red-fronted gazelle probably numbers no more than 20,000 in the wild.

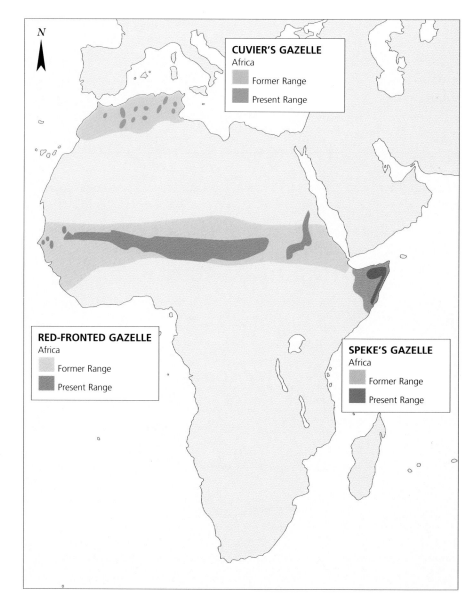

N

CUVIER'S GAZELLE
Africa
Former Range
Present Range

RED-FRONTED GAZELLE
Africa
Former Range
Present Range

SPEKE'S GAZELLE
Africa
Former Range
Present Range

Slender-horned Gazelle

(Gazella leptoceros)

ESA: Endangered

IUCN: Endangered

Weight: 44–66 lb. (20–30 kg)
Shoulder height: 25½–29½ in. (65–75 cm)
Diet: Grass, leaves, and twigs
Gestation period: 156–169 days
Longevity: 12–14 years
Habitat: Semidesert and desert
Range: Niger, Algeria, Libya, Egypt; possibly Sudan and Chad

THE SLENDER-HORNED gazelle is a medium-sized, delicately built animal. It is overall a light fawn color, which allows it to blend with its background very well. It has white markings on its rump and abdomen, some on the lower neck, and white flashings on the face.

As its common name implies, both males and females have long, slender horns. This species is also known by the names rhim gazelle and Loder's gazelle. Little is known about this animal in the wild because it has virtually not been studied.

It is known, however, that the slender-horned gazelle once roamed a large range encompassing most of the Sahara. Today this range has been reduced to small pockets. A small group of these gazelles was imported to Florida many years ago, but they did not thrive until they were moved to the San Diego Zoo's Wild Animal Park. There they have flourished.

Strong gene pool

Today there is a sizable herd living in the Wild Animal Park, and another herd is located at the Living Desert Museum in Palm Desert, California. These herds are important for the survival of the species, because there are thought to be fewer than 2,500 of these gazelles left in the wild.

To ensure the maintenance of a healthy captive population, more individuals are needed to increase the number of mating animals. This keeps the gene pool diverse and strong.

Soemmerring's Gazelle

(Gazella soemmerringii)

IUCN: Vulnerable

Weight: 66–132 lb. (30–60 kg)
Shoulder height: 29½–36 in. (75–92 cm)
Diet: Grass, leaves, twigs
Gestation period: 185–200 days
Longevity: 12–14 years
Habitat: Desert and semidesert
Range: Sudan, Ethiopia, Somalia, Djibouti, Kenya

SOEMMERRING'S GAZELLE is found primarily in the region known as the Horn of Africa, where the northeastern portion of the continent curves up underneath the Arabian peninsula. This is a fairly large gazelle, weighing up to 132 pounds (60 kilograms) and standing as high as three feet (0.9 meter) at the shoulder.

Widespread species

This species is the most numerous of the gazelle species in Somalia and much of Ethiopia, taking the place of the common Grant's gazelle and Thompson's gazelle. Its markings and body size are similar to those of Grant's gazelle, but its horns are not nearly as large and have strongly curved points. Its frontal appearance is significantly different from Grant's gazelle.

The glands that both male and female gazelles use for marking their territory are smaller in

Little is known about the habits of the slender-horned gazelle but it appears to travel in small groups, in the same way as many other species.

Soemmerring's gazelle, and this species does in fact mark its territory less than do other species. This gazelle will associate with oryx, hartebeeste, and even domestic camel.

Soemmerring's gazelle has experienced the usual problems of such species in northern Africa: it has been heavily poached in many of the areas where once it was numerous, and drought and domesticated livestock have reduced the size and quality of its habitat. The number of Soemmerring's gazelle left in the wild is near 10,000, few of which are in protected areas.

The soft golden color of the Soemmerring's gazelle helps to camouflage it among the brush from possible predators. Poaching and various encroachments on the gazelle's habitat have caused its decline.

Only a handful live in captivity—perhaps 40 in North America. This gazelle does migrate somewhat, stimulated by the seasonal rains. Births tend to take place in April and May, suggesting that breeding takes place during the light rains of fall.

There is an isolated group of gazelles that occurs on Kebur Island in Ethiopia's Dahlac Archipelago. These animals were isolated for so long from the rest of their species that they have become a dwarf form of the Soemmerring's gazelle (*Gazella soemmerringi berberana*).

Very little is known about this subspecies, although from the few descriptions that are available its habits seem to be the same as those of the larger mainland Soemmerring's gazelle, but modified to an island existence.

Speke's Gazelle
(Gazella spekei)

IUCN: Vulnerable

Weight: 33–55 lb. (15–25 kg)
Shoulder height: 20–23½ in. (50–60 cm)
Diet: Grass, leaves, and twigs
Gestation period: 195–210 days
Longevity: 10–12 years
Habitat: Semidesert and desert
Range: Northern Somalia

SPEKE'S GAZELLE is a small gazelle from the Horn of Africa, found primarily in the arid regions of northern Somalia with a few remnants in eastern Ethiopia. It prefers semi-arid bush and thorn bush, and its range extends even into pure

desert areas. Like most gazelles, the females usually collect in social groups, while the males are quite territorial.

Inflatable nose

The strangest feature of both males and females is that they have a large, inflatable area of skin along the bridge of the nose that inflates like a balloon when they get excited. This gives them a very bizarre appearance. The Speke's gazelle can combine this feature with a deep guttural tone, making for a unique display among gazelles.

Unfortunately, because of hunting and overgrazing, plus a devastating drought in their habitat, the number of Speke's gazelles has dropped alarmingly. Even worse, civil war has raged through this area for years, causing the numbers of Speke's gazelles to drop even further.

As with all species, the smaller the range, the more vulnerable the population.

New blood needed

The Speke's gazelle has come into captivity only a few times. In each case they bred well and, given proper management, they have done reasonably well. The most successful efforts so far in North America have taken place at the St. Louis Zoo, but managing these animals in captivity is not easy. Each gazelle has to be placed in an area with a fair

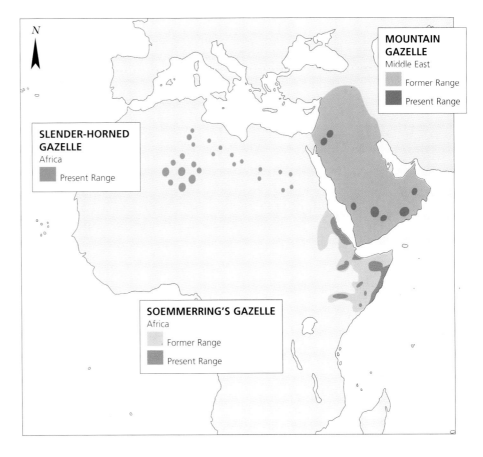

SLENDER-HORNED GAZELLE
Africa
Present Range

MOUNTAIN GAZELLE
Middle East
Former Range
Present Range

SOEMMERRING'S GAZELLE
Africa
Former Range
Present Range

amount of cover and protection. As positive as some of these efforts have been, the entire North American population in the early 1990s was less than 40 and represents a group bred from only one male and three females. This means the gene pool is too small and needs to be expanded if the Speke's gazelle is to continue breeding healthy stock. Fortunately, there are some gazelles from the Arabian peninsula that are kept in private collections, and a handful were recently sent to North America to help improve the stock.

Warren D. Thomas

The Speke's gazelle lives in the Horn of Africa in arid regions of Somalia and in eastern Ethiopia. The distinctive feature of this gazelle is an inflatable nasal region. It gives a loud sneeze, which is thought to be an alarm call. The sound is made by inflating and emptying the nasal sac.

GECKOS

Class: Reptilia

Order: Squamata

Suborder: Sauria

Families: Gekkonidae,

Geckos are the most primitive of all lizards. They are found on all major landmasses of the world and on many islands. Most geckos are small, about 6 inches (15 centimeters) long or less, and drab in color. However, a few larger species are big enough to feed on small birds and mammals, and some diurnal species are beautifully colored.

Most species are nocturnal and have eyes with vertical, slitlike pupils that can be expanded to accommodate darkness and let in more light. Most do not have movable eyelids, but instead have a clear scale, or spectacle, over their eyes to protect them. The voice of the gecko is one of its most unique features. It has the ability to vocalize more than most other lizards, usually in the form of chirps or squeaks, to defend themselves. Males also use the voice to establish dominance of a particular area or to attract females.

Geckos live on rocky outcrops or in trees. They are superb climbers, and many species have small toe pads made up of tiny hairlike scales that enable them to climb vertically or upside down. Geckos tend to lay their eggs in rock crevices or under bark, and almost all species lay a clutch of two eggs.

Geckos have some economic value to humanity because they feed on insects and spiders; some larger ones even eat young mice. Hence, the gecko has recently become a popular pet, commonly invited into the home to provide pest control for homeowners. Generally, the gecko species found in pet stores is the Tokay gecko (*Gekko gecko*) of Southeast Asia, often considered the largest known gecko. Another species, *Rhacodactylus leachianus*, may be bigger.

Several species of gecko are listed by the IUCN at this time: Gunther's gecko (*Phelsuma guentheri*) of Mauritius, Monito gecko (*Sphaerodactylus micropithecus*) of Isla Monito in the West Indies, and *Nephrurus deteani* of Australia are all endangered. The Paraguanan ground gecko (*Lepidoblepharis montecanoensis*) of Venezuela is listed as critically endangered. Rodrigues day gecko (*Phelsuma edward-newtonii*) of Mauritius, has not been seen for many years despite extensive searches, and is now listed as extinct. *Hopladactylus delcourti* of New Zealand is also extinct. Several other species of gecko are listed as vulnerable. Habitat protection will make the main difference to the survival of these geckos and prevent their slide into extinction.

Monito Gecko

(Sphaerodactylus micropithecus)

ESA: Endangered

IUCN: Endangered

Length: ½–1½ in. (17–26 mm)

Clutch size: Probably 2 eggs

Diet: Unknown

Habitat: Rocky areas

Range: Isla Monito in the West Indies

THE MONITO GECKO is endemic to tiny Isla Monito, which is halfway between Puerto Rico and the Dominican Republic.

Most plant life on the island is xeric, meaning it can survive without much water. Although little is known about the specific habitat preferences of the Monito gecko, it has been collected at sites described as rocky and open to the sun with little cover. This gecko is most commonly reported on the edges of the island, but individuals have been found on the interior of the southeast of the island.

There is no information about the specific diet of the Monito gecko, but it is probably similar to that of other geckos, consisting mostly of insects that are easy for it to catch given its small size. Little information is available about its breeding habits either, but observations suggest that reproduction occurs between March and November and is probably synchronized with climate changes.

As with many island species that have become endangered, the introduction of exotic, non-native species may have played a role in the gecko's decline.

Unknown population

Population levels of the Monito gecko are unknown. The species was first described in 1977, and although field surveys have been carried out since that time, they cannot be considered to give an accurate estimate. A total of 24 individuals were reported and six are preserved in museums.

Scientists looked for the geckos under debris spread across the island, but a number of small crevices that are inaccessible to human beings could well provide shelter to these geckos.

Reasons for decline

Because so little is known about the historical population trends and the ecologic requirements of the gecko, it is impossible to know the precise reason for its decline. Predation and habitat

MONITO GECKO
Monito Island

destruction have certainly reduced its numbers, but no observations have been reported. Monito Island is now protected, but after World War II it was used as a bombing range by U.S. military forces. Scattered debris suggests there has been significant habitat destruction. The Monito gecko is listed by biolo-

gists as an endangered species. Isla Monito is designated as its critical habitat, and because visits to it are not permitted, there is little threat of human interference. Because of the isolation of this island, there is a good chance that the gecko will be able to rebuild its population.

Elizabeth Sirimarco

GEESE

Class: Aves

Order: Anseriformes

Family: Anatidae

Subfamily: Anserinae

Tribe: Anserini

Geese winging across the sky in great, noisy skeins herald the changing of the seasons. They contribute significantly to the deep emotions people feel as autumn slips into winter and winter yields to spring. Their parental devotion to offspring and dedication to their mates kindle a special affinity between humans and geese.

Geese join swans and ducks to make up the large bird family known to wildlife managers as waterfowl. Despite the obvious differences among the various groups—for example, between a

swan and a teal—ornithologists have traditionally regarded their similarities as a compelling reason to classify all 147 species as one family. That family was then categorized into three subfamilies with several tribes. A reclassification scheme recognizes the whistling ducks as a discrete family (Dendrocygnidae), the magpie goose (*Anseranas semipalmata*) as a family by itself (Anseranatidae), and the remaining ducks, geese, and swans as a family (Anatidae) with several subfamilies. This system has not yet been widely accepted by ornithologists.

Geese are smaller than swans but generally larger than ducks and less aquatic than either. Many geese browse green plants on dry lands far from water. Typically, geese have deeper, more conical beaks than ducks. On some goose species, the beak extends onto the forehead and

may be knobbed. Geese and ducks also differ behaviorally. Ducks usually mate briefly, and the females are known to do all the rearing of offspring. Family groups soon disperse when the ducklings are grown. Geese mate for years, both parents tend the young, and family groups may remain together for years.

Many waterfowl species occur in reduced numbers. Less habitat is available to some species and more habitat available to others. Many goose species have experienced population declines on a regional basis, but their overall species populations remain high enough that they are not considered to be under any great threat. Two notable exceptions to this are the threatened Aleutian Canada goose (*Branta canadensis leucopareia*) and the endangered Hawaiian goose (*Branta sandvicensis*), discussed here.

Aleutian Canada Goose

(Branta canadensis leucopareia)

ESA: Threatened

Length: 22–43 in. (55.8–109.2 cm)

Weight: 3½–4½ lb. (1.6–2 kg)

Clutch size: Usually 6 eggs

Incubation: 28 days

Diet: Aquatic plants, grain, insects, crustaceans

Habitat: Meadows and marshes

Range: Breeds in the Aleutian Islands and winters in northwestern United States; rare in Japan

PUTTING FOXES on Alaskan islands seemed like a good idea to the people who trapped foxes for their fur, but the shuffling of wildlife nearly drove the Aleutian Canada goose into extinction.

One of 11 Canada goose subspecies, the Aleutian Canada goose looks like all the other Canada geese. It has a grayish brown body plumage, black neck and head, with a white strap running from cheek to cheek under the chin. A white "V" separates rump from blackish tail. The beak and feet are also black. Besides its small size, the Aleutian subspecies is distinguished from other subspecies by a white collar separating the black neck and grayish breast. This collar is not always well developed, and at least one other small subspecies shows a white neck ring. Aleutians are best recognized by their presence on their breeding grounds in the Aleutian Islands.

They once bred on many of the Aleutians but are now restricted to the far western islands of Buldir, Chagulak, Agattu, Nizki, and Amchitka. These islands are so remote that very little research has been done on the Aleutian Canada goose subspecies. Other subspecies that breed on the North American continent have been very thoroughly studied. Ornithologists do know that the Aleutian geese usually breed away from the coast on islands. They find marshes and meadows, where they build their nests. Pairs often nest in the same general area year

The Aleutian Canada goose is one of 11 subspecies of the Canada goose and has a similar appearance to its relatives. The release of foxes on the Aleutian Islands played a major role in the decline of the species.

after year. Like all waterfowl, the goslings hatch with a full coat of thick down. Their eyes are open, and they can walk and swim within an hour or so after hatching. For tens of thousands of years, the greatest threat to the goslings always came from the sky. Jaegers (*Stercorarius*) and gulls (*Larus*) steal eggs and snatch goslings.

In the nineteenth century, conditions changed for the Aleutian geese, when humans altered the balance.

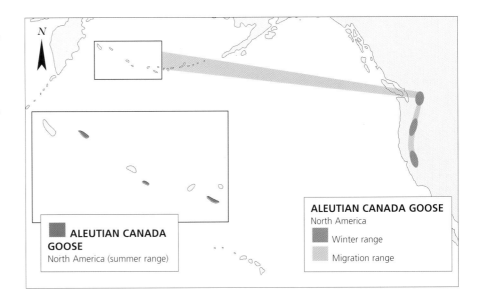

ALEUTIAN CANADA GOOSE
North America (summer range)

ALEUTIAN CANADA GOOSE
North America

Winter range

Migration range

Exotic introduction

During the 1830s, the Russian-American Company caught arctic foxes (*Alopex lagopus*) and released them on many Aleutian Islands. The Russian-American Company was in the business of procuring furs, so they usually trapped animals to kill them. The idea of catching and releasing the foxes was to establish fox populations in areas that had no native foxes. This would increase the total arctic fox population and improve the profits of trapping. Unfortunately, the only way for the foxes to survive was by preying on wildlife species that naturally occurred on the islands. Many islands supported no arctic hare (*Lepus timidus*), rodent, or shrew populations, so the foxes preyed on the birds. Goose eggs and goslings became such easy targets for hungry foxes that the geese disappeared.

Change in priorities

Eventually, fox populations grew so large that the Aleutian Canada geese suffered complete nesting failure. Island by island, the geese completely vanished. Either foxes were not released on all the

islands or else they did not survive on some islands. On the few islands without arctic foxes, the Aleutian Canada goose survived. In 1867 the United States bought Alaska from Russia, and conditions began to change. Alaska became the union's forty-ninth state in 1959. The Aleutian chain was designated the Aleutian Islands National Wildlife Refuge, and recovering the Aleutian Canada goose assumed greater importance than perpetuating arctic foxes.

Efforts in captivity

The U.S. Fish and Wildlife Service (U.S.F.W.S.) began raising Aleutian geese in captivity while simultaneously working to eradicate foxes from some islands. In 1965 the foxes were finally eliminated from Amchitka and not long afterwards from Agattu. Buldir Island may never have had arctic foxes, or if it did, they died out. In 1982 it harbored 300 breeding pairs of Aleutian Canada geese, by far the largest breeding population anywhere. The captive breeding program yielded less than satisfactory results, so it was discontinued. All

the captive birds were released on Agattu in 1982, and some of the birds were confirmed returning to the island five years later.

For establishing goose flocks on other islands, the USFWS now traps and moves wild birds with at least equal but usually better results than with the captive-reared geese.

Migration

Aleutian Canada geese migrate east and south rather than trying to endure the hostile winters on the Aleutian Islands. Some of the birds move no farther than British Columbia although most move as far south as northern California. In 1981, observers recorded 2,700 Aleutian geese in California, approximately three times the total seen in 1975.

The species would seem to be recovering, but now may not be the time to relax the vigil. Norway rats (*Rattus sp.*) have been found on some of the Aleutian Islands. They may eventually prove as disastrous as the arctic foxes if they can survive the winters. For now, though, the Aleutian Canada goose appears to be on the road to recovery. In

---

July of 1999 the Interior Department announced the good news of its intention to remove the Aleution Canada Goose from the endangered species list, pending a period of public comment. The goose's victory might well be that it managed to outlive the Russian-American Company.

Hawaiian Goose
(Branta sandvicensis)

ESA: Endangered

IUCN: Vulnerable

Length: 22–40 in. (56–102 cm)
Weight: Males to 5 lb. (2.25 kg); females to 4½ lb. (1.9 kg)
Clutch size: 1–6 eggs, usually 4
Incubation: 30 days
Diet: Green vegetation, small fruits
Habitat: Higher mountain slopes where ground is rocky and sparsely vegetated; does not associate with water as much as other geese
Range: Hawaii and Maui of the Hawaiian Islands in the Pacific Ocean

EVERY TERRIBLE CONDITION that can befall a bird did befall the Hawaiian goose. The consequence was near extinction, which has not been absolutely overcome despite a half century of dedicated effort.

Geese have long been hunted as game, and until laws were developed to protect them, the Hawaiian goose was killed without control. The goose was declining as early as 1778, when James Cook found the islands.

The Hawaiian goose only vaguely resembles the Canada goose. Its entire torso is silvery gray, more blue on the back, with a faintly browner breast and belly. Light feather edges give the wings and back a scaled or scalloped look. Dark feather tips make the sides and belly appear barred. The chin, front half of the cheek, around the eye, the entire crown, and upper nape are a deep chocolate brown. The back half of the cheek is buff, fading to a black-and-white streaked throat and neck. It is a distinctive goose found nowhere else but Hawaii.

Open season
At first the bird was hunted without restraint. When game laws were devised and applied, the hunting season was open during the goose's nesting period. Eggs

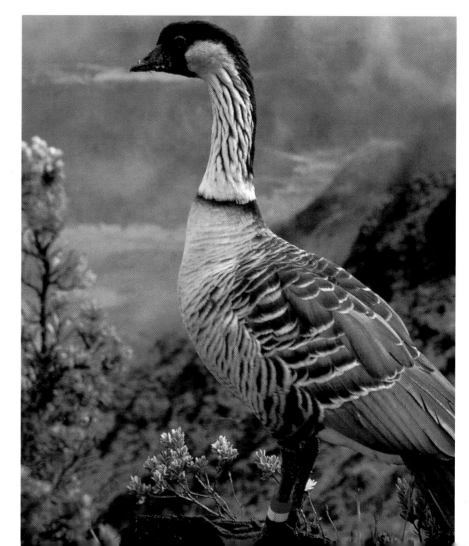

were collected and live birds were trapped for sale. The Hawaiian goose's primary feeding grounds were opened to livestock grazing. People who combed the mountain slopes to cut sandalwood often flushed birds from their nests. Housing developments and road construction eliminated some habitat. What habitat was left became a nightmare of exotic plants and mammals. The exotic plants out-competed and displaced the native plants and consequently diminished the goose's food supply. Livestock escaped so that domestic pigs (*Sus scrofa*), goats (*Capra sp.*), sheep (*Ovis sp.*), cattle (*Bos sp.*), horses (*Equus caballus*), and burros (*Equus asinus*) wandered freely over the landscape. Goats and sheep grazed the same food plants upon which the goose fed. Pigs

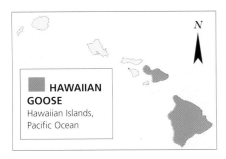

HAWAIIAN GOOSE
Hawaiian Islands,
Pacific Ocean

found nests and ate goose eggs and goslings.

Other exotic mammals included Polynesian rats (*Rattus exulans*), black rats (*Rattus rattus*), cats (*Felis silvestris*), dogs (*Canis familiaris*), and Indian mongooses (*Herpestes auropunctatus*). The Polynesian rats were introduced to the islands either unintentionally by the first Polynesian settlers or deliberately as a food source. The black rats were almost unavoidable compatriots of European settlers. Dogs and cats came with Europeans as pets.

Mongoose predation
The mongooses were reportedly introduced to control the black rats. The plan was ill advised, because the rats are nocturnal and the mongooses diurnal, so the mongooses never posed any threat to the rats. More likely, the mongooses were imported by sailors who kept them as pets. The rats, cats, dogs, and mongooses found the Hawaiian goose easy prey. The eggs and goslings are vulnerable, and the adult geese go through a yearly molt when they lose all their flight feathers at once and cannot fly for several weeks, making them easy prey.

Less adaptable
Besides this problem, Hawaiian geese are not as adapted to water as are other waterfowl. Their feet have less webbing than the feet of other geese, and they are obviously suited for a more terrestrial lifestyle. They have smallish wings for their body size, so they are not powerful fliers.

All of these traits have combined with habitat destruction and degradation to wreak havoc on this species.

Shrinking population
About the time James Cook found the Hawaiian Islands in 1778, the Hawaiian goose was already declining on Maui, probably as a result of the Polynesian settlers. The total Hawaiian goose population probably numbered around 25,000 birds.

The populations on both islands began to shrink more rapidly after missionaries brought European and American culture to the islands in 1820.

The Maui population was defunct by 1890. As few as 30 wild birds survived by 1952.

Recovery plans
Hawaiian wildlife officials began raising Hawaiian geese in 1949. An aggressive international breeding program was coordinated by the Severn Wildfowl Trust in England in the 1950s. That organization raised Hawaiian geese and distributed them to other zoos and aviaries for captive breeding.

Captive flock
Having more than one captive flock of geese ensured that the species would not perish from a single disaster. By 1982 about 1,800 captive-raised Hawaiian geese had been released on Hawaii and Maui.

Despite the steady influx of released birds from captive sites, the wild population still fails to sustain itself beyond about 400 birds. Two wild flocks now live on Hawaii and a separate wild flock inhabits Maui.

Partial success
In 1972 the U.S. Fish and Wildlife Service built nest enclosures at Hawaii Volcanoes National Park. The wings of adult geese were clipped so they could not escape, and the wire fencing excluded predators. Native plants were replanted outside the enclosures so that young birds could be released to feed. The technique has enjoyed limited success. Only half of the adult birds breed in any single year, and gosling mortality is very high. Under such conditions, the population cannot be expected to grow very fast. The population estimate in 1989–1990 was 555 individuals, and populations have the potential to increase as long as inbreeding, disease, poor nutrition, and predation do not become problems.

Heading for the hills
In general, the Hawaiian geese today live on higher mountain slopes where human activity is not so intense. They live above 6,888 feet (2,100 meters) on Maui and above 4,920 feet (1,500 meters) on the island of Hawaii. They nest in *kipukas*, which are patches of plant life surrounded by lava fields. Unless more can be done to improve the quality of the goose's habitat by eliminating exotic mammals, controlling exotic plants, and preventing human disturbance, the Hawaiian goose may forever depend on human assistance.

Kevin Cook

GERANIUMS (CRANESBILLS)

Phylum: Anthophyta
(flowering plants)

Order: Magnoliopsida

Family: Geraniaceae

Genus: Geranium

Cranesbills, or the true geraniums, belong to the genus *Geranium*, whereas the shrubby potted houseplants that are popularly known as geraniums are correctly named pelargoniums (in the genus *Pelargonium*), which also belongs to the family Geraniaceae.

The name *cranesbill* refers to the fruit, which is long, straight, and pointed, rather like the bill of a crane. The name *geranium* derives from the Greek work *geranos*, which means "crane." There are about 300 species of true geraniums in temperate and montane tropical regions of the world.

In the Hawaiian Islands in the North Pacific Ocean, there is a special group of six geranium species that grow nowhere else and have been treated by some botanists as a separate genus (*Neurophylloides*). They all have shrubby growth and unlobed leaves, with the main veins running parallel along the blade. These plants are often extremely rare in the wild, known from only a few populations with very few individual plants.

Conservation measures are urgently needed to ensure that these species do not decline to extinction.

Hawaiian Red-flowered Geranium

(Geranium arboreum)

ESA: Endangered

IUCN: Endangered

Size: 6½–13 ft. (2–4 m) tall
Leaves: Oval, unlobed, veined, with a toothed margin
Flowers: Singly or in clusters of 4–5 petals, deep purple-red with darker veins, ¾–1 in. (2–2.5 cm) long
Pollination: By birds
Seeds: Pointed, 1½ in. (4 cm) long. Cells at base contain purple seeds, 2.5 mm long
Habitat: Gulches in subalpine shrub lands
Range: Slopes of Haleakala, eastern Maui, Hawaiian Islands

IT IS THOUGHT THERE ARE only about 300 wild plants of the Hawaiian red-flowered geranium in existence. This very rare and beautiful plant is endemic to the island of Maui in the Hawaiian Islands of the North Pacific Ocean, where it is known in the local language as *nohoanu* or *hinahina*. The term *endemic* means that it grows wild nowhere else in the world. The plant was listed by the U.S. Fish and Wildlife Service as an endangered species in 1992, and there is now an officially approved recovery plan.

Hawaiian red-flowered geranium is unique in the cranesbill genus in having zygomorphic flowers (meaning they are symmetrical in one plane only), in which the upper three petals stand erect while the lower two are curved backward. This is thought to be an adaptation to pollination by birds, as is the flower color. This zygomorphic flower shape is an almost universal characteristic in the related pelargoniums, the widely cultivated potted plants that are popularly (but incorrectly) called geraniums. The shrubby habit of the Hawaiian red-flowered geranium is a good example of how normally herbaceous plants tend to evolve into shrubby or treelike forms when isolated for millions of years on oceanic islands.

Haleakala mountain on the island of Maui includes Haleakala National Park, which preserves the outstanding volcanic landscape of the upper slopes of Haleakala and many rare and endangered plant and animal species. This park was originally part of Hawaii Volcanoes National Park, but was redesignated as a separate entity in 1961. The park was designated as an International Biosphere Reserve in 1980, and almost 70 percent of its 28,655 acres (11,466 hectares) are wilderness. Haleakala mountain is the dominating feature of the whole island

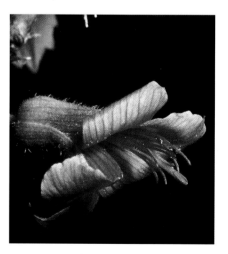

Red-flowered geranium (*Geranium arboreum*) is endemic to the Hawaiian Islands, where it is threatened by habitat destruction and collection.

Maui, rising to some 10,105 feet (3,080 meters) above sea level, but actually almost 26,250 feet (8,000 meters) high if measured from the ocean floor. These islands are really the summits of volcanoes rising from the abyssal depths. On the slopes of Haleakala mountain, there are conspicuous zones in the vegetation that are linked to the increasing altitude. Only the vegetation above 6,560 feet (2,000 meters) bears any likeness to what used to exist in the times before the European invasion of the Hawaiian Islands. Nowadays, pasture, planted forest, scrub of introduced lantana bushes (*Lantana camara*), and plantations have completely replaced whatever native vegetation once covered the lower two thirds of the slopes. Fortunately, though, the vegetation for most of the climb above 6,560 feet (2,000 meters) gives an excellent example of the high altitude shrub lands characteristic of the higher Hawaiian volcanoes. Hawaiian red-flowered geranium is now being conserved under the Maui Plant Cluster Recovery Plan. The plan deals with 20 endangered and one threatened plant species that currently grow (or used to grow) on the island of Maui, and in some cases on other Hawaiian islands too. The plants in the recovery plan are scattered around the island of Maui in various habitats, and twelve of them are endemic to the island.

Threats to Hawaiian red-flowered geranium include trampling, grazing, and habitat destruction by introduced livestock (such as cattle and pigs), trampling by humans along hiking trails, over-collection of

plants (mainly for scientific or horticultural reasons), destructive fires, insect pests, and plant diseases. The recovery plan details the life history, habitats, reasons for decline, and conservation efforts under way for each plant. Present and known historical ranges are also noted.

Critical plan
The goal of the plan is to be able to downlist the plants from endangered to threatened and eventually remove them from the protected species list altogether. In order for this to happen, the existing populations must be stabilized and their threats removed or limited so that they are able to reproduce and increase naturally in the wild.

Nohoanu
(Geranium multiflorum)

ESA: Endangered

IUCN: Vulnerable

Height: 3–6 ft. (1–2 m)
Leaves: Stalked, oval, unlobed, with 7–11 prominent veins
Flowers: Branching clusters of 25–50. Petals usually white with a purple base and veins, 10–15 mm long
Seeds: Pointed and beaklike, 15–20 mm long, with cells around the base containing dark reddish brown seeds, each about 2 mm long
Habitat: Montane grasslands, wet forests, shrub lands at 5,180–8,030 ft. (1,580–2,450 m)
Range: Maui, Hawaiian Islands

THE TOTAL WORLD population of nohoanu is thought to number only about 3,000 individual plants. This geranium is also endemic to Haleakala mountain on the Hawaiian island of Maui, where it is known by the same local Hawaiian names: *nohoanu* or *hinahina*. In some places it is known as many-flowered cranesbill. Like Hawaiian red-flowered geranium, the plant was listed by the U.S. Fish and Wildlife Service as an endangered species in 1992, and there is now an officially approved recovery plan for these plants.

Conservation plan
Like its red-flowered relative, nohoanu is currently being conserved under the Maui Plant Cluster Recovery Plan. The species face similar threats, including trampling, grazing, and habitat destruction by livestock, trampling by hikers, over-collection of plants by botanists and gardeners, fires, insects, and diseases. It is hoped that nohoanu will be downlisted by the U.S. Fish and Wildlife Service from endangered to threatened once its populations have stabilized and the plants are able to reproduce and increase effectively.

Nohoanu is probably pollinated by bees. Yellow-faced bees belonging to the genus *Nesoprosopis* have been seen visiting the flowers. Unlike the bird-pollinated Hawaiian red-flowered geranium, the flowers of this species are symmetrical in five planes, each plane corresponding to one of the five petals.

According to the IUCN 1997 Red List of Threatened Plants, the Hawaiian Islands have 623 globally threatened species, of

Many-flowered cranesbill (*Geranium multiflorum*) is threatened by habitat destruction, trampling, and collection.

which three are extinct, 99 are possibly extinct, 341 are endangered, 102 are vulnerable, 79 are rare, and 2 are indeterminate (insufficient details are known to assign a category). It is important to remember that the statistics are based on only the species that have been described for science over the past 250 years. They do not show how many unknown species became extinct before then.

Europeans arrived in the Hawaiian Islands at the end of the 1700s. People of the Polynesian culture first reached the islands in about C.E. 400. Archaeologists have discovered several species of animals that became extinct between this initial settlement and the arrival of Europeans, so one can only guess at how many plants became extinct during that same 1,400-year period. When the Polynesians first arrived, they brought with them water-control and slash-and-burn agricultural methods and introduced alien plants that they encouraged to grow in the islands' valleys. This type of land use caused erosion, altered the composition of native plant communities, and reduced the biodiversity in general.

Beginning with Captain James Cook in 1778, European explorers introduced livestock, which subsequently became feral, increased in numbers and range, and started to cause serious changes to the natural environment. These introduced mammals were, and still are, a major factor in altering and degrading natural vegetation and habitats. Feral livestock, such as cattle and pigs, trample and eat native vegetation and disturb and open up new areas. This causes erosion

NOHOANU
Hawaiian Islands

and allows the entry of aggressive alien plants. In addition, many slopes were stripped of native forests during the middle 1800s to supply firewood for whaling ships, plantations, and the residents of Honolulu; and sandalwood and tree ferns were also harvested in many areas, thereby changing the natural forest structure.

The provision for land sales to individuals in 1848 allowed large-scale farming and ranching to begin in Hawaii.

So much land was cleared for these ventures that the local climate began to alter and the quantity and distribution of rainfall were changed. Owners of plantations supported reforestation programs, with the aim of conserving the watershed, but these only resulted in many troublesome alien trees being introduced.

From the 1920s, systems for gathering and diverting water were built in upland areas in order to irrigate fields in the lowlands. These irrigation systems opened up new routes for the invasion of the native forests by alien plants and animals.

Of the four other shrubby endemic species of geranium or cranesbill on the Hawaiian Islands, three are endangered. They all share the local names: *nohoanu* or *hinahina*. The species are as follows: *G. cuneatum*, from Haleakala mountain, eastern Maui, and Hawaii; *G. hanaense*, from Hana Forest Reserve, eastern Maui (endangered); *G. humile*, also known as nohuanu, from western Maui (endangered); and *G. kauaiense*, from Kauai (endangered).

Nick Turland

GHARIALS

Class: Reptilia

Order: Crocodylia

As members of the order Crocodylia, the gharial has similar characteristics to alligators and crocodiles. One very different feature is a slender snout with a bulbous enlargement at the tip, especially on mature males. The body of the gharial is a light olive or tan above with faint markings. The belly is whitish or has a yellow tinge.

Gharials are found only in Asia. Like other crocodylia, the gharial likes to bask on river banks and to float in the water with only the tip of its snout and eyes above water.

These reptiles migrate to smaller rivers when the larger ones become flooded during the rainy season, but they are rarely seen in lakes or ponds.

The gharial and the false gharial should not be confused. Although they share a common name, they are members of different families. The gharial is usually classified as the only living member of its family (Gavialidae) in the order Crocodylia. However, the false gharial is more closely related to true crocodiles.

Gharial

(Gavialis gangeticus)

ESA: Endangered

IUCN: Endangered

Length: Males 23 ft. (7 m); females 14½ ft. (4.5 m)

Clutch size: 16–61 eggs

Diet: Fish

Habitat: Deep, fast-flowing rivers with high banks and deep pools

Range: Bangladesh, India, Nepal, and Pakistan

THE GHARIAL IS A large and slender-snouted crocodilian. Existing in clear, deep rivers with high banks, this reptile can also be found basking on undisturbed sandbanks at the river's edge. Two places that still maintain significant refuges for the gharial are the Chambal and Mahanadi Rivers in India. The Chambal has high banks. It also has numerous bends where depth exceeds 90 feet (27 meters). The remaining population in the Mahanadi river is concentrated in a slow-flowing gorge, which would normally not present the best habitat for the gharial. However, it does contain deep pools that offer the reptile an acceptable habitat. The gharial is thought to exist in relatively high populations in Himalaya-fed rivers that run from Nepal through India to the Ganges.

Two distinguishing features of the gharial are its long and very slender snout and the large number of slender teeth. These reptiles appear to feed almost exclusively on fish. A swimming fish is usually seized across the middle, then the gharial raises its snout out the water. With two or three snaps of the jaws, the prey is turned and swallowed head first. Occasionally the gharial is known to consume birds or even goats and dogs, but attacks on humans are virtually unheard of.

The gharial reaches sexual maturity at between 8 and 12 years when it has reached about 9 feet (2.7 meters) in length. The nesting season generally occurs from late March to mid-April. Nesting females excavate several "trial nests" the month before they begin laying eggs in the true nest. Nesting generally occurs only in sandbanks on the river's edge or in mid-river. There is a great deal of variation between clutch sizes among gharials. Different females produce different numbers of eggs, and the same gharial may have varying clutch sizes in any given year. The gharial's eggs are elliptical in shape and about 3⅓ to 3½ inches (8.5 to 9 centimeters) long and 2⅔ to 2¾ inches (6.5 to 7 centimeters)

This gharial (*Gavialis gangeticus*) shows the characteristic and distinctive, long, slender snout that ends with a pronounced bulbous tip.

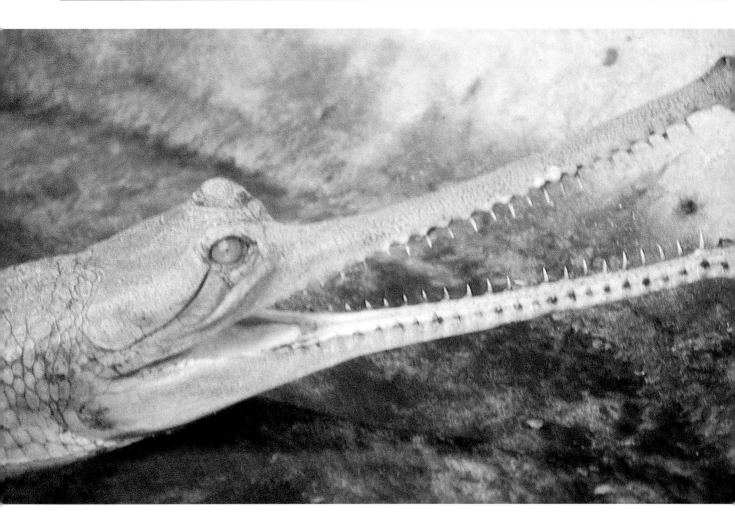

The long and slender snout of the gharial makes it an unusual looking member of the Crocodylia order. Notice the large, slender teeth.

wide. Incubation takes between 83 and 94 days, and the young measure 14¾ inches (37.5 centimeters) at hatching.

The female usually guards the nest site and attends the hatchlings for several months. For example, on Chambal River a female was seen lying in shallow water with hatchlings on her head and body; other young were seen swimming or basking on the bank beside her. At the time, this female had been with the hatchlings for three months. Eggs and hatchlings are heavily predated by fish, jackals, monitor lizards, birds of prey, or larger gharials.

The eggs are also eagerly sought by some tribal communities, and many nests are destroyed by monsoon floods.

Threats

The gharial's depleted status is largely attributed to habitat disturbance and to killing of the reptiles for skins and sport. In addition, the preferred habitat of the reptile—deep, fast-flowing rivers with high banks—offers optimal sites for the construction of dams and reservoirs for hydroelectric plants or irrigation schemes. The construction of such structures removes the deep pools and sandbanks that the gharial needs for nesting and basking. The construction itself also has a direct adverse effect on the animal. For example, during

the construction of one dam on the Ramganga river, heavy dynamiting along the riverbanks injured a number of gharials. Combined with the destruction of habitat, what was once a relatively large population of gharials has been reduced to only five adults in the few remaining pools along a stretch of nearly 16 miles (25 kilometers).

Hunting for hides is the other primary cause of decline. These reptiles have been captured using nylon nets, then drowned or killed to avoid damage to the expensive nets. The gharial now has legislative protection throughout its range, which has stopped the large-scale hunting. Unfortunately the protection came too late because hunting had already decimated the gharial population. Even today, the two most extensive gharial habitats show declining population numbers due to hide hunting.

Native use

A less critical cause of decline is the predation of gharial eggs by native groups. This practice affects populations that are already depleted. Because native people are quite efficient egg collectors, they collect more than they consume and use the excess in barter. In parts of India the gharial eggs are believed to have medicinal value.

Where are they?

The gharial is still found in Bangladesh, India, Nepal, and Pakistan. It is restricted to river systems that are fed by runoff from the Himalayas in the north of the Indian subcontinent. Although the species was once found in Myanmar (formerly Burma), there are no recent records suggesting that it still exists in that country. A survey party spent 26 days seeking the gharial on the Kaladan River in Myanmar to no avail. They were told by villagers that the reptile had long been absent.

Depleted populations

Reports indicate that some gharials were held by a Burmese animal dealer, but the origin of these animals is unknown. Records from the nineteenth and early twentieth centuries indicate that the gharial was once common, but today it has either been eliminated or is extremely depleted throughout its former range. In Bangladesh, for example, it was recently thought to be extinct, but there may be about 20 individuals in the lower portion of the Ganges and Brahmaputra Rivers. Nesting has also occurred on an island in the Padma river near the border of India. No precise number for the Bangladesh population is available. In Nepal the total gharial population is estimated at about 65–70 adults. Small numbers occur in each of several rivers that rise in the Himalayas and run through southern Nepal. The Pakistan population is critically endangered with estimates of only 20 surviving individuals. There is insufficient data to classify the false gharial.

The Indian population was reported to be on the verge of extinction in the 1970s, but since that time conservation measures have improved its chance for survival. The wild gharial population in India has been augmented by the release of young from wild-laid eggs hatched and reared in captivity. Animals of about 18 months in age have been released in protected sanctuaries. India now holds more individuals of this species than other countries within the species' range. There is optimism for the survival of the gharial—the only remaining member of its family, Gavialidae.

Some protection

There is nominal legislative protection for the gharial in all countries where it is known. It is also protected in several parks in India and Nepal, and there is a reserve that includes the species in Pakistan.

Elizabeth Sirimarco

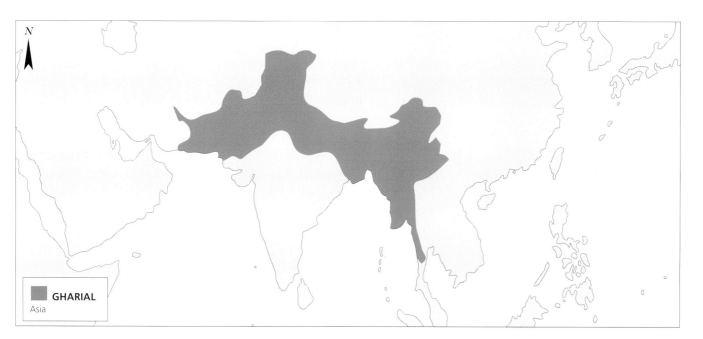

GHARIAL
Asia

GIBBONS

Class: Mammalia

Order: Primates

Family: Hylobatidae

Gibbons belong to the group of animals known as the "lesser apes." They are spectacular acrobats and supremely adapted to tree life. They are almost entirely arboreal, and their family name, Hylobatidae, is the Greek word for tree walker.

The gibbons live in areas of primary forest in Southeast Asia from Assam and China to Sumatra, Java, and Borneo in Indonesia. There are nine species of gibbon, some known by several different names. These include the black or crested gibbon; Kloss's gibbon; the hoolock, also known as the white-browed gibbon; the Javan or silvery gibbon; the pileated or capped gibbon; the agile gibbon; the Lar gibbon; the Bornean or gray gibbon; and the siamang (the largest gibbon). All are in need of conservation, but five species are threatened or endangered.

Gibbons are small tailless apes. Their fur is long, fluffy, and dense, varying in color from black to buff to golden and from brown to silvery gray. There is not much difference in size between the male and the female, but the black gibbon, hoolock gibbon, and the pileated gibbon have differences in coloration between the sexes. The males of these species are black, while the females are buff, golden, and brown or gray.

Male and female gibbons have long curved canine teeth, the other teeth are similar to those of apes. Gibbons differ from the apes in their smaller, more slender build and the presence of buttock pads.

Black Gibbon

(Hylobates concolor)

ESA: Endangered

IUCN:: Endangered

Weight: 13 lb. (5.9 kg)
Length: 17½–25 in. (45–64 cm)
Diet: Fruit, young leaves, small invertebrates
Gestation period: About 210 days
Longevity: Average 20 years
Habitat: Forest
Range: Laos, Vietnam, southern China

THE BLACK GIBBON is also known as the concolor, crested, or white cheeked gibbon. The male's coat is black with some varieties having white cheeks; the female is buff or golden, occasionally with black patches. The black gibbon goes through an interesting color change. Newborns are white and almost hairless, weighing about a pound (0.5 kilograms). Gradually, the infant becomes black. Males remain black, but as females reach maturity, they change back to the lighter phase of buff or golden.

As with other gibbons, this species lives in a family group that consists of a male, a female, and up to four offspring. Gibbons are unusual among primates in that they are monogamous and it is thought that they pair for life. Family groups defend territories through the use of loud vocalizations and dramatic displays of brachiation (swinging from branch to branch) and branch breaking.

Among all gibbons, including the black-handed gibbon, vocalizations are used to identify the species, sex, and individual identity of the calling animals.

This gibbon has a large, inflatable throat sac that is used to amplify communication and territorial calls. The male grunts, squeals, and whistles, while the female calls in a sequence of rising notes ending with a twitter.

The black gibbon is threatened because its population is restricted to an extremely limited area, with probably less than 25,000 individuals remaining in the world. Those remaining are threatened by major habitat alteration, severe hunting, and violent warfare that has plagued their region for decades.

Hoolock Gibbon

(Hylobates hoolock)

ESA: Endangered

IUCN: Data deficient

Weight: Male, 13 lb. (5.9 kg); female, 12 lb. (5.5 kg)
Length: Probably similar to the black gibbon
Diet: Mainly fruit
Gestation period: About 210 days
Longevity: Unknown
Habitat: Thick tropical forest
Range: Assam, Myanmar (formerly Burma), Bangladesh

THE HOOLOCK GIBBON is the largest of the gibbons after the siamang. The male hoolock has a

black coat, while the female's is golden with darker cheeks. Both have white eyebrows, and the infant is whitish in color.

Vocal calls

The male and female vocal calls are similar, but the female has a deeper tone than her mate and she alternates it with his calls. Aside from their exciting chatter, the most striking attributes of all gibbons, including the hoolock gibbon, are their long arms and short legs. These limbs have evolved as a direct result of the gibbon's highly specialized manner of locomotion. Its shoulders have a large range of movement resulting from the broad shape of its chest (in contrast with the monkeys, who have the greatest width from front to back). The elbow is fully extendable, and the forearm has a 360-degree range of movement. This amazing anatomy affords the gibbon remarkable arm-swinging ability; it swings effortlessly through the trees, grabbing hold of branches and propelling itself forward with accuracy and great speed.

Brachiation

The technical name for this type of swinging locomotion is "brachiation," and it is ideal for making both a fast retreat from predators and for reaching feeding spots inaccessible to less agile creatures. Gibbons also walk upright as they carry food along tree limbs. They have long curved fingers and toes, including an opposable big toe, which helps in grasping branches.

The hoolock gibbon is quickly becoming endangered as its population becomes more and more restricted to tiny pockets within

its range. It shares the problems of habitat destruction and hunting that affect all gibbons.

The Javan gibbon is a little-known species, but its endangered status is not questioned. There are less than 10,000 of these animals remaining.

Javan Gibbon
(Hylobates moloch)

ESA: Endangered

IUCN: Critically endangered

Weight: Male, 13 lb. (5.9 kg); Female's weight is unknown
Length: Unknown
Diet: Probably fruit
Gestation period: About 210 days
Longevity: Unknown
Habitat: Thick tropical forest
Range: West Java, Indonesia

THE JAVAN GIBBON is also known as the moloch or silvery gibbon. The coat is a silvery blue-gray, while its cap and chest are darker. The male's call is a simple hoot, while the female's call starts with long, low-pitched, rising notes and ends with a short trill.

All gibbons obtain the water they need from fruit, rain, and the dew from leaves. In their diet, gibbons prefer small scattered sources of pulpy fruit. This liking brings them in competition with birds and squirrels rather than with other monkeys. Their diet is mainly ripe fruit, but also includes young leaves, small lizards, and invertebrates such as termites—an important source of animal protein.

Feeding and foraging

During their daily active period (nine to ten hours), about a third of the time is spent feeding and a quarter of the time is spent traveling through the forest. Two-thirds of the feeding time is spent foraging for fruit and the rest of the time is spent picking and eating young leaves.

The one exception to this feeding pattern is found in the Kloss's gibbon, which eats virtually no leaves. The reverse is true for the siamang gibbon. This species depends on leaves for about 50 percent of its diet. By having more flexibility, the siamang can overlap with the ranges of the lar and agile gibbons. Generally, gibbon species do not have overlapping ranges and are geographically separated from one another by seas and rivers.

Low numbers

The Javan gibbon is listed by the World Conservation Union as critically endangered, with less than 10,000 individuals remaining and with no large population living in sanctuary. Unless measures are taken to protect this species habitat and reduce hunting pressure, the Javan Gibbon may not be able to survive for much longer.

Kloss's Gibbon

(Hylobates klossii)

ESA: Endangered

IUCN: Vulnerable

Weight: 12 lb. (5.4 kg)
Length: Probably similar to black gibbon
Diet: Fruit, invertebrates, leaves.
Gestation period: About 210 days
Longevity: Unknown
Habitat: Tropical rain forest
Range: West Sumatra

KLOSS'S GIBBON has been incorrectly named the dwarf gibbon or the dwarf Siamang.

Simple color

The Kloss's gibbon has a coat that is a glossy black color in the male, the female, and the infant. This is the only gibbon that shows such simple coloration. Weighing approximately 12 pounds (5.4 kilograms), the Kloss's gibbon lives on a diet of fruit, invertebrates and leaves.

The Kloss's gibbon is found in the tropical rainforests of western Sumatra where it can be detected by its distinctive call.

Sweet sounds

The male's call consists of a sort of a quivering hoot and a moan, while that of the female is a sequence marked by a slow rise and fall in pitch that lasts for about 30 seconds. Those who have heard these calls believe that

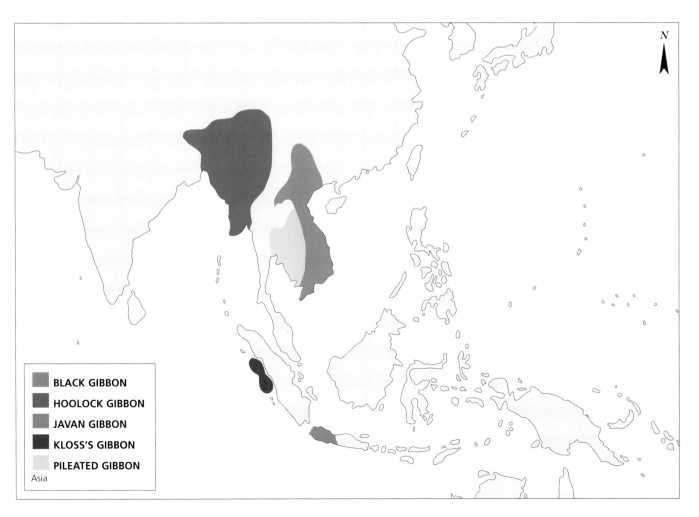

BLACK GIBBON
HOOLOCK GIBBON
JAVAN GIBBON
KLOSS'S GIBBON
PILEATED GIBBON
Asia

Offspring are excluded from the gibbon family group when they become sexually mature. They establish their own territories and family groups. In some species the parents help the offspring set up territories nearby. They also drive out potential rivals.

the female's calls are among some of the finest sounds that a mammal can make.

Sitting sleepers

Gibbons, unlike the great apes, do not build nests. They sleep sitting up in a fetal position, their knees bent up to the chest, hands folded on the knees, and their head buried between the knees and chest. The Kloss's gibbons have large horny pads on their buttocks, called ischial callosities, which make sitting for long periods more comfortable.

This adaptation illustrates one of the main lifestyle differences between gibbons and other apes.

Habitat problems

The Kloss's gibbon is considered vulnerable to extinction for the same reason that its relatives are: its habitat is disappearing and the animal is unable to defend itself against human hunters.

The World Conservation Union drafted an Action Plan for Asian Primate Conservation in the late 1980s, but without cooperation between governments with competing economic interests, such plans are hard to enact.

Endangered status

Kloss's gibbon is threatened, and will probably become a highly endangered species early in the 21st century unless a conservation program is instituted to protect it from the threat of habitat loss and hunting.

Pileated Gibbon

(Hylobates pileatus)

ESA: Endangered

IUCN: Vulnerable

Weight: Unknown
Length: Unknown
Diet: Fruit and young leaves, some invertebrates
Gestation period: 225 days
Longevity: Unknown
Habitat: Forest
Range: Southeast Thailand, Cambodia

THE PILEATED GIBBON is also known as the capped gibbon. There are differences in coloration between the sexes. The male is black with white hands, feet, and head ring, while the female is silvery gray and has a contrasting black chest, cheeks, and cap. The infant is gray.

The male's call consists of abrupt two-toned notes with an added trill in response to the female's call, which is usually an 18-second sequence of short notes that rise gradually to a rich "bubble" sound.

The pileated gibbon encounters exactly the same problems that other endangered gibbon species face: persecution by human hunters and persistent habitat destruction.

Today there are estimated to be less than 33,000 individuals remaining, and as the habitat continues to be degraded, the number will drop. Several species of gibbon may not survive very far into the 21st century.

Sarah Dart

Gila Monster

(Heloderma suspectum)

IUCN: Vulnerable

Class: Reptilia
Order: Squamata
Family: Helodermatidae
Length: 15–23 in. (38–58 cm)
Clutch size: 3–5 eggs
Diet: Eggs, small rodents, birds, small lizards
Habitat: Deserts with cactus or other spiny cover
Range: The southwestern United States (Arizona, New Mexico, Utah, Nevada, and California) and the Mexican states of Sonora and Sinaloa

THE GILA MONSTER is a venomous species of lizard that has two named geographic races or subspecies: the banded Gila monster (*H. suspectum cinctum*), found in the northern part of the range, and the reticulate Gila (*H. s. suspectum*), found in the southern part of the range. Only the reticulate Gila monster is said to be threatened. These reptiles, together with one other lizard, the Mexican beaded lizard, found in Mexico and Guatemala, and a few extinct forms, make up the family Helodermatidae. Members of this family are often called beaded lizards because their skin is studded with osteoderms—bony structures that give it a beaded appearance. Both the Gila monster and the Mexican beaded lizard may be called *escorpión* by Spanish-speaking people.

Gila monsters have large heads, small eyes, plump bodies, and thick tails. They are black or brown with irregular markings in red, yellow, or white. The tail is usually ringed with wide, dark bands. The short legs of the reptile have claws on each toe that are surprisingly strong. The Gila monster is most often found in Arizona and New Mexico with occasional sightings in California, southern Nevada, Utah, Arkansas, and a questionable record in Texas. They live in burrows and often take over the holes of small desert mammals. Little is known about the diet of these moderate-sized lizards, but it most likely consists of eggs of ground-laying birds. They may occasionally eat small lizards, rodents, and birds as well.

Venom

Both the Gila monster and the Mexican beaded lizard produce a potent venom in modified salivary glands found in the lower

The venom of the Gila monster contains an organic compound called serotonin that causes excruciating pain to the victim when the lizard bites. Unlike venomous snakes, this creature must use its exceptionally strong jaws to chew the venom into the wound.

jaw. These reptiles use this weapon only as defense and not to subdue prey. They are deceptively quick and can attack in a blink of an eye, especially when they are warm and active. Unlike venomous snakes, the Gila monster cannot strike and inject the venom, but must bite with its extremely strong jaws and chew the venom into the wound. In other words, the toxin must seep into the wounds, so the Gila monster has to hang onto its victim for at least a short while. Relatively few bites to humans have been reported because the animal is easy to avoid and a bite

629

is unlikely unless a person is in close contact. However, the venom affects the nervous system and respiratory organs, so a bite can be a serious problem. This beaded lizard is one of only two poisonous lizards in the world.

Although Gila monsters are desert creatures, they appear to like water and they are often seen immersing themselves in shallow bodies of water such as large puddles after a summer rain.

Water moves up through their beadlike scales to the mouth. These reptiles tend to be most active at night and during the rainy season; during the day they find shelter from heat under rocks. On warm spring days, they may be seen basking on rocks and even asphalt roads. During the winter they hibernate and live on fat they have stored in their tails. The tails of captive specimens tend to be much fatter than

those of their wild counterparts. When the temperature is particularly hot, the Gila monster can use its sharp claws to dig holes where it will lie to stay cool.

Unnecessary fear

Because of their size and their undeserved reputation for aggressiveness, Gila monsters are often destroyed when they are discovered, simply because people are afraid of them. For this reason they have never been particularly common. Construction of roads and real estate development in areas that were once desert have also affected the lizard by reducing its available habitat. Gila monsters are now under governmental protection because of their rapidly decreasing numbers.

Elizabeth Sirimarco

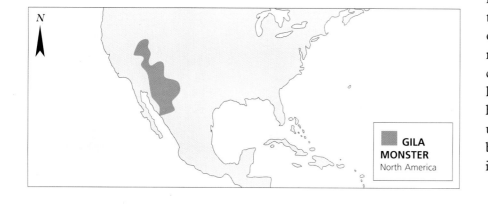

GILA MONSTER
North America

Ginseng

(Panax zingiberensis)

IUCN: Endangered

Family: Araliaceae
Height: 100–195 ft. (30–60 m)
Rhizome: Creeping, fleshy, gingerlike in appearance
Leaves: Palmately compound, around the top of stems
Flowers: 80–100 small, purple flowers grow in solitary umbels
Berries: Black with 1–2 seeds
Habitat: Evergreen, broad-leaved forest
Range: Yunnan, China

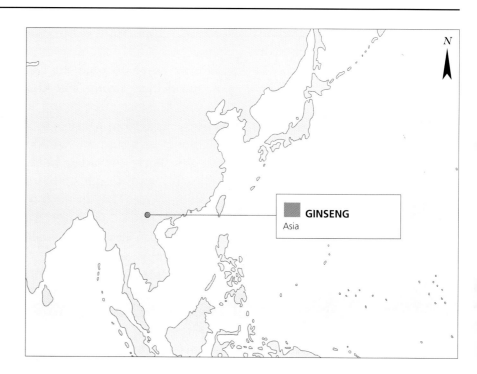

GINSENG
Asia

THIS SPECIES OF GINSENG occurs in China where it is confined to the south and southeast of the Province of Yunnan. It is a shade-loving plant growing in evergreen, broad-leaved forest on limestone mountains at altitudes of 3,280–5,600 feet (1,000–1,700 meters). The soils contain

American ginseng (*Panax quinquefolius;* right), is widely used in the preparation of herbal supplements. It is at risk of endangerment and is listed in appendix II of CITES.

red laterites, which are rich in organic material.

New shoots develop from the rhizomes each spring and the leaves unfold in May. The species flowers in June and the fruits ripen in October.

Panax zingiberensis is one of 5,000 Chinese plant species used in traditional herbal medicine. This species of *Panax* has the largest rhizomes of all the species in the genus.

The rhizomes are dug up as a substitute for *Panax* pseudo-ginseng, another species that is endangered in China. It grows also in Nepal, Bhutan, and northeast India.

The root of ginseng is highly regarded in China as a tonic, and it is used to treat a range of symptoms. Because of its importance, a protected area for this species is

---

American ginseng

American ginseng *(Panax quinquefolius)* is a woodland herbaceous plant that grows in southern Ontario, and southwestern Quebec to Oklahoma, Louisiana, and southern Florida. This species is widely cultivated in the United States, but wild specimens and wild-simulated ginseng (wild plants tended in their natural habitat) are more valuable.

P. quinquefolius prefers damp but well-drained soils on cool rocky slopes. The gnarled roots are dug up in the fall for export to East Asia. The United States exports an average quantity of 130,000 pounds (60 metric tons) of wild root a year, 90 percent of which goes to Hong Kong. *P. quinquefolius* is listed in Appendix II of CITES.

There is poaching of wild material, and trade is subject to licensing. With the huge increase of herbal supplements worldwide, American ginseng has been placed on a herbs at-risk list.

---

proposed in the Red Data Book of Chinese plants. The species is in cultivation and may be suitable for commercial cultivation. Propagation of the species is by seed, and saplings usually flower in their second year.

Sara Oldfield

GOLDENRODS

Class: Magnoliopsida

Order: Campanulales

Family: Asteraceae

Goldenrods belong to the Family Asteraceae (also known as Compositae), which includes asters, daisies, sunflowers, and coneflowers, among others. Goldenrods usually flower from late summer to fall. The flower heads, while they may superficially resemble single flowers, are actually composed of several to numerous tiny individual flowers. Goldenrod flowers are typically yellow and grow in small heads in arching, terminal clusters.

Goldenrods inhabit open or thinly wooded areas. While they are often blamed for causing hayfever allergies, the reputation is undeserved, as goldenrods are strictly pollinated by insects and their pollen is much too heavy to drift about on wind currents.

Goldenrods are also hosts to a number of gall-forming insects during their larval and pupal stages. A gall is a cancerlike swelling of plant tissue in response to an insect egg laid within it. One species of goldenrod, *Solidago odora*, is used to make a flavored herbal tea.

There are about 100 species of goldenrod, most of which are found in North America. Of these 100 species, 22 are currently listed by IUCN–The World Conservation Union. Many are threatened by habitat loss or by habitat disturbance caused by people using goldenrod habitat for recreational uses such as hiking and mountain biking.

Houghton's Goldenrod

(Solidago houghtonii)

ESA: Threatened

IUCN: Rare

Height: 8–30 in. (20–76 cm)

Leaves: Alternate, up to 8 in. (20 cm) long

Flowers: Yellow flowers in flat-topped clusters of 5–30 flower heads

Flowering period: August to October

Life Cycle: Perennial

Pollination: By insects

Habitat: Lakeshores

Range: Michigan and Ontario (around Lake Huron and Lake Michigan)

American monarch butterflies (*Danaus plexippus*) on goldenrod in St. Mark's National Wildlife Refuge in Florida.

HOUGHTON'S GOLDENROD is distinguishable by its large flower heads and slender stems 8–30 inches (20–76 centimeters) tall. Seven to fifteen hairless, 3-veined leaves, up to 8 inches (20 centimeters) long are located alternately on the stem, getting smaller toward the top. At the stem's pinnacle is a flat-topped, branched cluster of about 5 to 30 bright yellow flower heads.

Two other goldenrods with flat-topped flower clusters grow in the same habitat as Houghton's goldenrod and can be confused with it. These are the grass-leaved goldenrod, *Euthamia graminifolia*, and Ohio goldenrod, *Solidago ohioensis*. These three species are the only goldenrods with flat-topped flower clusters found along the shores of the northern Great Lakes. Grass-leaved goldenrod flower heads are markedly smaller than those of Houghton's goldenrod, and the grass-leaved goldenrod has many more leaves along the stem but lacks leaves at the base during flowering. Ohio goldenrod is a larger species with broader, flat leaves and dense flower clusters with smooth, non-hairy stalks and individual flower heads. Also, the yellow ray flowers in Houghton's goldenrod flower heads are noticeably larger than those in the other two goldenrod species.

Houghton's goldenrod is usually found in thinly vegetated areas on moist, sandy beaches,

N

HOUGHTON'S GOLDENROD
Michigan and Ontario

shoreline flats, and in damp depressions between sand dune ridges, called the interdunal wetland. It also occurs in waste areas directly behind lakefront dunes. The changing water levels of the Great Lakes play a role in maintaining this unique species. During high-water years, colonies of Houghton's goldenrod may be submerged. Some plants survive the flooding, and when water levels fall again, new seedlings take root on the freshly moistened sand.

Houghton's goldenrod sometimes grows among or nearby two other threatened plants, dwarf lake iris, *Iris lacustris*, and Pitcher's thistle, *Cirsium pitcherii*, as well as with Grass-of-Parnassus, *Parnassia glauca*, Kalm's lobelia, *Lobelia kalmii*, shrubby cinquefoil, *Potentilla fruticosa*, twig rush, *Cladium mariscoides*, and other goldenrods.

Houghton's goldenrod was originally discovered along the northern shore of Lake Michigan in Mackinac County during the geological survey of Michigan in 1839 by Douglas Houghton, a doctor, botanist, civic leader, and Michigan's first State Geologist. This species is believed to be a native resident of the northern shores of both Lake Michigan and Lake Huron. It is found at two sites in inland Crawford County, and in 18 shoreline populations in eight Michigan counties: Schoolcraft, northern Presque Isle, western Mackinac, northern Emmet, Delta, Chippewa, Cheboygan, and

Charlevoix. In addition, as of 1990, there were 25 populations on privately owned land. Colonies were also found in the Manitoulin District and on Bruce Peninsula near Cabot Head in Ontario. Despite a broad distribution, sudden declines in population have resulted in concern among botanists.

Houghton's goldenrod is threatened by shoreline development and by the increasing recreational use of dunes by off-

road vehicles and hikers. Beach houses are usually built behind the dunes, in the prime habitat of this species. Off-road vehicles severely disturb the sand, destroying mature plants and preventing seedlings from taking root. High water levels at some population sites have eroded beaches and destabilized dunes.

In addition to its federal threatened status, Houghton's goldenrod is also listed as threatened by the state of Michigan, a

Short's goldenrod, *Solidago shortii,* is found on a total of only five sites in Roberton, Nicholas, and Fleming counties in Kentucky.

designation that prohibits collection, possession, sale, purchase, and transport of the plants. The Nature Conservancy monitors population sites, and the U.S. Fish and Wildlife Service has approved a recovery plan for this species. The IUCN has listed the plant as rare. To conserve the remaining populations of Houghton's goldenrod, private, corporate, and public landowners and land managers who are likely to have this species on their property are being contacted and asked to assist in the preservation of this species.

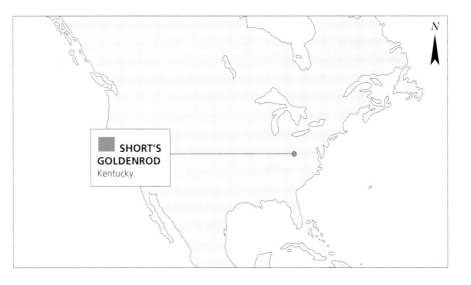

Short's Goldenrod

(Solidago shortii)

ESA: Endangered

IUCN: Endangered

Height: 24–30 in. (61–76 cm)
Leaves: Alternate, narrow, 2–4 in. (5–10 cm) long and 5–10 mm wide
Flowers: Tiny, yellow flowers borne on terminal heads
Flowering period: Mid-August to early November
Life cycle: Perennial
Pollination: Not known, but sweat bees have been observed visiting the flowers
Habitat: Cedar glades, openings in oak and hickory forests, pastures, and areas adjacent to roads
Range: Kentucky

SHORT'S GOLDENROD is a herbaceous perennial with alternately arranged narrow leaves. The biggest leaves are found near the middle of the stem. Tiny but brilliant yellow flowers are borne in terminal heads between mid-August and early November, with seed release starting in late September and continuing into late November. The plants have a creeping rhizome that produces from one to six stems during the growing season.

Short's goldenrod grows in cedar glades and openings in oak and hickory forests, in areas adjacent to the Old Buffalo Trace in Kentucky. It also grows in pastures and areas adjacent to roads. Disturbances caused by bison and fire may have been important in the past because they formed woodland openings in which Short's goldenrod could grow. Seed dispersal may have originally occurred via mud in the hair of passing bison. Although goldenrod seeds are normally wind dispersed, this species does not appear to be expanding its range by that method.

Distribution and protection

Short's goldenrod is endemic to Kentucky, where there are currently five populations located about 35 miles northeast of the city of Lexington near the junction of Nicholas, Robertson, and Fleming Counties. One population is found within Blue Licks Battlefield State Park, Robertson County; another population is just outside the park's boundary, in Nicholas County. The other three populations, located in Nicholas, Fleming, and Robertson Counties respectively, are within a 2-mile (3.2-kilometer) radius of the park. All populations outside of the park are on private property. The population in the Blue Licks Battlefield State Park includes about 2,000 individuals and is found primarily within a 1½-acre (0.6-hectare) area. This population represents about 50 to 60 percent of all the existing plants. The majority of the remaining plants are also found in the other population in Robertson County.

Fire threat

Threats to Short's goldenrod include accidental trampling, over-collecting for scientific purposes on privately owned land, habitat loss or modification, and destructive fires. The highly restricted distribution and limited numbers of this species increase its vulnerability and make any losses potentially more serious. Although fire may have been important historically in maintaining suitable habitat, in the current remnant habitat fire could destroy whole populations of Short's goldenrod. One known habitat loss occurred in the mid-1970s when a major portion of the Blue Licks Battlefield State Park population was lost during the construction of a new campground.

The area of the park that holds the greatest population has been dedicated as a nature preserve by the Kentucky Nature Preserves Commission.

The U.S. Fish and Wildlife Service (U.S.F.W.S.) believes that additional research is needed to determine proper management techniques for the maintenance of Short's goldenrod on this site, as well as on the four privately-owned sites.

Establishing additional populations within this species' historic range would also provide some measure of insurance against catastrophic loss.

The U.S.F.W.S. has established a recovery plan for Short's goldenrod.

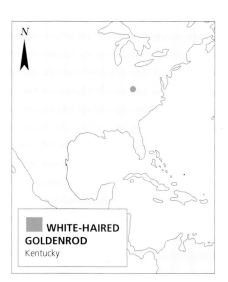

WHITE-HAIRED GOLDENROD
Kentucky

White-haired Goldenrod

(Solidago albopilosa)

ESA: Threatened

IUCN: Vulnerable

Height: Recumbent, grooved stems 8–22 in. (20–56 cm) long
Leaves: Alternate, 1–2½ in. (2.5–6.4 cm) long and 1¼–2 in. (3–5 cm) wide
Flowers: Yellow flowers located primarily in the leaf axils, 5–6.5 mm long, and more than 15 disk florets 3 mm in length
Flowering season: September through November
Life cycle: Perennial
Pollination: Pollination has not been investigated, but bees and syrphid flies have been observed visiting the flowers
Habitat: Behind the drip line of sandstone rock-shelters and on rock ledges
Range: Kentucky

THE WHITE-HAIRED goldenrod is distinguished by long, soft, white hairs that cover the leaves and stems. This perennial herb spreads in part via rhizomes, and its slightly zigzagged stems tend to lie prostrate on the ground. Its thin, soft leaves are alternate and are largest toward the base. They are somewhat egg-shaped or elliptic and pointed at the end, with slightly heart-shaped bases and coarse, serrate margins. Hairs cover both surfaces of the leaves, most densely along the veins. Flower heads are fragrant with bright yellow clusters composed of four or five (sometimes three) ray florets.

White-haired goldenrod flowers are reportedly pollinated by bees and syrphid flies, attracted by the bright color and fragrance of the flowers. The presence of fine, long hairs on the seeds of this species suggests they are dispersed primarily by wind. The plants have rhizomes, but the extent of vegetative reproduction from them is not known.

The white-haired goldenrod is similar to the broad-leaf goldenrod, *Solidago flexicaulis*, from which it is thought to have originated. These species are reported to hybridize with one another. White-haired goldenrod is shorter than the broad-leaf goldenrod, with smaller and thinner leaves and more dense hair. The habitats of the two species are also distinct. The white-haired goldenrod is found almost exclusively behind the drip line of sandstone rock-shelters. It is rarely on rock ledges or in sand by the side of a trail, while broad-leaf goldenrod is found primarily on the adjacent forest floor. Rock-shelters protect the plants from direct rain except during the most severe storms. The species appears to thrive in partial shade in dry, sandy soil.

Distribution

White-haired goldenrod is found only in Menifee, Powell, and Wolfe counties of east-central Kentucky. All occurrences of the species are found within the boundary of the Daniel Boone National Forest managed by the U.S. Forest Service. An occurrence is a group of individuals located beneath the same rock ledge. There are currently 90 known occurrences of white-haired goldenrod, containing an estimated 45,000 stems. Most are on land owned by the Forest Service, but a number of occurrences are on privately owned land within the Daniel Boone National Forest.

The primary threat to the survival of white-haired goldenrod is the many visitors to rock-shelters in the Red River Gorge area each year. Damage by visitors reached a peak in the 1970s, when 75 percent of the occurrences of this species were severely damaged, and 11 occurrences (3,422 individuals) were completely eliminated. The use of rock-shelters by hikers, campers, and rock climbers results in several types of damage to individual plants. Trampling can damage the current year's growth, or it can damage seeds or cause them to be dispersed to unsuitable sites. If trampling is severe, it may also damage the underground rhizomes, which often grow only just beneath the ground surface. Visitors also damage plants by dumping garbage, and building fires in rock-shelters. Plants that were damaged by trampling and fire building during the 1970s recolonized these areas once they were left undisturbed. However, in areas where disturbance continues for long periods, the plants may never recover, for even if plants recolonize trampled areas, their growth may be stunted because of soil compaction.

Another serious threat to the species is archaeological looters. About half of the rock-shelters in this area were once inhabited by Native Americans. As looters dig up soil in their hunt for artifacts, they also dig up stems and seeds of white-haired goldenrod. Plants are unlikely to recover from such extensive damage. All rock-shelters with both white-haired goldenrod, and Native American artifacts, have been disturbed by looters. Rock-shelter soils were also mined for saltpeter (potassium nitrate) in the past.

Protective measures

A number of actions have already been taken to help ensure the survival of white-haired goldenrod. Occurrences that are on Forest Service-owned land are protected from nearby logging by the Forest Service's Cliffline Management Policy, which restricts logging adjacent to cliff-lines. A portion of this policy is specifically aimed at protecting rare or sensitive cliffline plants.

Rick Imes

GOODEIDS

Class: Actinopterygii

Order: Atheriniformes

Family: Goodeidae

Found exclusively in the Mesa Central of Mexico and adjacent regions, the goodeids face severe challenges to their existence. About 35 species make up the group, and most are prized as aquarium fishes by hobbyists in the United States and other countries around the world. Threats posed by pollution, water diversion, and other habitat destruction caused by human activities, along with invasion and competition by non-native fishes, could spell extinction for many of the goodeids. These fishes are relatively small and only rarely reach a length of 8 inches (20 centimeters). Goodeids can be found in quiet lakes among dense mats of vegetation or in river rapids near bare rocks and boulders.

The shape of the body and fins of a species is a good measure of the kind of habitat it prefers. The river-dwelling varieties are streamlined to help them swim in currents; lake-dwelling types are more chunky and have long fins for flexibility. Goodeids eat a wide variety of foods. The meat-eating (carnivorous) species have rows of conical teeth to catch and hold prey. The vegetarian (herbivorous) species have teeth suitable for vegetation; those that eat a combination diet have both kinds of teeth.

Despite all the differences, goodeids have several common characteristics. All goodeids bear live young that derive nourishment directly from the parent before birth (they are known as viviparous). This process differs from that of fish that lay eggs fertilized outside the parent's body (oviparous), or from live bearers that produce eggs that are fertilized internally, remaining inside the parent, and nourished until birth (called ovoviviparous). Male goodeids develop a modification of the anal fin (just behind the anus) that may aid the sperm transfer process. The precise function of the modified anal fin in goodeid males has yet to be determined.

The most important characteristic of all goodeids is their bright coloration and their attraction as aquarium fishes. They will avoid extinction if protected from over-zealous collectors. Preservation of wild goodeid populations will require the securing of their historic range (including water rights) from polluters, non-native fishes, and from unscrupulous collectors.

Opal Goodeid

(Allotoca maculata)

IUCN: Critically
endangered

Length: 1½ in. (4 cm)
Reproduction: Live bearer
Habitat: Lake shoreline and
marshes
Range: Jalisco, Mexico

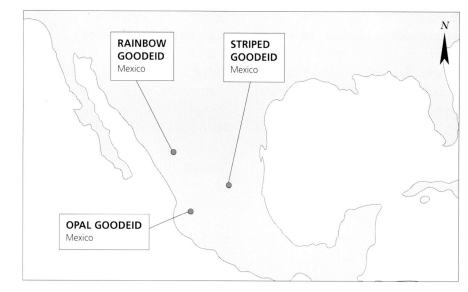

ALSO CALLED THE blackspot allotoca, the opal goodeid is native to western Mexico in the state of Jalisco and is part of a group of about 35 goodeid species contained in an area called the Mexican Mesa Central. This fish is so rare that some fisheries biologists believe it is now extinct in the wild, or at best critically endangered. The distinction is made here between absolute extinction and extinction in the wild because, like many goodeids, the opal goodeid is sought by fish fanciers and aquarists. Wild specimens of the opal goodeid have been found only in Laguna de Santa Magdelena and in a reservoir near Etzatlán.

The opal goodeid lives among other threatened and endangered fish of the area, such as various members of the group called charals. Like the charals, this species is threatened by non-native predators, specifically the largemouth bass (*Micropterus salmoides*). Because of its small range, any loss of suitable habitat

to competitors like the large-mouth bass is particularly damaging to the species as a whole. In addition, the opal goodeid is a prized aquarium fish. Probably, the demand for this fish as a show piece has also had a significant negative impact on the species in the wild. Nevertheless, any chance for a recovery may rest on the shoulders of those raising the fish for the aquarium trade.

The opal goodeid is an oddly shaped fish with some physical differences between the sexes. The female has a bulbous belly that gives it an almost awkward appearance, and a tail section that is much narrower than the

rest of the body. The male is more streamlined than the female but also has a tendency toward a more narrow tail. The dorsal fin, on the back, and the anal fin, just behind the anus and genitals, are well back on the body in both sexes; the tail fin is well rounded rather than forked. The anal fin of the male is modified to transfer sperm inside the female during courtship and mating. The background coloration of both sexes is a light gray-green on the back and upper sides and silvery on the lower sides and belly. The female has several vertical bars on the sides separated by blue blotches. The male is less showy but does

The rainbow goodeid is so called
because of the spectacular colors of
the male (top). The female (bottom),
by contrast, is not as bright.

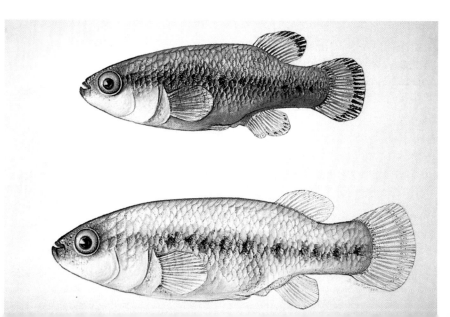

have smaller blue patches separating dark blotches on the sides. This fish derives its species name, *maculata*, which means "spot," from the prominent dark spot on the tail fin.

After an elaborate courtship and gestation period of up to several weeks the opal goodeid bears live young in broods ranging in size from 2 to 20. As the opal goodeid slowly moves through the quiet, warm waters of lake margins and marshes it uses several rows of uniform teeth within its stout jaws to hold its favorite prey—insect larvae and adult insects.

Rainbow Goodeid
(Characodon lateralis)

IUCN: Endangered

Length: 1¾ in. (5 cm)
Reproduction: Live bearer
Habitat: Stream pools among thick vegetation
Range: Headwaters of Rio Mezquital, Durango, Mexico

AT ONE TIME inhabiting the Mexican states of Jalisco and Coahuila, the rainbow goodeid is now restricted to the headwaters of the Rio Mezquital in Durango and faces a very uncertain future. This fish is a victim of a number of threats—all of them ongoing and formidable. Many factors have contributed to the rainbow goodeid's shrinking range: diversion of water from streams in the Coahuila Desert; pumping of desert groundwater for agricultural purposes; pollution from domestic sewage and industrial sources, which kills fish directly and destroys habitat; and introduction of the non-native common carp (*Cyprinus carpio*), which alters habitat and competes for food. Water diversion and pollution have been a fact of life for the rainbow goodeid for decades. In more recent years, this beautiful warmwater fish has been the target of fish fanciers and aquarists. There is a booming business in the capture and sale of colorful live-bearing fishes like the rainbow goodeid. Conservation plans for this species must address all of these areas of concern: water supply, pollution, competition from non-native fishes, and aquarium trade.

The males of this species are spectacularly colored. The dorsal fin on the back, the anal fin just behind the anus and genitals, and the tail fin display bands of red, yellow, and black; all other fins are gray or clear. The red on the anal fin extends onto the tail section of the body and onto the belly, and often up to the midsides. The head, neck, and back are olive-brown and the chin, cheeks, and gill covers are bright yellow; silvery patches mark the front half of the body. A row of dark blotches down the sides to the base of the tail of the male are well defined and easily visible.

While not as bright as the male, the female has similar olive-brown background coloration. Fin coloration patterns are somewhat similar but much more pale. Like the male, she has a row of prominent blotches on the side that run the length of the body. The female is more speckled across the body than her showier counterpart and is generally about 30 percent longer.

Breeding

The rainbow goodeid breeds during warm-weather months of spring and summer. After an elaborate courtship in which the male displays his brilliant colors and ability to ward off other suitors, the female is inseminated by the insertion of an extension of the male's genital tract or by forcing semen into the female after the genitals are brought together. In some other live-bearing fishes (for example, the Pecos gambusia, *Gambusia nobilis*, and all other gambusia) the male's anal fin is modified into a penis-like structure called a gonopodium. While the male rainbow goodeid shows some modification of the anal fin, biologists are not sure if it plays a role in reproduction.

The striped goodeid is a resident of stream pools and shallow lakes in Mexico. Its range is very small, which has presented problems.

The rainbow goodeid will eat algae and other vegetation, insect larvae, and aquatic invertebrates. In an aquarium it will feast on earthworms and brine shrimp.

Striped Goodeid

(Ataeniobius toweri)

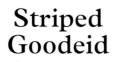

IUCN: Endangered

Length: 1¾ in. (5 cm)
Reproduction: Live bearer
Habitat: Streams and shallow lakes among vegetation
Range: San Luis Potosí, Mexico

THE STRIPED GOODEID is in extreme peril of extinction. This inhabitant of the Mexican state of San Luis Potosí in the northeastern part of the country is under attack from many directions. This fish has a very small and restricted natural range, and its habitat is being altered for agricultural reasons. Also, nonnative predators threaten the remaining specimens.

Survival challenge

Like other threatened and endangered fishes in Mexico, the striped goodeid is being challenged by the diversion of water from lakes and other wet areas for agricultural irrigation. As their homes shrink, fish are concentrated in ever-smaller areas and competition for food and adequate living spaces becomes fierce. The entire population suffers as well as the rest of the biological community. Adding insult to injury are more aggressive, non-native fishes that out-compete the striped goodeid for the meager surroundings.

Last resort

The only hope for the continued survival of the striped goodeid is a shift in priorities of local water users and the state and federal governments. Given that this is unlikely, the relocation of the remaining specimens and aquarium storage may be the only solutions of last resort for this endangered fish.

As with many threatened and endangered Mexican fishes, little is known about the striped goodeid, its habits, and its biological requirements. Additional study may help provide a solution to the plight of this fish.

William E. Manci

Goral

(Naemorhaedus goral)

ESA: Endangered

IUCN: Lower risk

Class: Mammalia
Order: Artiodactyla
Family: Bovidae
Subfamily: Caprinae
Tribe: Rupricaprini
Weight: 62–93 lb. (28–42 kg)
Shoulder height: 25 in. (63 cm)
Diet: Leaves, twigs, and grasses
Longevity: 15–18 years
Habitat: Forest and bush
Range: Asia

THE GORAL IS A relatively small, shaggy-coated alpine dweller that is found across Asia. Over the range are six or seven subspecies. The goral is seen among rock outcroppings and open meadows up to about 9,800 feet (3,000 meters) above sea level. This animal is related to the chamois, serow, and mountain goats.

Gorals tend to live singly or in small groups of four or five. They graze or browse on whatever is available—leaves, twigs, and shoots—and are active early morning and late evening. Their predators include wild dogs, leopards, lynx and, in some areas, wolves. Humans are their most dangerous predator. People have hunted the goral for fur, meat, and body parts that are used in both Chinese and Korean folk medicine.

However, the biggest problem facing the goral is habitat destruction. The animal is pro-

GORAL
Asia

lific and well adapted to its environment, but encroachment threatens several subspecies. These are Bailey's goral (*Naemorhaedus goral baileyi*) in Tibet; the Chinese goral (*N. goral arnouxianus*); the long-tailed goral (*N. goral caudatus*); and the red goral (*N. goral cranbrooki*).

Warren D. Thomas

See also Chamois and Serow.

GORILLAS

Class: Mammalia

Order: Primates

Family: Pongidae

Gorillas are the largest of the great apes, and one of humanity's closest relatives. There are three races or subspecies of gorilla living in western and east central Africa. They are the western lowland gorilla, the eastern lowland gorilla, and the mountain gorilla. Gorillas have long been the victims of bad publicity. Their ferocity has been greatly exaggerated, largely because of their intimidating appearance, enormous strength, and characteristic, Tarzan-style chest-beating.

The truth is, gorillas are shy and introverted by nature, and are more likely to hide away from people than attack them.

Despite their size, gorillas are almost wholly vegetarian, and their diet consists almost entirely of vegetation collected from the forest floor. Vast quantities of leaves, bark, coarse stems, roots, vines, bamboo, wild celery, thistles, and nettles must be consumed in order to maintain a gorilla's body weight. In addition to these foods, the western lowland gorilla eats greater quantities of fruit and an occasional termite.

Gorillas move stealthily through the dense forest on all fours. The last joints of their fingers are well-padded and covered in tough skin, aiding their knuckle walk. Their bulk discourages all but youngsters and smaller females from venturing high into the trees. There are exceptions, however. While mountain gorillas are more terrestrial than their cousins, they can climb trees. Gorillas build a nest to sleep in every night, and sometimes this nest is in a tree.

The coat of all gorillas is predominantly black, and the mature males of all three subspecies develop a silvery-gray "saddle"—a hair formation on their backs. In the western gorilla, this fur extends to the rump and thighs. The dominant male of a group is often referred to as a "silverback." Gorillas live in fairly stable groups usually consisting of one male silverback and one or two adolescent males, two to four adult females, and their offspring. Adult male gorillas are nearly twice the size of the females.

Gorillas are unusual primates in that both males and females tend to leave their family groups when they become sexually mature. Occasionally a silverback's adult sons will remain in a group and take over the leadership when the elder silverback dies. Most often, however, young males leave the group and wander alone, sometimes for several years. Eventually they attract other females and establish groups of their own. Since adult females tend not to be related (having come from different groups), they don't seem to show tightly knit bonds. The center of the group is the silverback—he is the one who maintains order.

Life within a gorilla group is usually peaceful, although when different groups meet there may be battles. Rival males attempt to attract females and become aggressive.

There is no fixed birth season. The menstrual cycle lasts 31 to 32 days. Females reach sexual maturity after about eight years, males in ten. This does not mean that they breed right away. Females generally are 10 and males 15 years of age before they first mate. Females give birth every 3.5 to 4.5 years. Youngsters cling to their mother's chest and later to her back until they are much older.

Eastern Lowland Gorilla

(Gorilla gorilla graueri)

IUCN: Endangered

Weight: 360 lb. (165 kg); females smaller than males

Standing height: 69 in. (175 cm)

Diet: Primarily ground plants

Gestation period: 250–270 days

Habitat: Tropical forest

Range: Eastern Democratic Republic of Congo (formerly Zaire)

THE EASTERN LOWLAND gorilla differs from its western cousin. Its coat is a more uniform black color with little variation. The mature male exhibits his silvery saddle, but only on its back. The eastern gorilla's hair is short on the back and long elsewhere, and its skin is jet black almost from birth. The jaws and teeth are larger, the face longer, and the body and chest broader and sleeker than the western lowland gorilla. This is the largest of the gorilla subspecies, reaching up to 69 inches (175 centimeters) in height. The males may weigh 360 pounds (165 killogramms).

Ghoulish souvenirs

It is estimated that between 3,000 and 5,000 eastern lowland gorillas remain in the Democratic Republic of Congo (formerly Zaire), living in three major national parks. The main threat to these gorillas is clear cutting of the forest. Cattle ranches and cultivation now stand where gorillas once thrived. Deforestation threatens to destroy gorillas

The eastern lowland gorilla has a more uniform black color than its western cousin. Mature males, like this one, exhibit a silvery hair formation on the back.

altogether. Other threats include the risk from wire snares set to capture small game. While not hunted for food or persecuted as crop pests, these gorillas are captured for export, and their skulls and hands sometimes sold as souvenirs to tourists, even though this barbaric practice has now been outlawed.

A gorilla monitoring program has now been established in the Democratic Republic of Congo. Its job is to better understand the distribution of eastern lowland gorillas, identify threats to their existence, and recommend action to protect them.

Survival hope

A tourism program to promote understanding about gorillas will bring in needed revenue for conservation. This offers hope for this subspecies' continued survival. More good news is that the population of the eastern lowland gorilla is increasing in this area.

Mountain Gorilla

(Gorilla gorilla berengei)

IUCN: Critically endangered

Weight: 343 lb. (154 kg); females smaller than males
Standing height: 68 in. (172.5 cm)
Diet: Primarily ground plants
Gestation period: 250–270 days
Longevity: Unknown
Habitat: Forest altitudes of 5,450–12,500 ft. (1,650-3,790 m)
Range: Rwanda, Democratic Republic of Congo, Uganda

THE MOUNTAIN GORILLA is found in the Virunga Mountains of Rwanda, the Democratic Republic of Congo, and Uganda. It is similar both in coat and form to the eastern lowland gorilla, but it has a thick coat of long black hair that is particularly noticeable on its arms. This coat is necessary to survive the cold at the high altitudes it prefers. Its jaws and teeth are even longer and more massive

than those of the eastern lowland gorilla, but its arms are shorter.

Most information on the social behavior of gorillas comes from studies done on this one subspecies. Mountain gorillas feed and move about during the day, when they also build their nests—usually out of vegetation—on the ground.

Dian Fossey

The mountain gorilla is critically endangered, and at the present time its total numbers are between 370 and 440. Naturalist Dian Fossey played a large part in the fight to save this gorilla. She lived in the Virunga volcano range in Rwanda for 18 years, struggling to protect the mountain gorilla and its habitat from hunters, farmers, and cattle. Her ongoing field study added much to the knowledge of these creatures. Sadly, her work was interrupted by her death in 1985. However, her work continues at the Karisoke Research Center, which she founded.

Until Fossey came along, the mountain gorilla was in grave danger of total extinction. In 1978 another project was begun to preserve the gorilla in Virunga National Park, which is home to about one-third of its remaining numbers. This campaign was originally called the "Gorilla Habitat Protection In Rwanda," but it was later renamed "The Mountain Gorilla Project."

Good news

UNESCO has declared the Virunga National Park part of its Man and Biosphere program, and has cited the park as a role model to be followed in the management of such reserves. The

Virunga National Park attracts many visitors, meaning that the mountain gorillas, while encroaching on precious agricultural land in one of the poorest countries in Africa, are at the same time supporting a tourist industry, which is one of Rwanda's top three sources of foreign currency. In other words, the gorillas are earning their keep through tourism, and that generates funds for conservation in the national park.

There are still areas of concern, however. While direct poaching has been reduced by the conservation laws, some gorillas are inadvertently trapped in snares that are illegally set for other game. Gorillas caught in snares can die or lose their limbs trying to get free. Antipoaching patrols (first established by Dian Fossey) work to release any gorillas found in these traps.

Disease

Rwanda is the most densely populated country in Africa. The mountain gorilla's habitat cannot be considered completely safe. In addition, increased tourism may bring more humans in closer contact with the gorillas and could transmit human diseases to the wild gorillas, although these gorillas are now routinely vaccinated against certain diseases such as measles.

Western Lowland Gorilla

(Gorilla gorilla gorilla)

IUCN: Endangered

Weight: 307 lb. (140 kg); females less than males
Standing height: 66 in. (167.5 cm)
Diet: Fruits and vegetation, occasionally termites
Gestation period: 250–270 days
Longevity: Unknown, probably 35 years in the wild; 53 years is the record in captivity
Habitat: Forest
Range: Western equatorial Africa

THE WESTERN LOWLAND gorilla is found in southeastern Nigeria, Cameroon, mainland Equatorial Guinea, Gabon, Congo, and parts of the Central African Republic and Angola. This gorilla is the smallest of the three subspecies. The only other significant difference is the

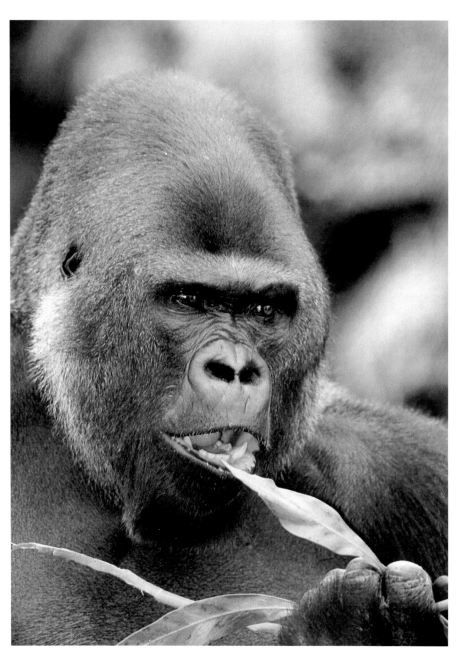

The incredible size of the male gorilla, or silverback, makes him an impressive, even intimidating creature. However, these animals are known to be rather shy and are more apt to hide from people than attack them.

643

over-hanging nose tip, absent in the two Eastern forms. In adulthood, the western lowland gorilla is grayish or brownish with a silvery hair formation that extends all the way down the back to the thighs and is not sharply distinct from the overall body color. This subspecies is the variety of gorilla that is most commonly found in zoos.

Threats

The future for this gorilla looks the brightest of the three gorilla races. In places where the human population is low and huge areas of forest still remain intact (for example, in Gabon), the prospects are best. The commercial value of trees in this area is not high, so clear cutting of their range is less of a threat than local hunting for gorilla meat. This hunting is by no means under control. Furthermore, habitat loss due to forest exploitation remains a threat for the gorilla wherever the human population is increasing.

Some countries, such as Congo, need international support to help maintain protected areas properly.

Recent successes in captive breeding offer hope for survival of the western lowland subspecies. The last census taken in Gabon between December 1980 and February 1983 estimated the gorilla's numbers at 35,000.

Sarah Dart and Thaya du Bois

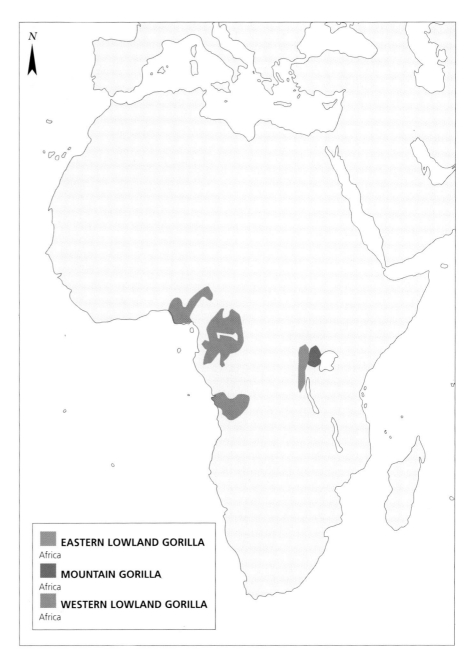

EASTERN LOWLAND GORILLA
Africa

MOUNTAIN GORILLA
Africa

WESTERN LOWLAND GORILLA
Africa

There is a tight bond between this mother, a western lowland gorilla, and her child. Offspring will cling to their mother's chest when young. As they grow older, they will cling to her back. Male gorillas do not carry their children, but they are sometimes seen playing with them.

Slender-billed Grackle

(Quiscalus palustris)

ESA: Endangered

IUCN: Extinct

Class: Aves
Order: Passeriformes
Family: Icteridae
Subfamily: Icterinae
Length: Male, 14 in. (35.6 cm);
female, 11½ in. (29.2 cm)
Weight: Unknown
Clutch size: Unknown
Incubation: Unknown
Diet: Probably insects
Habitat: Marshes
Range: Headwaters around Rio
Lerma, near Mexico City

GRACKLES ARE NOT the most attractive birds. They sport no pretty colors—in fact their plumage is all black, although it does shine with a little iridescent color. They offer no lovely song but utter a harsh cackling and squeaking call from which they get their name. They gather with other blackbirds, sometimes by the hundreds of thousands or even by the millions. Such congregations create severe nuisances for people who live in the vicinity. Grackles also play the role of bully at backyard bird feeders. All the cute little birds with bright colors get out of the way when grackles come to feed.

So when grackles suffer the threat of extinction, most people are inclined to ask, "Who cares?" The slender-billed grackle faced severe pressures from human activities for many decades. Now, if it is not already extinct, it is at least severely endangered.

Purple sheen

The slender-billed grackle is very similar to the great-tailed grackle (*Quiscalus mexicanus*), but it is smaller and has a thinner beak. The male is black overall with a purple sheen, becoming a slightly redder purple on the head, neck, and breast. The female is dusky brown, darker on the wing, rump, and tail. Her underparts are also lighter and paler. Outwardly the slender-billed grackle resembles any other large-tailed grackle. For many years ornithologists considered the large-tailed grackles as just one species. Then, in the 1970s, differences between inland and coastal forms were accepted as sufficient enough to justify two species. The coastal form remained the boat-tailed

The slender-billed grackle is not noteworthy for its appearance, and its call can be loud and high pitched. Because of this, the bird has received little sympathy for its plight.

grackle (*Quiscalus major*), and the inland form was referred to as the great-tailed grackle.

The slender-billed grackle was first described in 1827, but its relationship with the great-tailed grackle has never been resolved

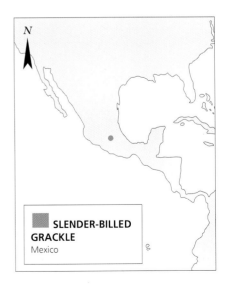

SLENDER-BILLED GRACKLE
Mexico

This boat-tailed grackle (*Quiscalus major*), which is related to the slender-billed grackle, is also a relative of the blackbird. It inhabits coastal areas.

Habitat under threat

The slender-billed grackle inhabited a marshy complex at the headwaters of the Rio Lerma in Mexico. The river originates at a small lake and wetland area southwest of Mexico City. This locality probably explains the slender-billed grackle's demise.

Mexico City lies at about 10,000 feet (3,048 meters) above sea level. To the north and east stretches the Sierra Madre Oriental mountain range, and to the north and west sprawls the Sierra Madre Occidental. The city was built by the Aztec people, probably around 1325 C.E. Their great city, Tenochtitlan, was built on and around Lake Texcoco. Stone causeways were built for crossing the water to the city. The Aztecs farmed, fished, and hunted but they left some of the land as it was. The slender-billed grackle may have inhabited a larger area during the days of the Aztecs. Today, Tenochtitlan lies beneath Mexico City and more than 15 million people live where the lake once was. Some think it is on the way to becoming the world's largest city.

Polluted environment

So many people at such an elevation inevitably causes problems. Mexico City's air and water pollution are among the worst in the world. The city's many impoverished inhabitants, desperately hungry, scour the landscape looking for food and firewood. The result is wholesale destruction of wildlife and wildlife habitat.

Limited resources

This social climate is where the slender-billed grackle has fought for survival. If the slender-billed grackle is extinct, it cannot be brought back. If it is still alive, it probably cannot be saved.

It is difficult to justify spending precious national resources to save a plain, black, noisy bird when there is so much human squalor and abject poverty.

Kevin Cook

with certainty. Some ornithologists have regarded it as a distinct species, while others have considered it to be a small form, possibly a subspecies, of the great-tailed grackle. Its exact status as a species may remain academic. Several books on endangered birds published in the late 1980s and early 1990s do not mention the slender-billed grackle. Either it was discounted as a valid species, or it was thought to be already gone.

This female common grackle is quite attractive, being much lighter and paler than the male of the species. She is a dusky brown, with a darker wing, rump, and tail.

Australian Grayling

(Prototroctes maraena)

IUCN: Vulnerable

Class: Actinopterygii
Order: Salmoniformes
Family: Retropinnidae
Length: 9 in. (23 cm)
Reproduction: Egg layer
Habitat: Large rivers and associated lakes
Range: Southeastern coastal rivers and Tasmania

THE AUSTRALIAN GRAYLING is another victim of short-sighted thinking by people and of a disregard for the needs of native fish species. Local fisheries biologists consider it one of the four most seriously threatened fish on the continent. Specifically, the Australian grayling faces competition from non-native fish and is likely to suffer predation by the brown trout (*Salmo trutta*), a fish that was introduced to satisfy fishers. It faces barriers to migration, such as dams and other stream-control devices, and habitat alteration caused by agriculture and deforestation.

The Australian grayling relies on rivers that have a silt-free bottom to ensure that its eggs are not smothered by sediment. Agricultural activities and logging promote soil erosion and sedimentation in rivers, which severely reduce the reproductive success of this fish.

This fish has a rather irregular distribution throughout its home range, which extends in a broad swath across the southeastern coast of Australia and to the coastal and inland areas of Tasmania. While the overall range is relatively large, this species is found only in isolated population patches. Such distribution arises because this fish tends to group together in schools. In the early 1970s concern for the Australian grayling's future was increased because, besides its rarity, there is a lack of knowledge about its general biology. It was argued that any plan to aid in this fish's recovery was meaningless without better understanding its habits and requirements. Today more is known about this species, and the prospects for its recovery are much improved.

Hope for this fish's survival is improved by its ability to produce large numbers of eggs. A single female can produce from 30,000 to 60,000 eggs each year. If fisheries scientists take advantage of this characteristic in a hatchery or ensure higher reproductive success in the wild, the species may have a bright future.

The Australian grayling is the largest of Australia's fish within the order Salmoniformes, reaching a maximum length of about 9 inches (23 centimeters). However, compared to better known salmoniform fish, such as the sockeye salmon (*Oncorhynchus nerka*) and chinook salmon (*Oncorhynchus tshawytscha*) of North America, the Australian grayling is relatively small. Many other salmon reach lengths in excess of 20 inches (51 centimeters). The Australian grayling does, however, have many characteristics in common with its larger cousins. This fish has the capability to move from fresh water to salt water during various stages of its life. After the Australian grayling hatches from its gravel nests within freshwater streams in the month of May, the juvenile fish is washed many miles downstream to estuaries or into the ocean. It spends as many as nine months in this saltwater environment, feeding and grow-

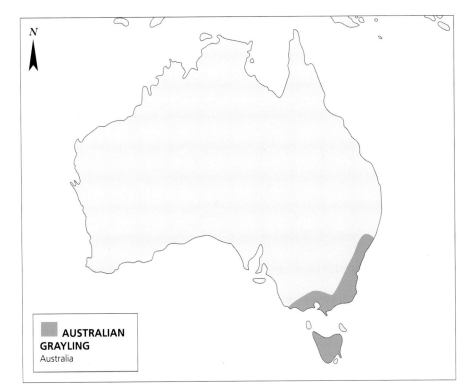

N

AUSTRALIAN GRAYLING
Australia

ing, before it moves back upstream into fresh water for the remainder of its adult life. This transition from fresh water to salt water (called diadromy) requires profound internal changes of which most fishes are not capable. This sequence varies from the salmon in that, after moving downstream to the sea, the salmon spends its adult life in a marine environment and only returns to the stream to spawn.

Salmonlike fish

The Australian grayling is a beautiful fish with a distinctively plump, generally gold-bronze body as an adult. Its torpedolike shape makes it a most efficient swimmer. The back is somewhat darker and the sides show a slightly greenish hue, but the belly is silvery to white. The gill covers are steel blue in some fish, and the dorsal fin on the back and the highly forked tail fin are gray. Other body fins are a much lighter yellow color with some tones of gray. The snout is particularly pointed, and the head is small compared to the rest of the body, much like that of a smelt. However, the small fatty adipose fin halfway between the dorsal fin and the tail leaves no doubt that this fish is, in fact, closely related to the salmon. The body of the Australian grayling is well scaled, but the head and gill covers are nude. During breeding season, the scales of the male become covered with microscopic nodules called tubercles.

Initially biologists believed that tubercles helped to increase the male's sense of touch during courtship and to stimulate spawning, but the tubercles are so small that this kind of heightened sensitivity seems rather unlikely. Now it is thought that they are most probably a result of elevated levels of sexual hormones in the blood.

Vegetarian diet

Despite its physical and behavioral similarities with salmon, the diet of the Australian grayling is quite unusual. Instead of an adult diet consisting primarily of smaller aquatic animals, the Australian grayling prefers to scrape algae off rocks with its comb-like teeth. It will eat insects if they are available, but the bulk of its diet is vegetarian. This preference is unique for a salmoniform fish and sets it apart as a distinct and interesting species.

William E. Manci

GREBES

Class: Aves

Order: Podicipediformes

Family: Podicipedidae

Grebes resemble birds such as loons, ducks, and some auks; but they do not belong to any of these species.

During the 19th century grebes were erroneously grouped with various other birds. In the early 1900s, however, they were recognized as an order by themselves.

A recent reclassification system groups the grebes together as a family in a larger order that contains the shorebirds, pelicans, hawks, storks, tubenoses, and some others. This new classification is intriguing but it has not yet been accepted by ornithologists.

Generally, the grebes differ from other aquatic birds in having no webbing between the toes. Instead, each toe is lobed, with a flat pad of fleshy skin. Working together, the lobed toes also serve as webs.

Compared to ducks, grebes do not have such a flattened beak. They have no plates along the sides of the beak for straining tiny food bits from the water. Instead, they have unusually thin, pointed beaks, well suited for capturing aquatic invertebrates and vertebrates.

Most grebes perform elaborate courtship rituals characterized by head bobbing, neck weaving, and peculiar dancing. The courtship varies depending on the species. Some species simply rise up on the water surface and patter in place, but other species race across the water and end up plunging beneath the surface.

Some species also go through displays in which mates present strands of algae or other aquatic plants to each other.

Human activities have both helped and hurt some grebe species in North America. For example, the destruction of natural wetlands has cost vital nesting habitat.

On the other hand, the prolific construction of reservoirs has created some new nesting habitat and habitat for birds in migration. No detailed studies have examined the net gain or net loss of grebe habitat or how grebe species have been affected by habitat shifts.

Two grebe species have been affected by human activities, which have damaged habitat. At issue is not the presence or absence of habitat as a result of humans, but how well the existing habitat provides for the life needs of the grebes.

Alaotra Grebe

(Tachybaptus rufolavatus)

ESA: Endangered

IUCN: Critically endangered

Length: 10 in. (25.4 cm)
Weight: Unknown
Clutch size: Unknown
Incubation: Unknown
Diet: Unknown
Habitat: Lake
Range: Lac Alaotra (Lake Alaotra) in northeastern Madagascar

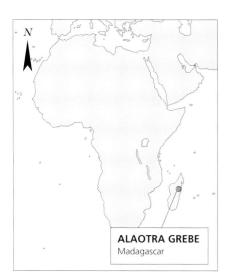

ALAOTRA GREBE
Madagascar

SO MANY UNUSUAL PLANTS and animals have been found on Madagascar that finding a unique grebe should hardly be a surprise. Fifteen specimens of a small grebe were collected in 1929 and soon thereafter were described as a species distinct from the little grebe (*Tachybaptus ruficollis*). This newly discovered species was named the "Alaotra grebe" for the lake where it was discovered. The little grebe enjoys an expansive range from Africa through parts of Europe and Asia. The Alaotra grebe, having smaller wings, cannot move around so easily. Ornithologists originally thought that it was restricted to shallow Lake Alaotra. Through the years up to the 1970s, however, Alaotra grebes were collected or reported from many localities around Madagascar. Those sightings and records are now being questioned for their accuracy of identification.

Aggressive relative

Apparently, for some time the Alaotra grebe has suffered encroachment by its relative, the little grebe. The two grebes mate, breed, and produce hybrid offspring. These hybrids could easily be the grebes that have been seen around Madagascar away from Lake Alaotra. The hybrids raise more than identity questions. They challenge a species' survival.

The little grebes are hybridizing the Alaotra grebes into oblivion. Some ornithologists question whether any pure strains of Alaotra grebe still exist. If they do survive, their population must be very low, but no estimates are available. An estimated 50 birds were seen at Lake Alaotra in 1960. Only 12 Alaotra grebes were seen on the lake in 1982. The last sighting of this bird was in 1985, when two individuals were seen.

If little grebes have been on Madagascar for centuries or even thousands of years, why did they not hybridize the Alaotra grebe into extinction earlier? If the little grebe is a recent arrival on Madagascar, what happened to encourage its rapid spread on the island? Even without thorough research to document explanations with certainty, some assumptions of natural history are probably valid. First, some aspects of the aquatic and wetland habitats around Lake Alaotra favored one grebe over another. Presumably, for many thousands of years the Alaotra grebe enjoyed a survival advantage there. Second, habitat conditions changed and the competitive balance tipped in favor of the little grebe. As the little grebe increased in number, the probability that an Alaotra grebe would encounter a little grebe during the breeding season likewise increased. The ultimate question is what caused the habitat conditions to change? Only two answers are possible. Either the changes were the consequence of a natural process, or people instigated the changes.

History of the land

The fourth largest island in the world, Madagascar became a French territory in 1896. The island became independent as the Malagasy Republic in 1960. Political turmoil followed, and the nation renamed itself the Democratic Republic of Madagascar. Civil strife created desperate economic conditions. Driven by the need to employ and feed its people, the Madagascar government encouraged forest cutting, mining, and agriculture. All these activities change plant communities, which are the habitat of animals. Lake Alaotra and its wetlands became an area of rice and fish farming, which affect the character of the lake. Further, some of the farmed fish were tilapia (*Tilapia* sp.). Exotic to Madagascar, the tilapia are vegetarian; and all of them are protective as parents. They reproduce prolifically and grow rapidly. Good documentation is not available, but the similarities between Lake Alaotra and other places with similar circumstances suggest a likely scenario.

Rice farming changed the water cycles of the lake. Tilapia consumed native aquatic vegetation, thus changing the habitat for the Alaotra grebe and for its normal prey fishes. Because the tilapia are exotic species on Madagascar, the native grebe was less skilled in capturing the small tilapia as food, and the large tilapia were simply too big. The little grebe, which has a natural range that overlaps with native tilapia populations, already knew how to avail themselves of the tilapia as prey. Consequently, natural conditions favored the little grebe over the Alaotra grebe.

Madagascar is home to the critically endangered Alaotra grebe (pictured here). The plight of Madagascar's endangered wildlife is magnified by the isolation of this island environment.

JUNIN GREBE
Peru

Certain elements of this hypothetical explanation may be inaccurate, but the basic scenario has been repeated thousands of times around the world.

Ornithologists now believe that nothing can be done to protect a wild population of Alaotra grebes. The species is doomed to be obscured by hybridization. The only hope would seem to be a sort of protective custody through captive breeding, but even with the instigation of such a program, this species may end up with nowhere to live.

Junin Grebe
(Podiceps taczanowskii)

IUCN: Critically endangered

Length: 14 in. (35.6 cm)
Weight: Unknown
Clutch size: Unknown
Incubation: Unknown
Diet: Fish
Habitat: Lake
Range: Lake Junin in Peru

AS A SPECIES GROUP, grebes are specifically adapted for life on and in the water. They have small pectoral muscles, which are the main muscles for flying, and they have small wing areas considering the weight of their bodies. Not surprisingly, a few grebes have become so specialized to water that they have either lost their ability to fly or their capacity for flight has been greatly reduced.

Flightless grebes
The Junin grebe is one of three flightless grebes in Central and South America. The others are the Titicaca grebe (*Rollandia microptera*) of Lake Titicaca on the Peruvian-Bolivian border, and the Atitlan grebe (*Podilymbus gigas*) of Lake Atitlan in Guatemala. The Atitlan grebe may already be extinct, and the Junin grebe may soon follow.

Lake Junin lies high in the Andes Mountains northeast of Lima, Peru. There a small grebe found a way to survive without ever having to leave the lake. Eventually, ornithologists discovered the Junin grebe after it had spent hundreds of thousands of

years in isolation from similar grebes in other parts of the Americas. Its unique identity is quickly apparent.

The Junin grebe, named for the only lake it inhabits, cannot fly. It has a larger, heavier body than related, flighted grebes. The extra size is probably an advantage for retaining body heat in the lake's cool water. It sports a larger beak than its relatives, which probably helps it prey on the large, fast fish that live in Lake Junin. The fish usually stay in deep, open water, so that is where the Junin grebe is typically found. Grebes that prefer to eat aquatic insects or other small prey usually swim closer to shore.

Although essentially incapable of flight, the Junin grebe still has wings. They are not long and paddlelike as those of penguins, so the grebe does not use them for propulsion under water. The grebe swims by kicking its feet and using its wings to stabilize itself in the water.

Harsh winters

Because the Junin grebe cannot fly, it cannot seasonally migrate to escape harsh weather or find abundant food supplies. It must spend winters and summers on the same lake, so abundant food must be available year-round. Another complication of flightlessness is the inability to escape a deteriorating habitat.

Polluted lake

Lake Junin has become polluted, presumably with agricultural chemicals, but possibly from other sources as well, such as human sewage or mine tailings.

The lake has also been tapped as a source for irrigation and domestic water. Fluctuating water levels and chemical pollution combine to degrade the habitat quality for the grebes.

Critical situation

In 1987 only 100 Junin grebes were found on the lake, while by 1993 the population count was down to 50 individuals. The specialization that enabled the Junin grebe's survival for thousands of years is now a disadvantage.

The grebes cannot escape Lake Junin to seek refuge in other places. The species cannot survive anywhere else. Unless conditions at Lake Junin are regulated to improve the water quality to accommodate the grebe, the species will perish.

Kevin Cook

GREEN-PIGEONS

Class: Aves

Order: Columbiformes

Family: Columbidae

Green-pigeons have yellow-green to olive-green plumage. About two dozen species in the genus *Treron* make up the green-pigeon group, which is part of the larger fruit-dove complex of birds. They eat whole fruits rather than seeds. Many fruit-eating birds do not digest seeds but pass them in their feces, helping to scatter them. Green-pigeons, however, have powerful gizzards that grind the seeds within the fruit pulp, so they pass no seeds.

Large Green-pigeon

(Treron capellei)

IUCN: Lower risk

Length: 14 in. (35.6 cm)

Weight: Unknown

Clutch size: Unknown

Incubation: Unknown

Diet: Fruits, particularly large figs (*Ficus*)

Habitat: Forests and woodlands

Range: Malay Peninsula, Sumatra, Java, and Borneo

A SMALL TROUPE of stout birds wings in from some unseen place and quickly settles in the upper branches of a tall tree. The biggest species of its clan, the large green-pigeon seems unusually robust. With its stout beak and portly physique it could belong to another family. The heavy beak is suitable for taking large figs. These large green-pigeons want the fruits of the strangler fig, a felon among trees.

Strangler figs (*Ficus aurea*) now occur around the world in tropical latitudes. Many of them start life high in a tree where some bird or mammal passes a seed that comes to rest in a crotch or fork. The seed germinates, and the seedling begins to grow both vertically and horizontally. It sends leaf-bearing branches upward to mingle with the crown of its host tree and sends strong, rootlike branches down the host's trunk. Like twining arms, the strangler fig's branches weave round and round the trunk of the host tree. After a

651

few years, the trunk may be completely encircled. As more years pass, the host tree becomes inhibited by the fig until it finally succumbs to strangling. The fig continues to grow long after its host dies, and it eventually gains tree stature on its own. It grows the fig fruits of its kind, and gives them up to more birds that will also disperse the seeds to other trees. The large green-pigeon, however, does not cooperate.

Because the large green-pigeon has been studied so little, not much is known about its natural history. However, it probably behaves as most other green-pigeons. It is probably strongly arboreal except for short stints on the ground, where it eats the grit that helps its gizzard grind food. When thirsty, it probably descends to water by working its way down branches or roots that extend into the water. Many green-pigeons feed for a while each morning and then again each afternoon. They often follow traditional flight paths. Such tradition could make them vulnerable to hunting pressure.

No one seems certain about its status, but at the close of the 1990s it had improved to near threatened. Many ornithologists suspect the bird has more to fear from human activities than from natural predators. It has not been seen on Java for many years. The rate of forest clearing in other countries where the species is known to occur indicates overall habitat loss. A species cannot lose habitat indefinitely without being affected. The large green-pigeon apparently prefers older, slightly open forests. Such forests are often cut first in forestry management because they are viewed as

decadent, or overly mature and less productive. Before any meaningful protective measures can be initiated, ornithologists must study the bird, its habitat, and its population.

Sumba Green-pigeon
(*Treron teysmannii*)

IUCN: Lower risk

Length: Unknown
Weight: Unknown
Clutch size: Unknown
Incubation: Unknown
Diet: Presumably small fruits and seeds
Habitat: Lowland forest
Range: Sumba of the Lesser Sunda Islands of Indonesia

PART OF INDONESIA'S Lesser Sunda Islands, Sumba lies east of Java, beyond Lombok and Bali. All told, Sumba covers 4,306 square miles (11,196 square kilometers). Most of the island is mountainous, rising to its highest at 2,913 feet (888 meters). A narrow coastal plain separates ocean

Sumba Island harbors several unique species of birds. Among them is the Sumba green-pigeon. Little is known about the bird, although it is thought to be at low risk of endangerment.

coast from mountain slopes. The Sumba green-pigeon inhabits lowland and lower montane forests up to about 1,640 feet (500 meters). Native forest survives only in isolated patches on Sumba. Most have been cut either for sandalwood or for clearing land for agriculture. A dozen Sumba green-pigeons were found eating figs in one tree in 1987. This sighting indicates the bird still survives, but no one has studied the species enough to know if it can survive in altered habitat. Some birds adapt to secondary forest or shrub land habitat that replaces forests, but some do not. Until significant research can be done on the Sumba green-pigeon, and on other birds unique to the island, the exact status cannot be known. Ornithologists prudently suspect that the long-term habitat alteration on Sumba has caused the Sumba green-pigeon to decline even if some individuals manage to survive in the secondary plant communities.

Timor Green-pigeon

(Treron psittacea)

IUCN: Vulnerable

Length: Unknown
Weight: Unknown
Clutch size: Unknown
Incubation: Unknown
Diet: Presumably small fruits and seeds
Habitat: Unknown
Range: Timor, Roti, and Semau in the Lesser Sunda Islands of Indonesia

THE TIMOR GREEN-PIGEON lives on the largest and driest of the Lesser Sunda Islands. The Lesser Sundas trail off into the sea east of Java. They form a broken line that separates the Java and Flores Seas from the Indian Ocean. Timor lies at the end of this island chain.

The island's prevailing winds blow northward off the hot, dry, northern reaches of Australia. Consequently, Timor experiences a drier climate than most of the other Sundas.

The dry climate supports a different plant community. It grows more grass and shrubs, with scattered sandalwood (*Santalum* sp.) and coconut palms (*Cocos nucifera*). The people of Timor grow cotton, rice, wheat, wool, and sandalwood.

Loss of habitat

Timor used to have some lowland areas of deciduous forest where the Timor green-pigeon lived. This green-pigeon is generally light gray-green. Its throat and rump are yellow-green.

Its dark gray wings have yellow edges to the feathers. The breast and belly are mostly white with some green hue. Its central tail feathers are yellow green, but its outer feathers are more gray.

The few deciduous forests that remain in Timor are small and fragmented. Because of habitat destruction and degradation, the island cannot support as many green-pigeons as in the past, and civil strife on Timor has had a noticeable impact on the island's animal life.

Portugal retained control of East Timor until civil war forced that European country to pull out. Indonesia, which ruled the western end of Timor, annexed East Timor in 1976. Political turmoil began, and the conflict was still continuing at the close of the 1990s. During the civil war, the Timor landscape sustained severe damage.

Recovery means intensive farming to feed the island's people. This could mean more loss of the remaining forests that harbor Timor green-pigeons.

Inaccessible islands

The social and political circumstances of civil war and the struggle by East Timor for independence from Indonesia do not encourage field studies of endangered birds, and the Lesser Sunda Islands, such as Timor, are far removed from usual travel corridors. They are not easily accessed for long-term or repetitive studies. Ornithologists know more about the geography of these islands than about the wildlife living there.

The Timor green-pigeon has not been specifically studied beyond the details reviewed by taxonomists to determine that it is a unique species. Protecting available habitat from further destruction is the only hope for this little known bird's survival.

Kevin Cook

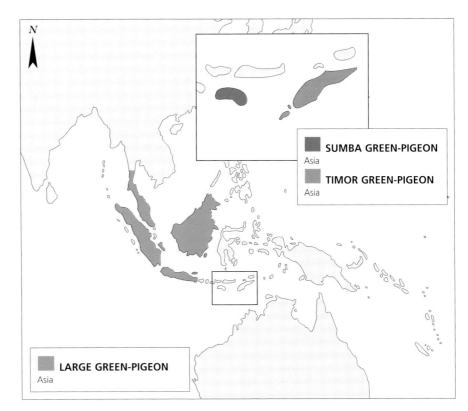

SUMBA GREEN-PIGEON
Asia

TIMOR GREEN-PIGEON
Asia

LARGE GREEN-PIGEON
Asia

GRYLLOBLATTIDS

Class: Insecta

Order: Grylloblattodea

Family: Grylloblattidae

Grylloblattids are commonly known as rock crawlers or ice crawlers. These common names refer to their wingless condition and their preferred habitats, which are rocky slopes and caves on snowcapped mountains. The grylloblattids are members of the insect order Gryloblattodea, related to grasshoppers and crickets (Orthoptera), plus mantids and cockroaches (Dictyoptera).

Unlike most insects, which are active in warmer regions of the world or during warmer seasons of the year, rock crawlers prefer cold temperatures. Living at higher altitudes, ranging from 3,500 to 10,000 feet (1,067 to 3,050 meters), and often at the edges of glaciers or snowpacks, their optimal temperature for activity is near freezing. Some species live in icy caves. During warmer periods, grylloblattids have been observed to burrow several feet down into crevices among rocks and boulders.

Rock crawlers have three main body regions: a head, thorax, and abdomen. Grylloblattids resemble rove beetles (Coleoptera) and earwigs (Dermaptera). They are elongated and cylindrical in shape, but somewhat flattened, which helps them crawl under rocks and into cracks and crevices. They range in size from ½ to 1¼ inches (14 to 30 millimeters). Their bodies have a leathery texture and are covered with fine hairs that probably act as insulation in the cold temperatures.

Although rock crawlers lack wings, their legs are well adapted for running. They are usually pale brown, gray, or yellow in color.

They possess long, slender antennae, and a pair of tail-like appendages known as cerci. Both the antennae and cerci are multisegmented. Because grylloblattids live under rocks or in caves where they don't have to rely on their visual senses, eyes are often absent or are greatly reduced.

The immature stages of rock crawlers are called nymphs, and they closely resemble adults except that they lack developed reproductive organs. Unfortunately, the life history of rock crawlers is poorly known, but it is known that they require several years to mature.

Both adult grylloblattids and nymphs are scavengers that feed on the remains of other insects and invertebrates that have died on the montane snowfields. Rock crawlers are nocturnal and during the daytime can be found in crevices or under the snow.

Species that live in caves are often found in more open areas, such as on the walls or floors. Habitat conditions in caves are characterized by relatively high and constant humidity, plus cool temperatures, but without the extreme fluctuations expected in more exposed alpine areas.

Alpine regions

In contrast to many insect orders, which typically have numerous species, only about 20 species of grylloblattids are known worldwide, and they represent the last of an ancient lineage in the evolutionary tree of insects. Species diversity for most insect orders is usually greatest in

The *Grylloblatta camphodeformis occidentalis*, like others of its order, is commonly called a rock crawler or ice crawler. It is related to grasshoppers, crickets, mantids, and cockroaches.

tropical regions of the world, but rock crawlers are known only from the alpine regions of Siberia, Japan, and northern North America. Ten species of grylloblattid have been described from the United States and Canada. All are characterized by limited ranges and relative rarity.

A threatened species

The Mount St. Helens grylloblattid (*Grylloblatta chirurgica*) exists only in a single lava flow on Mount St. Helens in the state of Washington. The lava flow is known as Cave Basalt, because of its many lava tube caves. Individuals are usually found under rocks near the entrances of the caves, but have been seen inside some of the caves on this flow. Presumably, the rock crawlers also live in the rock fissures that surround the tube caves.

Restricted range

Distribution of the Mount St. Helens rock crawler is limited, as this lava flow is only 6¼ miles (10 kilometers) long and ½ to 2 miles (1 to 3 kilometers) wide. Because of its restricted range, the rock crawler is susceptible to loss and degradation of its habitat. Threats to the species include the volcanic activity of Mount St. Helens and the development of lands owned by the U.S. Forest Service. The rock crawler has disappeared from Ape Cave. Today, the largest known population is associated with Spider Cave.

Conservation efforts are complicated by a lack of information on the life history and ecology of this species. Until this information is at hand, protection of essential habitats is the way to save this grylloblattid.

Richard A. Arnold

GUANS

Class: Aves

Order: Galliformes

Family: Cracidae

Guans hop from limb to limb and run along larger branches as if living a terrestrial lifestyle up in the trees. They all have strong feet and toes that make them good runners. Most guans are adorned with brightly colored dewlaps, crests, or both. One species sports a hornlike growth unique among birds. These birds make their homes only in the forests of Central and South America—one species or another inhabits portions of northeastern Mexico southward into southern Brazil and Uruguay.

Traditionally, guans have been placed in the family Cracidae with curassows and chachalacas. Combined with the brush-turkeys, or megapodes (Megapodiidae), the pheasants (Phasianidae), and the peculiar hoatzin (Opisthocomidae), these birds make up the order Galliformes. Today there is some question about the classification of the guan. A more recent analysis elevates the family to its own distinct order, called Craciformes, but this arrangement has not been widely accepted by ornithologists as yet.

In the most widely accepted classification, nine species in the genus *Ortalis* are called chachalacas. Another dozen species in the genus *Crax* are the curassows. Eighteen species in the genus *Penelope* make up the guans, but not all ornithologists agree on the classification of the birds in this family. Many guans live in areas and habitats that are

almost inaccessible. The forests in which they live are so dense that ornithologists would have difficulty spotting the birds even if they could reach their habitat.

In 1988 the International Cracidae Specialist Group (ICSG), as part of the World Conservation Union (IUCN) and the International Council for Bird Preservation (ICBP), was formed. The ICSG developed a plan to help ornithologists coordinate their efforts to protect the guans and their relatives. The plan emphasizes resolving taxonomic questions about the entire group, conducting basic natural history research both on wild birds and captives, assessing causes of population declines and the magnitude of the threat facing the endangered species, prioritizing recovery work, and developing recovery strategies.

Black-fronted Piping Guan

(Pipile jacutinga)

ESA: Endangered

IUCN: Vulnerable

Length: 22 in. (56 cm)
Weight: 3 lb. (1.4 kg)
Clutch size: 3 eggs (from 1 nest in captivity)
Incubation: 28 days (from 1 nest in captivity)
Diet: Probably fruit
Habitat: Forests, particularly gallery forests
Range: Portions of Brazil, Paraguay, and Argentina

WITH DAWN AN HOUR away, a buzzy drumming sound awakens the morning forest. Then a rising scale of clear whistles pierces the darkness, followed by more buzzy drumming and more whistling. The black-fronted piping guans are awake and ready to begin a new day. The breeding season is here and they are eager to signal their intentions to other guans.

It makes a good story, but no one knows for sure if it is accurate. Perhaps the native people who live within the black-fronted piping guan's range know something of its ways. If they do, they have not written it down to share with the world. Consequently, ornithologists know very little

The black-fronted piping guan is black overall, with a purplish blue sheen to its plumage. One thing that makes this species unusual is the peculiar buzzing sound that its wings make while the bird is gliding.

about the the black-fronted piping guan. However, some useful assumptions can be drawn from knowledge of closely related piping guans.

Most guans have specially modified flight feathers on the outer part of the wing. When they rapidly fan their wings, a drumming or whirring noise results. Piping guans have particularly narrow outer flight feathers that are more like a quill than a vane. When they fan their wings, the drumming sound also seems to have a buzzing quality. To create the noise, the guans climb to the top of a tree, launch themselves into the air, glide a second or two, then rapidly fan their wings while gliding. Thus the drumming comes from birds gliding over the treetops. Within the family, only guans grow these modified feathers and perform the flight display. Because other piping guans perform the flight display, one can reasonably expect that the black-fronted pip-

ing guans do, too. Unfortunately the display is becoming less common in the forests of Paraguay and southern Brazil because the black-fronted piping guans are dwindling in number.

The black-fronted piping guan is black overall, with a purplish blue sheen to its plumage. The feathers of the throat, breast, belly, and sides, have thin white borders that give the underparts a peculiar pattern. The small feathers on the fleshy part of the wing are white and together form a large white patch. The crown sports a dingy white, shaggy crest that usually lies flat but can stand erect. A ring of bare skin around the eye is blue, as is the base of the beak. The beak's tip is black. A bright red dewlap shading to blue and lilac dangles from the throat. The feet are likewise dark red. This is one of many birds that for centuries was killed by native people for food. Using Stone Age hunting techniques and implements, people caused

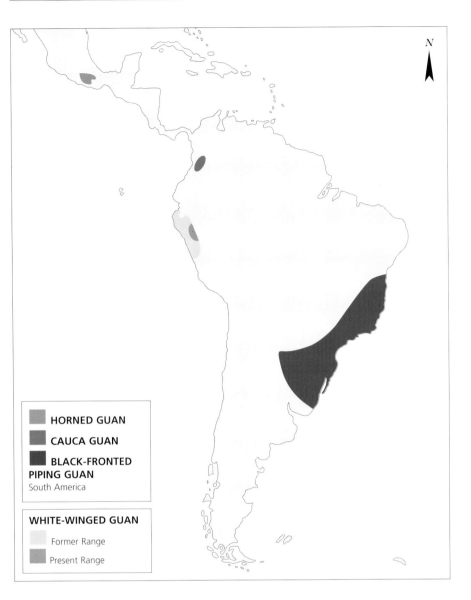

HORNED GUAN

CAUCA GUAN

BLACK-FRONTED
PIPING GUAN
South America

WHITE-WINGED GUAN

Former Range

Present Range

across its former range. Some observers reported seeing it in the gallery forests that had not been cut. Gallery forests are strips of tall trees with interlocking crowns that grow along streams. Ornithologists suspect that the gallery forests used by the black-fronted piping guans may represent the last portions of forests that were once much larger. As forests were cut, the only guans to survive were those in the patches still left uncut. Birds in these patches probably visit the gallery forests because no other habitat is left to them.

As the guan's population declines, each group becomes more vulnerable to hunting. People now use rifles and shotguns rather than arrows, and the impact of hunting is very severe on the guans.

Fortunately, in protected areas, populations are apparently managing to survive.

Cauca Guan
(Penelope perspicax)

IUCN: Endangered

Length: 30 in. (76.2 cm)
Weight: Unknown
Clutch size: Unknown
Incubation: Unknown
Diet: Unknown
Habitat: Humid montane forests from 4,264–6,560 ft. (1,300–2,000 m)
Range: Colombia

THE HUMAN CRAVING for drugs to alter the senses claims many victims. Could the demand for drugs have claimed an entire bird

only minor damage to this species. In predator-prey relationships, predators never kill all their prey. First, the prey outnumbers the predators. Second, prey species develop behaviors that help them avoid predators, so Stone Age people could hunt guans indefinitely.

As people from other continents filtered into South America, however, they brought great changes to the landscape and the culture.

The first wave of Europeans brought simple improvements such as wheels and refined metals. Later cultural influences brought medical care, tractors,

and chain saws. Medical care meant that fewer infants died and people lived longer, resulting in a growing human population. When hunting and gathering and subsistence farming could no longer provide enough food for the inhabitants, modern agricultural practices were introduced, which required clearing the land and plowing the soil for crops. A growing society needs lumber products, which necessitates cutting forests.

The black-fronted piping guan is one bird that cannot survive without the forests. In the 1970s and 1980s the guan's distribution became fragmented species as well? Is the Cauca guan a victim? Perhaps not, but considering where the bird lives, the question comes to mind.

The Cauca guan is a mixture of different shades of brown. Its head and neck are medium to dark brown, grading to a rich cinnamon back, wing, rump, and tail. Throat and breast feathers are edged with tan or buff, producing a scaled look; this pattern is less conspicuous on the upper back and nape. The skin around the eye and lore is bare and gray. Its crest is slight, and its chin is slung with a bright pinkish red dewlap. Its feet and toes, are dark pink. When adult, this guan reaches about 30 inches (76.2 centimeters) in length.

Only in Colombia

Unique to Colombia, the Cauca guan takes its name from a valley in the Colombian Andes. The Cauca Valley stretches through the departments of Cauca and Valle (departments are similar to American states). The Cauca guan once inhabited the forested eastern slopes of the central Andes and the slopes of the western Andes. It might once have inhabited forests at the head of Magdalena Valley and possibly still does.

The Cauca guan survives in three protected areas, although poaching occurs in two of them. Recent population estimates are unavailable.

Will the deforestation end?

If forest cutting does not stop, the habitat needed by the Cauca guan may deteriorate further. Certainly the world needs lumber products that forest trees can provide. Also, people need space

for grazing cattle and sheep. They need space for planting crops. But why were the montane forests of Colombia cut? Were they cut to make room for coca? Could the human craving for cocaine have been so strong that a species became extinct so people could grow more coca to produce more cocaine? In any case, a connection between the cultivation of coca to produce cocaine and the loss of bird habitat is purely speculative.

Horned Guan
(Oreophasis derbianus)

ESA: Endangered

IUCN: Vulnerable

Length: 32–36 in. (81.3–91.4 cm)
Weight: Unknown
Clutch size: 2 eggs
Incubation: Unknown
Diet: Young leaves, berries and other fruits, some insects
Habitat: Humid montane forests 7,000–9,000 ft. (2,134–2,744 m)
Range: Western Guatemala, southern Mexico

FEW BIRDS ARE as unusual yet as attractive as the horned guan. It is thought of by some as the "unicorn" among birds.

The horned guan is black overall with a greenish sheen on its nape and a blue sheen to its wing. Its long tail has a single, narrow, white band closer to the base than to the tip. The throat and breast are white and finely

streaked with black. A tuft of feathers at the base of the beak projects forward over the nostrils. The white eyes set in a black face give the bird a bright-eyed expression. The horned guan's most remarkable feature arises from its crown. A single, bright orange pink or scarlet horn grows up to 2¼ inches (5.5 centimeters) long and protrudes straight upward from the middle crown.

Arboreal bird

Observers report the horned guan as being very tame. This may be because the bird seldom sees people. It lives where most people do not. It avoids dry forests dominated by pines (*Pinus*) and oak (*Quercus*) in favor of cloud forests that are perpetually wet and contain broad-leaved trees. Undergrowth in the cloud forests can be very dense where the canopy is not completely closed and thick. Where the canopy is fuller, the undergrowth can be quite sparse. The horned guan spends most of its time in the trees, but is not exclusively arboreal. Some observers have seen it scratching on the ground, where it presumably searches for some portion of its food.

Prized delicacy

Local people also search for the horned guan as food. It is much prized for eating. However, live birds would seem to be of greater value. For many years, horned guans attracted recreational bird watchers. Several tours a year brought people to Mexico and Guatemala, and they relished seeing rare tropical birds such as the horned guan. Political uncertainties of Central America have dampened some enthusiasm for traveling there, but the potential for tourist dollars still exists.

Wildlife tourism

Local support for protecting horned guans could be nurtured by developing an international interest in wildlife tourism. Many rare species of plants and animals would coincidentally benefit from protecting the horned guan's habitat. Populations in more remote regions within its range appear to be secure.

White-winged Guan

(Penelope albipennis)

ESA: Endangered

IUCN: Critically endangered

Length: 22 in. (56 cm)
Weight: Unknown
Clutch size: Unknown
Incubation: Unknown
Diet: Small fruits and plant shoots
Habitat: Historically, coastal forests including mangroves
Range: Northwestern Peru

In 1977, a Peruvian farmer shot a couple of large, dark birds near his farm. The event was ordinary in all respects except for the identity of the birds. The farmer had killed two white-winged guans, a species presumed extinct for

The horned guan is often thought of as the unicorn of birds. It has a single, bright orange pink or scarlet horn that protrudes straight upward from the crown.

decades. Subsequent fieldwork by ornithologists proved that a small population survived.

Distinctive coloring

White-winged guans grow up to 22 inches (56 centimeters) in length and are dark olive brown overall. Their back, wing, and tail show a bronze sheen. Their underparts are orange-brown with some darker brown mottling. They sport a slight crest that is not as bushy as those of other guans.

Orange dewlap

The bird is essentially tan, with grayish white feather edges. The bare skin around the eye and lores is lilac. Like other guans, they have a dewlap dangling from the throat, which is orange or reddish orange. They take their

name from the flight feathers of the wing. The wing is mostly white, with a bit of brownish smudging toward the inner tips. This white wing confused matters for years.

Some ornithologists of the late 1800s and early 1900s suggested that the white-winged guan was not really a distinct species but merely an abnormal bird of some more common guan species. Perhaps, they speculated, the white-winged guan was just an unusual example of a partially albino bird.

Near extinction

The bird was never abundant, and for many years it was only known from three specimens. Before the issue of the strange, white-winged bird's identity could be resolved, however, it

seemed to slip into extinction. When that farmer shot those two birds, the mystery of the white-winged guan was reopened.

White-winged guans are now recognized as a full species. They inhabit only a small portion of their former range, which was never very large. They seem to favor dry, forested slopes and ravines in the western foothills of the Andes Mountains.

Water lovers

These birds almost always associate with pools or streams. Observers usually report seeing them at elevations between 984 and 1,640 feet (300 to 500 meters). The entire known population, which at the close of the 1990s was thought to number less than 100 individuals, resides in the department of Lambayeque. (In Peru, departments are similar to American states.) Early reports of the species were from coastal swamps.

The bird's presence in the foothills cannot be explained with absolute certainty, but two reasonable possibilities exist. First, the birds were never really abundant in coastal habitat. They might have occurred there incidentally rather than by preference. Second, the species once ranged over a far greater area but disappeared from much of this range as human activities disturbed their lowland habitats.

Last habitat

In this case the foothills do not represent a preferred habitat so much as they represent the last available habitat for a species that has nowhere else to go. The International Cracidae Specialist Group has identified and recognized the white-winged guan as a species in need of research.

The organization will investigate the effectiveness of preserves to determine how well they suit the needs of the species. The International Cracidae Specialist Group also plans to revise the description of white-winged guan habitat by carrying out more thorough field work.

Public awareness

Finally, education programs oriented toward local citizens to improve awareness must be evaluated and improved as necessary.

So long as people continue shooting the rare white-winged guan for food, the species' chance for survival is small.

Kevin Cook

GUAYACÓNS

Class: Actinopterygii

Order: Cyprinodontiformes

Family: Poeciliidae

Of the approximately 20 species of the family Poeciliidae that live in North America, five are members of the genus *Gambusia* and are listed as vulnerable or endangered. In the United States they are commonly called gambusia, while in Mexico they go by the name guayacón. Several of these fishes are rapidly disappearing. The Clear Creek gambusia and the San Marcos gambusia recently have become extinct in the wild.

Like all fishes of the family Poeciliidae, guayacón are known for their ability to give birth to live young. The most familiar member of this family is the guppy (*Poecilia reticulata*). In habitat, guayacón prefer dense vegetation and exhibit a specific taste for adult and larval mosquitos. This characteristic has made gambusia and guayacón desirable in many regions and localities that have mosquito problems. Despite the sometimes catastrophic results caused by their domination of less-aggressive fishes, they often are used as a weapon against malaria and other mosquito-borne diseases.

One characteristic feature of the guayacón is an upturned mouth that enables it to catch insects easily. It has large scales on the body but not on the head (the head usually is bare), a dorsal fin that is positioned far back toward the tail, and a tail fin that is rounded rather than forked.

Guayacón de Cuatro Ciénegas

(Gambusia longispinis)

IUCN: Vulnerable

Length: 1½ in. (4 cm)
Reproduction: Live bearer
Habitat: Shallow marsh pools and lakes among vegetation
Range: Cuatro Ciénegas basin, Coahuila, Mexico

SOUTH OF THE U.S.-Mexican border near the center of the Mexican state of Coahuila is a basin called Cuatro Ciénegas (meaning "four marshes"). This unusual area was formed by the uplifting of surrounding mountain ranges that isolated the basin and its animals from neighboring

Guayacón de Dolores

(Gambusia hurtadoi)

IUCN: Vulnerable

Length: 1⅛ in. (4 cm)
Reproduction: Live bearer
Habitat: Shallow pools among dense vegetation
Range: Chihuahua, Mexico

river drainages. The action of groundwater-fed springs on sediments of the basin floor created an environment that is unique.

Unfortunately, the Cuatro Ciénegas basin and its marvelous diversity of wildlife are under attack from farmers and ranchers eager to use the basin's water resources. Quite a few canals have been constructed to divert water from Cuatro Ciénegas to nearby fields and ranches for irrigation and livestock watering. As more water is diverted from the area, shallow marshes and pools will dry out and fish and other animals will be forced to live in smaller and smaller tracts.

Nearby towns also demand water from the Cuatro Ciénegas region. The relatively small amount of water that is returned from these towns contains sewage and other pollutants. Overall, reduced water levels in Cuatro Ciénegas streams and marshes tend to increase average temperatures and destroy fast-flowing stream riffles and other critical habitat.

If allowed to continue, this reduction in water levels may cause the extinction of unique fish species like the guayacón de Cuatro Ciénegas.

The guaycón de Cuatro Ciénegas, like other gambusia, is a small fish. It has fairly uniform body coloration, with a light yellowish green skin tone. The entire body, including the head and cheeks, are well scaled. All fins except for the male's anal fin are rounded at the ends and slightly small relative to the body size; the dorsal fin on the back is set well behind the fish's center and toward the tail. The anal fin of the male is quite long and pointed and, undoubtedly, was the inspiration for the genus name *longispinis*. This modified anal fin, called a gonopodium, is used during mating and aids in the insertion of a sperm-containing sac into the female.

As with all gambusia, the favorite foods of this guayacón are mosquitoes and other surface-dwelling insects.

National park?

Efforts are under way to declare the Cuatro Ciénegas basin a national park to reduce the use of water for outside purposes. Also, proponents of a conservation plan hope to acquire funds for continued biological research of the unique plants and animals that occupy the region.

DESPITE THE ALREADY small range of the guaycón de Dolores in the Chihuahuan Desert of northern Mexico, the range of this fish continues to diminish. Pollution of the fish's water supply from industrial, domestic, and agricultural sources and its diversion for agriculture create concern for the well-being of this species. In fact, the status of this handsome live-bearing fish continues to deteriorate. Water, a precious commodity in the desert, is being diverted from this fish's range at an alarming rate. Without a plan to conserve water and habitat for this guaycón, it is headed for extinction.

The guaycón de Dolores has a bulbous belly and a fairly uniform body coloration of a light yellow-green skin tone. There is a hint of blue below the eyes and on the sides. A pair of dark horizontal stripes accent each side from just behind the head to the base of the tail.

Live-bearers

Live-bearing fishes like guayacóns do not lay eggs like most fishes. Instead, they hold the eggs within the body. Males are, therefore, required to fertilize eggs within the female. Male guay-

Guayacóns are part of the same genus as gambusia, fish that give birth to their young instead of laying eggs. This is a guaycón de San Gregorio.

acóns use a penis-like structure (a modification of the anal fin called a gonopodium) to insert a sperm-filled sac into the female. The female is not required to use the sperm immediately; the sperm sac may be carried for up to ten months. As eggs mature for fertilization, the female may then release sperm from the sac to fertilize the eggs.

After several weeks the eggs hatch and the young emerge from the mother's abdomen. This reproduction is called ovo-vivipary, which means "live birth from eggs." This guayacón feeds on surface dwelling insects such as mosquitoes.

Guayacón de San Gregorio
(Gambusia alvarezi)

IUCN: Vulnerable

Length: 1½ in. (4 cm)
Habitat: Shallow pools
Range: Chihuahua, Mexico

THE GUAYACÓN DE San Gregorio suffers from habitat degradation and depleted resources. Pollution from industrial and agricultural waste and the diversion of its water supply are this guayacón's biggest threats.

Its body is light yellowish green. The fins, except for the male's anal fin, are rounded and small relative to the body size. Like all other guayacóns, the guayacón de San Gregorio give birth to live young.

Without a plan to conserve water and habitat for this guay-con, the outlook looks dim.

William E. Manci

GUENONS

Class: Mammalia
Order: Primates
Family: Cercopithecidae

Guenons are without doubt the most common monkeys in Africa. They are found in many different habitats throughout what is known as sub-Saharan Africa. Guenon comes from a French word meaning "fright," for a guenon's grimace-like facial expression does indeed give it a frightened look.

Guenons are all longtailed, and inhabit forests, woodlands, and savannahs near rivers and streams. The coats of both sexes are brightly colored, but patterns are more apparent in the males. Many species are known for their beautiful coloration and luxurious fur. Because the guenon has colorful fur markings, it is hunted both for its skin and because it often raids crops. Guenons have cheek pouches for storing food. They are omnivorous, eating leaves, green shoots, flowers, small invertebrates, birds, and eggs.

The social organization of the guenon varies by species. Some species may travel together for long periods, with adult males emitting loud "distance calls" to keep the group together. These groups can vary from small, one-male harems to larger associations with many adults of both sexes. Males may leave their group when they reach sexual maturity.

Guenon species live side by side because they have habitat needs that do not overlap. Different species prefer to forage at different heights in the forest canopy. Even so, guenons can be territorial.

Diana Guenon
(Cercopithecus diana)

ESA: Endangered

IUCN: Vulnerable

Weight: Approximately 11–15 lb. (5–7 kg)
Body length: 16–21 in. (41–53 cm)
Diet: Fruit, leaves, seeds, insects
Gestation period: 150–180 days
Longevity: Unknown
Habitat: Rain forest
Range: Sierra Leone, southwestern Ghana, Liberia, Ivory Coast, Guinea

THE DIANA GUENON is a medium-sized species that is generally considered to be one of the most beautiful. It prefers to live in high canopy forests, mature secondary forest, and some semideciduous forest.

This guenon ranges in medium-sized groups with a single adult male. Its coat is a gray and mousy color with a chestnut back; its extremities and tail are black, and it has a white stripe on its thighs and chest. The rump is red or cream, and the face is black, surrounded by a white ruff and beard.

Two subspecies are recognized: *C. diana diana* is found west of the Sassandra River, and *C. diana roloway* to the east.

No population estimates are available for this guenon and, although it is not a crop pest, it is hunted extensively for meat. Ironically, the typical hunters are those workers employed to destroy its habitat.

The Diana guenons are vulnerable to hunting because their coats are conspicuously colored, they make loud and frequent noises as they travel in the high canopy, and they have a fairly large body size.

Further studies are necessary, but hunting should be banned and the remaining habitat must be protected.

L'Hoest's Guenon

(Cercopithecus lhoesti)

ESA: Endangered

IUCN: Lower risk

Body length: Up to 22½ in. (56 cm)
Diet: Fruit, leaves, insects
Habitat: Montane forest,
Range: Eastern central Africa

FOUND ON THE borders of the Democratic Republic of Congo, Uganda, Rwanda, and Burundi,

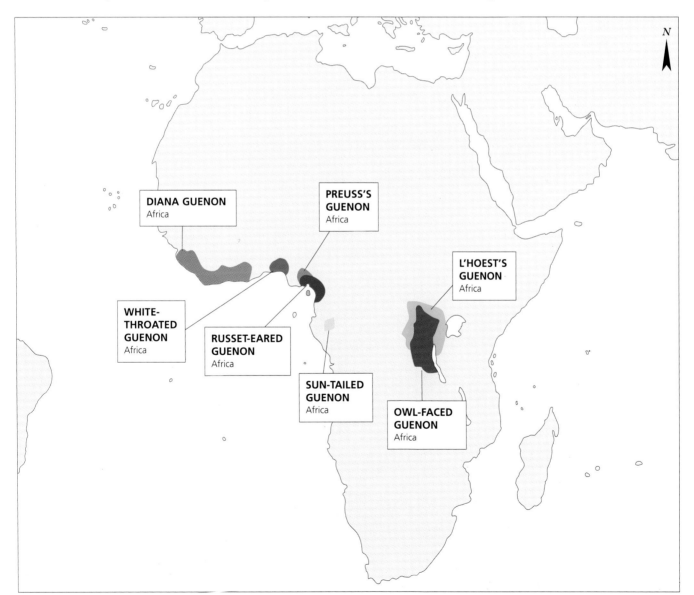

L'Hoest's guenon has a dark gray coat with a chestnut saddle and dark underparts. The eastern form has a white bib, while the western form has less striking markings—a smaller bib, light gray fur on its cheeks, and a whitish "moustache." The weight of this species is unknown. L'Hoest's guenon lives in groups of 10 to 17 individuals, although larger groups have been seen. These groups will occasionally venture down from the canopy onto the ground to raid crops.

It is not unusual to see different guenon species foraging and traveling together, including other monkey groups such as the colobuses. It is uncommon, however, for chimpanzees or baboons to associate with guenons, even though they may be seen feeding in close proximity. Little is known of the lifespan or breeding habits of L'Hoest's guenon.

The total numbers of this guenon are unknown. It is a fruit eater, and is dependent on undisturbed thick forest habitat for survival. Destruction of this environment, and hunting, despite restrictive laws, are the main threats. L'Hoest's guenon inhabits reserves, and there are no protective measures in place.

Owl-faced Guenon

(Cercopithecus hamlyni)

IUCN: Lower risk

Weight: Unknown
Body length: 22½ in. (56 cm)
Diet: Fruit, insects, leaves
Gestation period: Unknown
Longevity: Unknown
Habitat: Lowland rain, montane, and bamboo forest
Range: Eastern Democratic Republic of Congo, parts of Uganda, possibly Rwanda

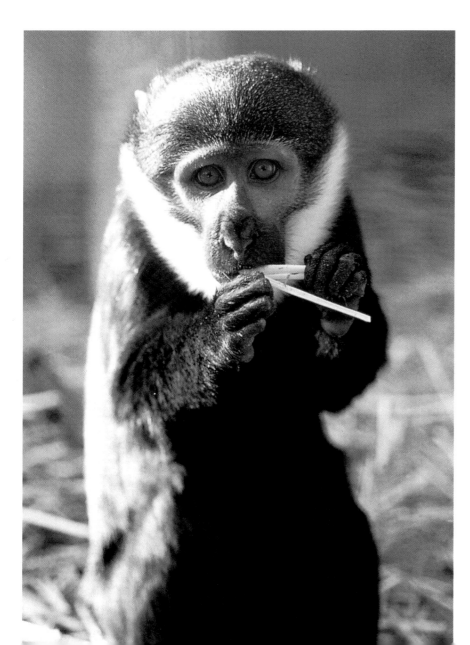

THE COAT OF THE owl-faced guenon, or Hamlyn's monkey, is olive buff, with darker extremities. Its scrotum and perineum are bright blue. It has a black face, with a yellowish crown and a thin white stripe down its nose. It lives in small groups of less than ten, with a single male. They often spend time on the ground.

Low population in the wild

Little is known about this guenon. Surveys of the owl-faced guenon's status and distribution are urgently needed, because no estimates of its numbers exist, but they are not abundant. The guenon's habitat is being destroyed by deforestation.

This guenon breeds well in captivity, and is found in several zoos. The owl-faced guenon will become endangered in the early 21st century if no further conservation measures are taken.

At least eight species of guenon, including L'Hoest's guenon (pictured here), face serious threats from habitat destruction. The total number of L'Hoest's guenon is unknown.

Preuss's Guenon

(Cercopithecus preussi)

Weight: Unknown
Body length: 22½ in. (56 cm)
Diet: Fruit, insects, leaves
Gestation period: Unknown
Longevity: Unknown
Habitat: Primary and old secondary montane forest at about 3,200 ft. (1,000 m)
Range: Southern Nigeria, Cameroon, and Bioko Island

PREUSS'S GUENON has dark fur, with lighter cheeks and beard. It is sometimes considered to be the same species as L'Hoest's guenon. It lives in small, one-male groups of two to nine individuals, and is seen in the presence of other guenon species.

Instant recognition

Many guenon species live near each other, and recognizable features on the the face, head, tail, thighs, and rump prevent interbreeding.

Unlike other primates, there is no sexual swelling in the female during estrus (peak mating receptivity).

No population estimates exist for this guenon, but it has a limited range and its numbers are believed to be declining. The reasons for the decline are habitat destruction and hunting. Surveys

The owl-faced guenon (*Cercopithecus hamlyni*) is one species that is not considered threatened at this time. Because of the constant changes to the African environment, however it may one day face the problems of its endangered relatives.

are needed as well as full protection of its remaining habitat and enforcement of hunting regulations. None of these guenons are known to exist in captivity.

Russet-eared Guenon

(Cercopithecus erythrotis)

Weight: 9–11 lb. (4–5 kg)
Body length: 14½–20½ in. (36–51 cm)
Diet: Fruit, insects, shoots, leaves
Gestation period: Unknown
Longevity: Unknown
Habitat: Rain forest
Range: Southern Nigeria, western Cameroon, Bioko Island

ALSO CALLED THE RED-EARED or nose spotted guenon, the russet-eared guenon has a brown, mouse-colored coat with gray limbs. Part of its tail is red, its face is blue around the eyes, its nose and ear tips are red, and its cheek fur is yellow. Little else is known about this monkey.

Subspecies

Three subspecies are known: *C. erythrotis camerunensis, C. erythrotis erythrotis,* and *C. erythrotis sclateri.* They are all arboreal, typically observed in groups of 4 to more than 30 individuals. Sometimes males are seen by themselves. This animal associates with other guenon species.

Further study needed

This guenon is threatened by hunting and habitat destruction and, although it is protected within forest reserves, more stringent enforcement is needed to prevent further decline. Further study of the russet-eared guenon is required, and data on its habitat and ecology are especially necessary.

No estimates are available of the remaining population of this guenon, but it has been known to breed in captivity. It is hunted across its range.

Sun-tailed Guenon

(Cercopithecus solatus)

IUCN: Vulnerable

Weight: Unknown
Body length: Unknown
Diet: Fruits and vegetables in captivity; crops in the wild
Gestation period: Unknown
Longevity: Unknown
Habitat: Tropical lowland rain forest
Range: Gabon

THE SUN-TAILED GUENON was only discovered in 1984. Its discovery, and the fact that it is only present in one forest, emphasizes the importance of tropical rain forest as a source of genetic reserves.

There is little known about this animal and no population estimates are available.

The sun-tailed guenon has been hunted for its meat and the species was, unfortunately, only discovered after many had been shot for food by hunters.

Logging is less likely to be a problem for these guenons than the danger from hunting. Fortunately, the trees removed from its environment are not its source of food. But restricted distribution, rarity, hunting, and logging make the sun-tailed guenon vulnerable to decline.

Six animals are reportedly in captivity (three in Gabon, and three in France), but as it is a rel-

Another endangered guenon is the white-throated which is sometimes refered to as the red-bellied guenon. This species has been adversely affected by habitat destruction.

atively new species, no protective legislation yet exists, and studies of both its distribution and its biology are needed.

White-throated Guenon

(Cercopithecus erythrogaster)

ESA: Endangered

IUCN: Vulnerable

Weight: 13 lb. (6 kg)
Body length: 18 in. (26 cm)
Gestation period: Unknown
Longevity: Unknown
Diet: Fruit, possibly insects
Habitat: Lowland rain forest
Range: Southwest Nigeria

THE WHITE-THROATED guenon is a little known species. The guenon is mousy brown, with a black face, a white throat ruff and a reddish to gray belly.

While little is known about the russet-eared guenon in the wild, it has been known to breed in captivity, thus improving its chance for survival.

Total numbers of the guenon are unknown, but thought to be declining. The white-throated guenon is threatened by habitat destruction as the forest is thinned out. It is also hunted for meat and is not specifically protected by hunting regulations. Its remaining range must be protected to save this species.

Lack of information

The social and mating behavior of this guenon are not documented. It is thought to live in one-male groups of over 30 animals. Smaller foraging groups numbering just five individuals are more commonly seen. This guenon spends much time in the trees in dense vegetation.

Sarah Dart

See also Colobuses, Langurs, Macaques, Mandrills, and Mangabeys.

White-breasted Guineafowl

(Agelastes meleagrides)

ESA: Threatened

IUCN: Vulnerable

Class: Aves
Order: Galliformes
Family: Phasianidae
Subfamily: Numidinae
Length: 18 in. (45.7 cm)
Weight: Unknown
Clutch size: Unknown
Incubation: Unknown
Diet: Plant and animal foods
Habitat: Forest undergrowth
Range: Western Africa

THE SEVEN GUINEAFOWL species form a subfamily (Numidinae) of the pheasant family (Phasianidae). The guineafowls include the common domesticated helmeted guineafowl (*Numida meleagris*) and the endangered white-breasted guineafowl.

The domesticated helmeted guineafowl are kept for food, and they eat insects and warn of intruders. They are adaptable and face no threat of extinction.

In contrast, the white-breasted guineafowl does not adapt well to human-made habitats. Like other guineafowls, it forms small flocks, and is primarily terrestrial. It resembles other guineafowls in that it has the bare, brightly colored head and upper neck. Its head is bright rose-red and it has a white lower throat and breast. The white extends up and over the upper back, like a shawl. Unlike most other guineafowls, it had a naturally small distribution.

Historically, it inhabited primary rain forests in Ghana, Ivory Coast, Liberia, Sierra Leone, and Guinea. The trees of such forests grow very tall and dense, forming a canopy. The canopy foliage is usually so dense that little light reaches the forest floor. Without sunlight, few plants thrive on the floor of the forest. The white-breasted guineafowl lived among the few plants that form the sparse undergrowth of these primary forests. When the forest trees are cut, more sunlight reaches the forest floor, and plants invade the forest. The dense growth does not appeal to the white-breasted guineafowl. It fails to reproduce, and its population declines.

People have been cutting trees and destroying primary forests for decades in west Africa. Unfortunately, the rain does not stop falling as the forests disappear. Some areas of coastal west Africa receive 16 to 18 feet (488 to 549 centimeters) of rain a year. Without the forests to deflect the rain and to absorb the water, erosion begins immediately. Before new vegetation can become established, soil washes out to the Gulf of Guinea. When new vegetation does become established, it does not include the structure essential for white-breasted guineafowls.

The forests are cut as a prelude to mining activities, to open up land for farming and grazing, for the lumber market, or for firewood. These activities provide basic materials for modern civilization, but the cutting has been excessive with the assumption that animals will find somewhere else to go, when in reality there is no other place for them.

Poachers and predators

Some preserves and national parks have been established in the west African nations where the white-breasted guineafowl lives, but they are largely ineffective. The forests are still cut both legally and illegally, and people still hunt the guineafowl for food. A healthy population of any species can withstand some predation but a depleted species with only a fraction of its population cannot sustain any extra predation. The white-breasted guineafowl must contend with its natural predators, and hunting by humans hastens the bird's approach to extinction. Ending poaching within parks and reserves is difficult in a society that largely accepts hunting as part of normal human behavior.

Saving the white-breasted guineafowl will depend on a captive-breeding program, but before captive birds can be released into the wild, the wild lands must be made safe. West African nations must control forest cutting and indiscriminate hunting. At the close of the 1990s, there was some hope for the overall population.

Kevin Cook

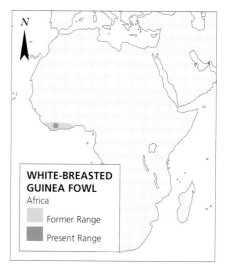

WHITE-BREASTED GUINEA FOWL
Africa

Former Range

Present Range

Mindanao Gymnure

(Podogymnura truei)

IUCN: Endangered

Class: Mammalia
Order: Insectivora
Family: Erinaceidae
Weight: Unknown
Head-body length: 5–5¾ in.
(13–15 cm)
Diet: Carnivorous
Gestation period: Unknown
Longevity: Unknown
Habitat: Forest vegetation
Range: Mindanao Island,
Philippines

THE MINDANAO GYMNURE is known to occur only on the island of Mindanao. There is only one other species in the genus, and it occurs on Dinagat Island, also in the Philippines. It is uncertain how widespread or numerous the Mindanao gymnure once was, but logging and slash-and-burn agricultural techniques threaten it today.

The Mindanao gymnure is a small, shrewlike creature with a long, narrow snout and well-developed canine teeth. The long, thick body fur ranges in color from gray to a reddish brown above, while the underparts are a paler, whitish gray tinged with brown. The tail hair is thinner and ranges from a yellow-brown to purple in color.

The Mindanao gymnure has been collected on three different mountains at elevations ranging from 5,250 to 7,550 feet (1,600 to 2,300 meters). It has been caught among mossy tree roots, in dense fern undergrowth, and near logs and boulders in dense vegetation.

Little is known of the natural history of this small mammal. Its diet seems to consist of insects and earthworms, based on the stomach contents of one individual, with the speculation that its feeding biology may be similar to that of shrews. No data exists about its reproductive biology, predators, or population. The rapidly increasing population of the Philippines has led to habitat loss, and it is vital that we learn more about this tiny creature to ensure its continued survival.

Terry Tompkins

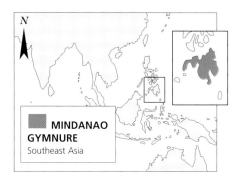

MINDANAO GYMNURE
Southeast Asia

HARES

Class: Mammalia

Order: Lagomorpha

Family: Leporidae

Animal biologists sometimes question the casual way people use terms for different species. There are some species that are properly called *rabbits*, while others should be called *hares*, but the names are often used inter-changeably. The term *hare* usually refers to a mammal that is larger than a rabbit, and a hare normally has longer ears with black tips. There are some variations in the shape of the skull, too. Hares are also born fully furred and ready to move within minutes of birth.

Hispid Hare

(Caprolagus hispidus)

ESA: Endangered

IUCN: Endangered

Weight: 5½ lb. (2.5 kg)
Body length: 14¾–19½ in.
(38–50 cm)
Diet: Herbivorous
Gestation period: Unknown
Longevity: Unknown
Habitat: Grass thickets,
woodland
Range: Northern India

THE HISPID HARE was feared to be extinct during the early part of the 19th century. However, scattered discoveries during the late 1950s through the early 1970s indicated that the species still survived in several small populations. The survivors were scattered throughout its former range in the southern foothills of the Himalayas.

In jeopardy

Even though this hare is now found in several locations, its future is still in jeopardy. Most often considered to be a potential meal by hunters, or a destroyer of crops, this slow-moving relative of the common rabbit is considered by many to be the most at risk of all the endangered mammals in the world.

The hispid hare (sometimes called a bristly rabbit) is one of

the largest members of the order Lagomorpha, a group that includes rabbits and pikas as well as hares. While biologists are still not in complete agreement, it is now fairly standard to refer to members of the genus *Lepus* as hares, while all other lagomorphs (besides the pikas) are properly called rabbits. This species, however, is still usually referred to as a hare and that name is used here to avoid confusion.

Unique features

The hispid hare has some features quite unlike those expected from a member of its family. The ears are very short and wide, unlike the long ears normally associated with rabbits. In addition, the hind legs are short and stocky—in fact, they are not much longer than the front legs. Both of these features may be adaptations to living in the thick thatch grassland of India. The hispid hare probably relies on stealth and its ability to sneak through the dense undergrowth to escape predators.

Another unusual feature of this species, the one which led to its common name, is its pelage or coat of fur. Covering the short, fine inner fur is a layer of very coarse, almost bristlelike, guard hairs. The hispid hare is a dark brown color on the back, while the underside of the body is a pale brownish white.

Thatched home

The few studies of the hispid hare give biologists a clue as to why this species in danger. Historically, this species apparently

A greater study of the hispid hare is necessary to design a recovery plan that would attempt to save what is left of one of the most primitive of the surviving lagomorph species.

lived much of the year within thick stands of thatch, using it as cover from predators. The thatch, which reaches heights of from 3 to 5 feet (1 to 1.5 meters) during the monsoon season, is also a major food source. The roots and soft interior part of the stems are the bulk of the hare's diet. It is believed that the hispid hare only left this dense, relatively secure area when, at the height of the rains, the thatch became too waterlogged to inhabit.

Smoked out

This lifestyle seems to have served the hare well until large numbers of humans arrived on the scene. During the dry part of the year, at the very time when it appears the hispid hare was bearing young, the dry thatch was burned by local people to increase the yield of thatch for use as a roofing material. In addi-

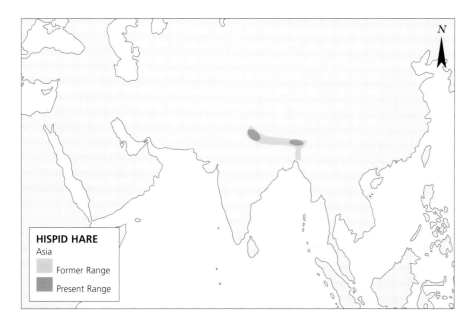

HISPID HARE
Asia

Former Range

Present Range

tion the burning served to clear the thatch lands and adjacent woodlands for agricultural purposes. This activity was harmful to the hare; it fled the burning areas, moving to adjacent cultivated fields and irrigation embankments. There, farmers found it easier to kill the hispid hare for food. Also, it was mistakenly believed that the hispid hare damaged crops.

Easy prey

After its thatch cover had been burned, domestic dogs probably found the slower hispid hare easy prey. The exposed hare is also easier prey for its own natural predators, the leopard-cat (*Felis bengalensis*), the Indian civets (*Viverricula* sp.), the Indian fox (*Vulpes bengalensis*), and the jackal (*Canis aureus indicus*).

Shrinking communities

The hispid hare survives today only in northwestern Assam and in a few populations along the India-Nepal border.

Many of these areas are protected, but because of the small sizes of the populations, the future for this species does not appear promising.

Space needed

Because an individual hare is intolerant of all other hispid hares except its mate, it does not make its home in large warrens or colonies like some other species of lagomorph, and each individual requires quite a large area for itself.

Home ranges for the hare of 1 to 2 acres (0.4 to 0.8 hectares) have been reported. Considering the lack of tolerance for hares other than its mate, and its shrinking habitat, it is unlikely that this species will survive without taking some drastic measures to halt its decline.

Further study

To save the hare from extinction, it would be necessary to reduce or completely eliminate thatch burning and to enforce the Indian Wildlife Protection Act. Lastly a program should be instigated to educate local people about conservation. At the same time, greater study of this species is necessary to design a feasible recovery plan.

N

TEHUANTEPEC HARE
Southern Mexico

Tehuantepec Hare

(Lepus flavigularis)

IUCN: Endangered

Weight: Unknown
Head-body length: 21 in. (53 cm)
Diet: Probably herbivorous
Gestation period: Unknown
Longevity: Unknown
Habitat: Shrub forest on coastal sand dunes
Range: Southern Mexico

ONE OF 23 SPECIES of hares contained within the genus *Lepus*, the Tehuantepec hare is in serious danger of extinction. It has a very limited distribution, being found only in the 2½ to 3 mile (4 to 5 kilometer) wide strip of shrub forest on the coastal sand dunes bordering the Gulf of Tehuantepec in the Mexican states of Oaxaca and Chiapas. Compounding the danger to any species with such a small range are some additional problems. This hare is hunted at night for food by people using guns and fishing throw nets. Its habitat is being cleared for agricultural purposes.

The Tehuantepec hare, like nearly all members of the genus *Lepus*, has long ears and large hind legs and feet. The species is gray in color over much of the body, but the fur on the back is a light reddish brown with some black hairs. There is a black stripe on the nape of the neck that runs up to the ears. The lower sides and belly are white. Both the large ears and the large hind limbs are important in this species' defense system. Hares neither dig nor occupy burrows, they have come to rely on early detection of danger, hence the large ears. They combine this early detection with their ability to run quickly and for prolonged distances in order to avoid predators. Hares are nocturnal, and sit motionless to avoid detection.

Hares bear young that are fully furred, with open eyes and the ability to move about shortly after birth. Rabbit offspring are born blind, partially furred, and unable to move. Although there are no direct reports about the diet, it is believed that, like other members of the genus *Lepus*, the Tehuantepec hare eats grasses and forbs (a broadleaved, flowering plant), as well as the buds, twigs, and bark of woody plants. This diet compounds the other threats to the hare: if it survives habitat loss and being hunted for food, it is still in danger of being killed by farmers who believe they are protecting their crops from pests.

Sand dune habitat

It is important that a habitat protection plan be developed and put in place for the coastal sand dunes. With human populations growing rapidly in the area, accompanied by greater land cultivation to feed that growth, the future for this secretive mammal is very much in question.

Terry Tompkins

See also Pikas, Rabbits.

HARTEBEESTS

Class: Artiodactyla

Family: Bovidae

Subfamily: Bovinae

Tribe: Alcelaphini

Hartebeests are a large group of antelope found in savanna habitats south of the Sahara desert in Africa. This group includes the true hartebeests (genus *Alcelaphus*); the topis, tsessebes, bontebok, and blesbok (genus *Damaliscus*); and the gnus (genus *Connochaetes*), or wildebeests. Since hartebeests are found over a wide area (from northern to southern Africa), there are many subspecies that share similar characteristics. Some of these traits include long faces; heavily ringed horns on both males and females; shoulders that are higher than the rump, giving their bodies a sloped appearance; and color that varies from light brown to mahogany. Some subspecies sport black flashings on the legs and face.

There is some confusion about the origin of the name *hartebeest*. This was the term given these antelope by early Dutch settlers. Some translated the name as "deerbeast," while others thought the word was *hardbeast*, meaning that it was difficult to kill. In fact, the Dutch ranchers often tried to run them down on horseback, without success; the hartebeest is not only one of the swiftest antelope in the world but by far has the most stamina. Even the best thoroughbred horse could not catch or run down a hartebeest.

Hartebeests are found in small groups of from six to twelve individuals. Occasionally males make up part of the group, but more often males are either solitary or found in bachelor groups. The males prefer high ground (often a termite mound) that they can climb onto to survey the surrounding veldt. When breeding season comes, the males will find favored territory and each male stakes out his own personal territory to defend. Fighting males will butt their heads together, push and shove with their horns, and even drop down to their knees to try to hook their opponent.

Some hartebeest species still have large populations; two subspecies, however, do not and are now endangered. Unfortunately, the North African hartebeest (*A. buselaphus buselaphus*) is already extinct.

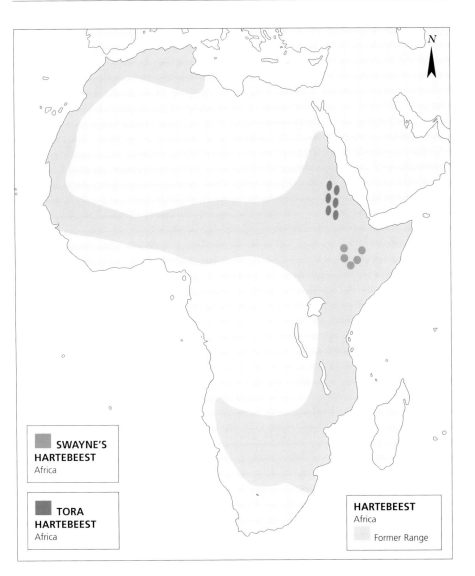

SWAYNE'S
HARTEBEEST
Africa

TORA
HARTEBEEST
Africa

HARTEBEEST
Africa

Former Range

Swayne's Hartebeest
(Alcelaphus buselaphus swaynei)

ESA: Endangered

IUCN: Endangered

Weight: 275–400 lb. (125–182 kg)
Shoulder height: 47–53 in. (120–135 cm)
Diet: Grass, leaves, and twigs
Gestation period: 240 days
Longevity: 18–20 years
Habitat: Wooded grasslands
Range: Ethiopia, Somalia

THE SWAYNE'S hartebeest used to be found in Ethiopia and Somalia; however, except for some isolated pockets, this subspecies was virtually eliminated from Somalia by 1930.

If this hartebeest did manage to persist into the 1970s, the last remaining individuals were probably wiped out by the disastrous civil war.

Shared characteristics

Swayne's resembles the other hartebeests, the tora and the korrigum, and is about the same height. It tends to have a slightly redder coat than other hartebeests, and the front of its upper limbs are dark, while the whole forehead is dark down to the nostrils. Swayne's hartebeest also has a lunette- or lyre-shaped pair of horns.

The red, or Cape, hartebeest (*Alcelaphus buselaphus caama*), is a true hartebeest. It roams the grasslands of Angola, Botswana, Namibia, and South Africa. This species is at lower risk of extinction.

Swayne's hartebeest is normally wary of the approach of humans; however, if a human is in the area, the animal's curiosity will sometimes allow the human to approach fairly close.

Contested territory

This hartebeest ranges amid thorny savanna, usually in small groups. There is often a male and a number of females with their young. The males tend to be territorial, and there are quite a few fights that go on between the males, which can get savage.

Scarce commodity

Water is normally scarce in the bush veldt this hartebeest prefers; although water holes are available this species can tolerate drought very well. Despite disastrous droughts in Ethiopia, Swayne's hartebeest got along reasonably well.

Limited range

The biggest threat to Swayne's hartebeest is its small range, caused by the encroachment of people and the destruction of habitat that so often accompanies the presence of humans. The adjacent cultivated areas of Ethiopia have large human populations with equally large numbers of sheep, goats, cattle, and horses. These domesticated animals are, unfortunately, allowed to overgraze, which affects the hartebeest range. The livestock also compete for the same water as the hartebeest. Despite protection by the Ethiopian government, poaching is still common.

None in captivity

Swayne's hartebeest has never been in captivity, so there is no population reservoir in captivity to support the wild population. A hartebeest is not the easiest animal to manage in captivity because it needs considerable room to range. Male hartebeests are particularly antagonistic to other males when it comes to territory, and even the females have a combative nature over dominance. If a few hartebeests were taken into captivity and properly managed, there is no reason why Swayne's hartebeest shouldn't do reasonably well.

Uncertain existence

The existence in the wild of this hartebeest is extremely precarious. One of the largest groups was located in the Senkelle reserve in central Ethiopia. In 1990, the numbers on this reserve were about 2,000. All the political and drought problems that Ethiopia has experienced over the years have taken their toll. For example, during a recent political revolution, a population estimated at between 2,000 and 3,000 was reduced to a mere 200 by armed bands of local people hunting the species as an easy source of food. For this reason alone, Swayne's hartebeest is considered to be endangered.

Tora Hartebeest
(Alcelaphus buselaphus tora)

ESA: Endangered

IUCN: Endangered

Weight: 287–397 lb. (130–180 kg)
Shoulder height: 47–57 in. (120–145 cm)
Diet: Leaves, twigs, and grasses
Gestation period: 240 days
Longevity: 18–20 years
Habitat: Wooded grassland
Range: Northwestern Ethiopia, east Sudan

THE TORA HARTEBEEST comes from the open scrub and thorn bush country of northwestern Ethiopia and eastern Sudan, but once it ranged into southeastern Egypt as well. This hartebeest once numbered literally in the thousands. Unfortunately, due to excessive hunting and competition from the local herds of livestock, their numbers have been reduced to less than 5,000.

Even though it has been afforded official protection over most of its range, this protection has existed more on paper than in reality, so this animal stays in great jeopardy.

Lyre-shaped horns

The tora hartebeest, like all other hartebeests, has the typical body conformation of high shoulders, sloping hind quarters, and a slender neck with a long head. Both sexes have widely spread, lyre-shaped horns that are slightly ribbed.

Its color is similar to other animals in this group, such as Swayne's hartebeest, but it has a much darker coat overall. The forelegs, base coat, and forehead are also much darker.

Damaliscus hunteri, or Hunter's antelope, is also called Hunter's hartebeest by some who classify these animals. By whatever name they are called, they are strong and elegant creatures.

Dominance and predators

The tora hartebeest is a grass-land-dwelling animal, and males establish territory and defend it forcefully while they are trying to attract females.

On some of the most favored sites, much fighting goes on between males, not only for dom-inance in breeding but for the best territory where they are likely to attract females. These battles are sometimes vicious. Horns can snap and animals can be maimed or injured; then they run the risk of being killed later by a predator.

Adaptation to drought

The tora hartebeest is tolerant of dry conditions, and can manage to exist for long periods of time without drinking water. This har-tebeeste can sustain itself on whatever moisture it can extract from the leaves, twigs, and grasses which form its diet.

Calves are born during the time of the spring rains after a gestation of about 240 days. Within a short time the newly born calves are strong enough to follow the mother. Besides human hunters, the tora harte-beest is preyed on by most local predators, including lions, leop-ards, and certainly hyenas.

The tora hartebeest has rarely been kept in captivity. There has never been a sufficient number to establish a captive population.

Until there is a sufficient pop-ulation reservoir in captivity to draw on, it will be impossible to establish a thriving and increas-ing wild population.

Warren D. Thomas

See also Antelopes and Kor-rigum.

HARVESTMEN

Class: Arachnida

Order: Opiliones

Family: Phalangodidae

Harvestmen are the spiderlike creatures known as daddy-longlegs. Most harvestmen found in temperate regions of the world are active animals that run rapidly on stiltlike legs, which in some species may be 30 times as long as the body. Worldwide there are between 3,500 to 5,000 species of this spiderlike insect.

The scientific name for this order, Opiliones, is derived from the Latin word *opilio*, meaning "shepherd," and may refer to the fact that in some countries, shepherds walk about on stilts to better count their flocks. The family name is from a Greek word, *phalangion*, which means spider. There are several harvestmen in the family Phalangodidae known to be endangered.

The animal class Arachnida consists of several orders. They are different from other arthropods such as insects by having an oval body divided into only two parts. The parts are the anterior cephalothorax or prosoma, and a posterior abdomen. Six pairs of leglike appendages attach to the prosoma. One pair is called the chelicerae, which are jawlike appendages used for biting and holding; another pair, called the pedipalps, function chiefly as tactile organs (but also help grasp food); and four pairs of legs are used for locomotion.

Unlike insects, arachnida lack wings, antennae, and strong biting jaws. Their eyes, if any, are simple rather than the compound form found in many insects and crustaceans. The bodies of harvestmen are usually covered with numerous spines and bristles.

Most harvestmen measure less than ½ inch (about 5 to 10 millimeters) in length and have very long, thin legs. Although they are often mistaken for spiders, harvestmen can be distinguished from true spiders by their legs, the absence of a waist or pedicel between the abdomen and cephalothorax, and a multi-segmented abdomen.

It is the legs that serve harvestmen as their primary sources of information. In addition to the fundamental purpose of walking, harvestmen use their legs for climbing, seizing prey, and digging. The first, third, and fourth pair of legs are used for walking, while the second pair are more sensory in function. Their legs are covered with numerous tactile sensory organs in the form of spines, hairs, and bumps, as well as chemical receptors and even hearing organs. The legs also function much as the nose, tongue, and ears do for other animals. In addition, the tactile organs on the legs supplement the function of the eyes, which can do little more than distinguish between light and dark. Because their legs serve many vital functions, they are kept in good condition.

Harvestmen are primarily carnivorous and feed on fresh or recently dead animal tissue. Some species are omnivores and feed on fungi, spores, and other plant matter. They eat a wide variety of animal matter, but more often prey on smaller invertebrates such as mites (Acarina) and insects such as springtails (Collembola). The legs and other limbs are important for prey capture and feeding.

Water is very important to harvestmen, so many species live in areas characterized by high humidity. For this reason, tropical regions of the world support the greatest number of harvestmen species and certainly most of the largest ones. In temperate regions, harvestmen tend to be smaller in size and live in habitats where moisture is conserved, such as under rocks or in caves. Also, many species are active primarily during wetter seasons of the year.

Larger harvestmen have a natural camouflage. They are colored in such a way that allows them to hide from potential predators. Some harvestmen species secrete a repugnant fluid that is distasteful to predators.

Smaller, ground-dwelling harvestmen are probably preyed upon by other arachnids and insects. If a harvestman is gripped by an aggressor, its legs readily break (not unlike a starfish), which allows them to escape. The detached limb may make its own rhythmical movements for as long as an hour, which serves to distract the would-be predator's attention from the real prey. Unlike starfish, lost appendages are not regenerated.

Most species of harvestmen are believed to have an annual life cycle, although several are known to have longer life cycles. Some species are known to reproduce by sexual means, while others reproduce partheno-genetically, a type of asexual reproduction.

Endangered species

Some members of the harvestmen family have been recognized or proposed for endangered status in the United States. The Bee Creek Cave harvestman (*Texella reddelli*) and the Bone Cave harvestman (*Texella reyesi*) live in six small caves and sinkholes of the Edwards Limestone formation near Austin, Texas. The largest of these caves is only about 200 feet (60 meters) in length. This species measures about 2 millimeters in length, is yellowish brown in color, and is blind. These caves, which also harbor two endangered beetles, a pseudoscorpion, and a spider, are threatened by urban and industrial development. One cave was filled when a new road was built, and it is feared that further development near the caves will result in these species' destruction by changing the natural drainage patterns. Land clearing, digging, and blasting have caused other caves in the area to collapse or have hidden their entrances.

Nothing is known about the biology of this harvestman, so protection of its habitat is essential for its conservation.

Limestone caves

Another limestone cave dweller is the Melones Cave harvestman (*Banksula melones*) of California. This species is proposed for vulnerable status, and currently lives under rocks in the twilight and dark regions of about 15 caves. These caves are associated with the Stanislaus River in the Sierra Nevada mountain range. Construction of a new dam and reservoir threatens the survival of this species. The Melones Cave harvestman measures about 2 millimeters in length and probably feeds on springtails (Collembola), but little else is known about it. For this reason, habitat protection will be essential until more biological information on its life history and ecological requirements can be obtained.

In the greater San Francisco-San Jose Bay area of California there are thought to be seven species of harvestmen. These are the Edgewood blind (*Calicina minor*), Edgewood Park micro-blind (*Microcina edgewoodensis*), Hom's micro-blind (*Microcina homi*), Jung's micro-blind (*Microcina jungi*), Lee's micro-blind (*Microcina leei*), Lum's micro-blind (*Microcina lumi*), and Tiburon micro-blind (*Microcina tiburona*).

All of these harvestmen live in serpentine grassland habitat and have restricted ranges, and most are known from only one or two locations. They live under rocks and are active during the winter rainy season. Habitat destruction due to housing and highway developments threaten their survival.

Richard A. Arnold

HAWKS

Class: Aves

Order: Falconiformes

Family: Accipitridae

Hawks inhabit almost every terrestrial habitat from prairies through forests to tundra.

No specific biological criteria distinguish hawks from eagles, but eagles are generally larger and have stouter physiques.

The two largest groups of hawks are the bird hawks in the genus *Accipiter* and the soaring hawks in the genus *Buteo*. American bird enthusiasts have adopted *accipiter* and *buteo* into common usage as group names.

The accipiters are called bird hawks because many species feed primarily or even exclusively on birds. Typical accipiters have short, round wings and long, narrow tails. These features give them quick bursts of speed and high maneuverability for pursuing small birds in forests and woodlands.

The buteos have longer wings than accipiters, and short, fan-shaped tails. These traits allow them to soar on air currents with little wing flapping.

Buteos frequently hunt in areas where no perches are available. They compensate by soaring high above the ground, then dropping on their prey. Soaring as opposed to flapping allows them to hunt with only a minimal use of energy.

Many accipiters have suffered range changes as people have cut woodlands and forests. Buteos have, likewise, shifted their range or entirely disappeared from some areas as prairies and savannas have been converted to agriculture. The most severely threatened hawks live on islands from which naturally small populations cannot escape when habitat disappears.

For at least three centuries, beginning in the 1600s, people deliberately and methodically persecuted hawks and other birds of prey. Governments have paid bounties to hunters or other people who killed hawks and then turned in the feet as proof. There was a mistaken belief that hawks killed poultry and other livestock as well as game animals that were important food sources for humans.

Ironically, hawks actually eat more insects and mice than anything else, and in fact they function as natural pest controllers by protecting crops from insect and rodent damage.

Hawaiian Hawk

(Buteo solitarius)

ESA: Endangered

IUCN: Lower risk

Length: 16–18 in. (40.6–45.7 cm); females larger than males
Weight: 15–17½ oz. (420–490 g) based on broad-winged hawk; females larger than males
Clutch size: Usually 1–2 eggs
Incubation: Unknown
Diet: Insects, birds, rodents
Habitat: Woodland
Range: Hawaii

BEFORE HUMANS DISCOVERED the Hawaiian Islands, a small hawk settled there. Although perfectly capable of flight over the open sea, the hawk, as a species, was content to live on Hawaii, the largest of the islands. Being 2,397 miles (3,835 kilometers) southwest of San Francisco, California, Hawaii enjoyed a unique isolation from most continental influences. No predators such as amphibians, reptiles, and mammals—except a species of bat (*Lasiurus cinereus*), could cross the Pacific ocean and establish themselves on the island. Consequently, the hawk was able to capture large insects and small birds with little competition.

Then people found the islands. They also found the hawk. The Polynesians called it *io*, perhaps for the piercing cry it gives, while American ornithologists know the species as the Hawaiian hawk. As people settled the islands they exposed them to

When the island of Hawaii was still undiscovered by humans, the Hawaiian hawk prospered. Once this beautiful land was inhabited by humans, the bird's habitat was changed forever.

changes that had enormous implications. The Polynesians brought the Polynesian rat (*Rattus exulans*) to the islands. Europeans and Americans brought many new species—intentionally and otherwise, including black rats (*Rattus rattus*), Norway rats (*Rattus norvegicus*), and house mice (*Mus musculus*). Polynesians also began clearing lowland forests to grow crops and provide building materials. European and American settlers carried the destruction even further. The later settlers brought mosquitoes to Hawaii, and those insects carried the germ for avian malaria. All of these events influenced the sur-

Hawks facing the gravest problems are those found isolated on islands, such as Ridgway's hawk, which is found on Hispaniola in the Greater Antilles. When their habitat is destroyed, they will have nowhere to go.

astated the native bird population. Despite the habitat changes, the Hawaiian hawk has survived.

Exotic prey

Exotic mammals became an alternative food supply for the hawk. Whereas native songbirds succumbed to malaria, exotic birds did not. Birds such as the common myna (*Acridotheres tristis*) and the Japanese white-eye (*Zosterops japonicus*) became well established on the Hawaiian Islands and became a new food source. Even some introduced spiders and insects now figure prominently in the Hawaiian hawk's diet. In this respect, the hawk shows more adaptability to habitat alterations than do most native birds.

Color phases

As with many buteos, the Hawaiian hawk shows two distinct color phases. In the dark phase, the hawks are dark brown overall. Light phase birds contrast with rufous brown upperparts and white underparts streaked brown on the breast. Both color phases show a grayish tail, faintly banded with dark brown. Within the total Hawaiian hawk population the light and dark phases occur in almost equal proportions. These color phases do not represent discrete species or subspecies: just as some humans grow brown, red, or blond hair, buteos have variable genes for plumage color. In natural situations, color phases probably

vival of the Hawaiian hawk. Basically a woodland species, the bird hunted over most habitat types on Hawaii except the densest rain forests. As grasslands and shrub lands were converted to sugarcane plantations and other

agricultural uses, the hawk lost necessary habitat for both nesting and hunting. Forest and woodland clearing also diminished the habitat available for small birds, the hawk's principal food. Avian malaria further dev-

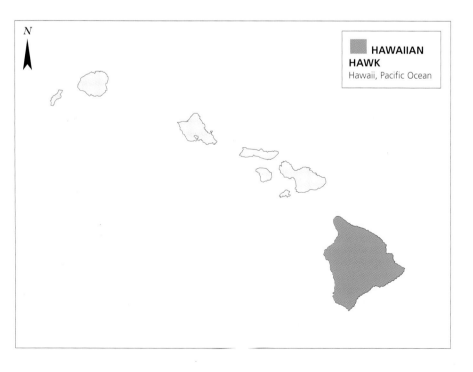

N

HAWAIIAN HAWK
Hawaii, Pacific Ocean

contribute to a species' ability to accommodate to changing habitat conditions.

As well as rodents, birds, and insects, many exotic plants and a variety of exotic grazing mammals have become established on the island. The grazing mammals, such as cattle, sheep, goats, horses, burros, and deer, plus pigs that root in the soil, spread the seeds of exotic plants by passing the seeds in their feces. These plants quickly grow and outcompete native plants. They have spread over the island and degraded the quality of the last patches of native forests and woodlands. The grazing animals, meanwhile, eat the native plants, consuming fruits, seeds, seedlings, saplings, and foliage. Between the exotic plants and the exotic animals, Hawaii's native habitats are drastically altered even though they look green and healthy.

Healthy population

No one knows for sure how Hawaiian hawks are affected by these disturbances. Because so many other native Hawaiian birds became extinct or now face extinction owing to human-caused problems, prudence urges monitoring the Hawaiian hawk population and protecting it from further disturbance. Some ornithologists in the 1980s found that the hawk was at that time occupying many diverse habitats between sea level and the uppermost limit of trees on Hawaii. Its population appeared healthy enough and its distribution was broad enough to justify the IUCN revising its status from endangered to lower risk.

The success of the Hawaiian hawk in adapting to altered conditions on Hawaii must not be misconstrued. Many other Hawaiian birds, notably the Hawaiian goose (*Branta sandvicensis*) and the Hawaiian crow (*Corvus hawaiiensis*), have failed to thrive in the modified environment of present-day Hawaii. The Hawaiian hawk prospered on Hawaii before human settlement; it will continue to survive in those areas where the native character of the island is recovered. The hawk's avian kin cannot survive without the recovery and preservation of native habitat. This hawk's success should not lull people into accepting less effort to restore Hawaiian islands.

Ridgway's Hawk
(Buteo ridgwayi)

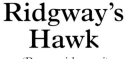

IUCN: Endangered

Length: Probably 14–19 in. (35.6–48.3 cm); females larger than males
Weight: Probably 15–17½ oz. (420–490 g); females larger than males
Clutch size: Unknown
Incubation: Unknown
Diet: Probably reptiles, birds, and mammals, but very few insects
Habitat: Forests, woodlands, shrub lands
Range: Hispaniola in the Greater Antilles of the West Indies

A QUIET SENTINEL watches from its perch. Early morning sun washes its gray-brown back, highlighting its rufous shoulders. Its white chin quickly blends into a pale rufous breast. Dingy white bars cross its belly. Suddenly intent, the sentinel weaves its head fluidly side to side. It quickly rises up on its pine-twig perch and exposes its bare and golden-colored feet and toes. With graceful ease it drops from the twig. Building deceptive speed, it keeps its broad, rounded, black wings slightly

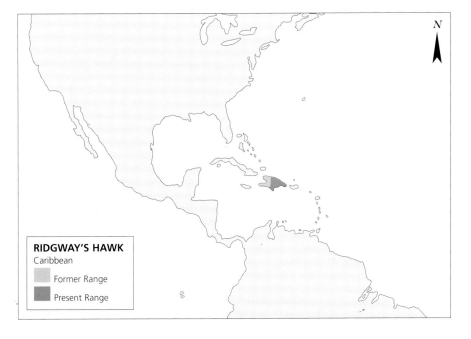

RIDGWAY'S HAWK
Caribbean

Former Range

Present Range

folded as it silently glides out and down. Its legs drop and its taloned toes flare at the same instant it unfurls its wings and picks a small lizard from a rock. Moments before, the lizard was basking in morning sunshine. Now, it has become breakfast for a Ridgway's hawk.

The lizards of Hispaniola have less to fear nowadays. The decline of Ridgway's hawk has made basking much less hazardous. The plight of the hawk is the plight of Hispaniola island and its people.

Discovery in 1492

Christopher Columbus reached the New World when he dropped anchor off the coast of Hispaniola and went ashore in 1492. Since then, Spain, France, and the United States have exercised some rule on Hispaniola. Today the Republic of Haiti occupies 10,714 square miles (27,856 square kilometers), on the island's western end—an area the size of Maryland. The Dominican Republic occupies the remaining 18,704 square miles (48,630 square kilometers) of Hispaniola, an area the size of Vermont and New Hampshire combined. Political dissent and repression have marred both countries, and Haiti suffers the most severe human poverty in the Western Hemisphere.

More than 12 million people now live on Hispaniola, more than half of them Haitian. Desperate for basic fuel for heating and cooking, Haitians cut all the wood they can find to burn for making charcoal. People in both countries graze livestock on the island. Additionally, crops such as sugarcane, rice, coffee, tobacco, and cocoa replace native plant communities with habitat less suited to wildlife. Mountains in the Dominican Republic rise more than 10,000 feet (3,049 meters) above the Atlantic Ocean to the north and the Caribbean Sea to the south, making it the highest island in the West Indies.

In this setting, the Ridgway's hawk struggles to survive. It once ranged over most of the island's forest and woodland. Coastal and lower montane forests were mostly broadleaf species. Pines replaced them at higher elevations. Early observers of the Ridgway's hawk gave mixed reports on its habitat preference. Nearly all reported seeing the hawk in lowland forests and shrub land. Some found it in the pine forests and others did not. Today, nearly all of Haiti's forests have been cut. Most of the low shrub lands have been cleared for agriculture or have been cut for firewood, so that most of the shrub lands are second growth. Some primary broadleaf forest persists in the Dominican Republic, and the pines remain at the higher reaches. Not surprisingly, then, recent observations of the hawk have been mostly in the pine zone of the Dominican Republic. Some ornithologists suspect that Ridgway's hawk may have completely disappeared from Haiti.

This small, rare hawk used to inhabit several forested islets near the Hispaniolan coast. None has ever been found on more distant islands. Other Buteo hawks do not live as permanent residents on Hispaniola, and only a very few hawk species migrate through or across the island. Losing Ridgway's hawk to extinction would not only be a loss of a species, it would be a major loss of an important predator on Hispaniola. At the close of the 1990s the majority of the population existed in a poorly protected National Park (Los Haitises).

In many ways Ridgway's hawk resembles the much more common and widespread roadside hawk (*Buteo magnirostris*). The roadside hawk lives only in Central and South America. It takes many larger insects as part of its regular diet. The Ridgway's hawk has a larger, more stoutly built foot, which suggests it specializes in larger prey. Vertebrates such as lizards, small rodents, and birds probably make up most of the hawk's diet. Feral house cats (*Felis sylvestris*) and Indian mongooses (*Herpestes auropunctatus*) have probably assumed much of the predatory role once filled by the Ridgway's hawk.

Preservation

The only solutions to preserving the Ridgway's hawk are not easy and may ultimately be impracticable. Research must be done to determine more of the hawk's natural history. Field work needs to verify the hawk's presence or absence on the neighboring islets. What little natural habitat that remains on Hispaniola must be preserved since it is diminishing at an alarming rate. Also, an aggressive program to restore habitat must be undertaken. Finally, captive breeding of the Ridgway's hawk could preserve the species; but unless some of the wild nature of Hispaniola is recovered, Ridgway's hawks could represent a species without any habitat in the wild.

Kevin Cook

Java Hawk-eagle

(Spizaetus bartelsi)

IUCN: Endangered

Class: Aves
Order: Falconiformes
Family: Accipitridae
Length: Unknown
Weight: Unknown
Clutch size: Unknown, but related species lay 1–2 eggs
Incubation: Unknown
Diet: Unknown
Habitat: Montane forests
Range: Java, Indonesia

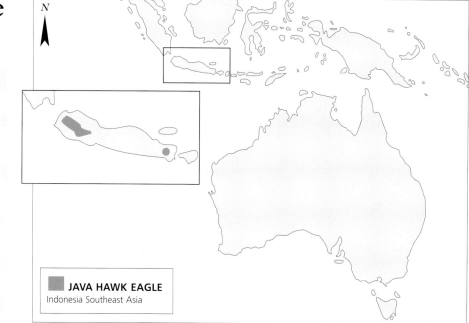

JAVA HAWK EAGLE
Indonesia Southeast Asia

IN THE EAST INDIES, tea (*Camellia sinensis*) is an exportable crop. A few plantations would cause only a minor impact on most birds, but many countries also cultivate kapok, coconuts, cocoa, coffee, rubber, bananas, rice, and sugarcane. People need space to live, to work, and to grow food for their own consumption. Unfortunately these are needs that can devastate island habitats.

The Indonesian island of Java covers 48,900 square miles (1,271,400 square kilometers). Nearly 100 million people live there and the eagle is not considered when their plantations are developed. Little is known about the hawk-eagle's preferred habitat, and it is surmised that these plantations adversely affect it.

The Java hawk-eagle has not been well described. Specimens of the Java hawk-eagle collected in the 1820s were originally described as the changeable hawk-eagle (*Spizaetus cirrhatus*). One specimen collected in 1907 was at first misidentified as a mountain hawk-eagle (*Spizaetus nipalensis*). By comparison to these related species, the Java hawk-eagle probably measures 26 to 27 inches (66 to 68 centimeters). Wingspans and weights cannot be so easily deduced because such information is not available for the related species.

The Java hawk-eagle sports a crest of two or four crown feathers about 3½ to a little over 4 inches (9 to 11 centimeters) long. These feathers are surrounded by a mop of shorter feathers. The crest is basically dark brown, with whitish tips to the individual feathers. Otherwise, the bird is overall brown above, with a black jawline separating a brownish cheek from the pale, rusty throat.

The underparts of the Java hawk-eagle blend from pale rust on the throat to rusty brown on the breast and a darker brown belly. The pattern is a light lower throat and breast, with darker brown barring, with a darker belly with white barring. The barring extends under the tail and onto the foot.

Short, rounded wings and a long tail allow forest-dwelling eagles and hawks to maneuver quickly in the tight spaces among the tree limbs. Presumably, the species' size and physique mean that it captures medium-sized prey, from the forest floor and from branches of trees.

The Java hawk-eagle belongs to a group of 30 species known as the "booted eagles," with a feathered leg and foot and a bare toe. It probably once ranged throughout most of Java when its habitat was more expansive but now inhabits only the forests of Java. During the 1980s, eagles were seen at or near 3,300 feet (1,000 meters) over tea plantations, but no one has reported seeing an eagle catch prey in a plantation.

Without sufficient information, specific recommendations for the bird's preservation cannot be made. In 1989 the population was down to between 50 and 60 pairs. To save the Java hawk-eagle, the last of Java's native forests must be preserved.

Kevin Cook

Hook-billed Hermit

(Ramphodon dohrnii)

ESA: Endangered

IUCN: Critically endangered

Class: Aves
Order: Apodiformes
Family: Trochilidae
Length: 4½ in. (11.4 cm)
Weight: ⅕–¼ oz (6–7 g)
Clutch size: Probably 1–2
Diet: Nectar and insects
Habitat: Lowland forests
Range: Brazil

HUMMINGBIRDS COMPRISE one of the largest families of birds. They have brilliant, often glittery plumage, aerobatic skill, a dainty size, pugnacious behavior, and an appetite for the nectar of flowers.

The hook-billed hermit differs from, yet resembles, other hermits. Not all ornithologist agree how it should be classified. Hermit species live in forest habitats of northern South America. The hook-billed hermit occupied only a very small range in southeastern Brazil, where a unique forest

system once extended through three states from the Bahian plateau in southern Bahia through the coastal vegetation zone of Espirito Santo into Rio de Janeiro. The primary forest has been heavily cut for timber and agriculture. In 1939 this unique forest probably exceeded 14,000 square miles (35,000 square kilometers), but by 1990 only 2½ square miles (6.5 square kilometers) remained on Klabin Farm near Conceicao, and another 14 square miles (35 square kilometers) in Monte Pascoal National Park in southeastern Bahia. Only about 20 hook-billed hermits were known to live on Klabin Farm in 1977. At that time the bird was uncommon but more numerous in Monte Pascoal National Park.

The hook-billed hermit does not look like a hummingbird, but it is a member of the hummingbird family.

Another population has since been discovered at the Porto Seguro Preserve, but no population estimates have been offered.

Based on related species, the hook-billed hermit probably lays 1 to 2 eggs, but more field research needs to be carried out to gain accurate information of its behavior and habits.

To preserve the hook-billed hermit, its remaining habitat must be secured. The challenge for Brazil would seem to be to improve production on the land they already have, rather than try to produce more goods by destroying more habitat.

Kevin Cook

White-bellied Heron

(Ardea imperialis)

IUCN: Endangered

Class: Aves
Order: Ciconiiformes
Family: Ardeidae
Subfamily: Ardeinae
Tribe: Ardeini
Length: 50 in. (127 cm)
Weight: Probably 5–5¾ lb. (2.2–2.6 kg); males usually larger than females
Clutch size: 4 eggs, based on 1 nest
Incubation: Unknown
Diet: Unknown, but probably crustaceans, fish, amphibians, and small mammals
Habitat: Wetlands including swamps, marshes, lakes, rivers
Range: Bangladesh; northeastern India (Assam); Nepal; extreme southern Xizang, China (formerly Tibet); some of mainland Myanmar

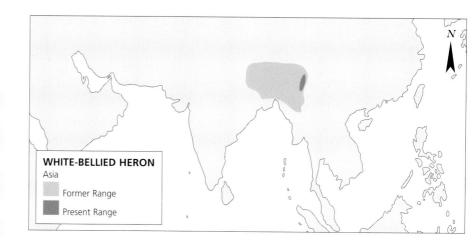

WHITE-BELLIED HERON
Asia
Former Range
Present Range

A GRAY WRAITH of a bird stands in the water. Slowly, it steps forward, placing each foot carefully. It cocks its head ever so slightly. With patient ease it lowers its neck down and leans a little forward. Like a coiled spring suddenly freed, it jabs its great beak into the water. Swinging its neck and head up, the bird works a fish the size of a man's shoe around before swallowing it head first. A white-bellied heron has just captured another meal. Apparently sated, the bird stands motionless.

The trim build, long foot and leg, and kinked neck indicate that the bird must be a heron. The white-bellied heron has not been seen in recent years. Where observers once saw it occasionally, it is no longer seen at all. In the areas where it probably lives now, it has not yet been specifically described, but it has been casually mentioned in northern and in central Myanmar.

Compared to other heron species that have been intensively studied, such as the gray heron (*Ardea cinerea*), the white-bellied heron has been either overlooked or completely ignored.

Second largest of all heron species, behind only the goliath heron (*Ardea goliath*), the white-bellied heron stands over 4 feet (1.2 meters) tall. It has dark gray upperparts washed with a little brown or olive. The neck is gray all around except for a white chin. The head appears a little browner, and the crown is dark. A pale gray breast fades to a white belly. The heron has a dark gray leg and foot. The skin around the lore and eye is bare and greenish yellow. The beak is massive and dagger shaped, mostly dark with a bit of yellow at the base, and the lower half is a little greener. Such a large beak

The white-bellied heron has not been seen in recent years, but there is no conclusive evidence to indicate that it is already extinct.

684

certainly must allow the white-bellied heron to swallow big fish and other sizable prey.

White-bellied herons are solitary birds, as are many herons. Because nests have not been described, ornithologists are not sure whether they nest in colonies in the same way as some species in the genus, or whether they nest in isolation like others. When these herons are spotted, they are invariably solitary, although as many as five birds have been reported scattered about a single lake.

Wetland dweller

An inhabitant of swamps and streams or pools in forests, the white-bellied heron appears to avoid coastal wetlands. In India the bird once frequented the *terai*, a vast region of wetlands containing mostly the elephant grass (*Typha* sp.) that Americans call cattails. The *terai* extended over much of northeastern India below the foothills of the southern Himalaya Mountains. Interspersing the wetlands were patches of forest that grew on higher, drier ground. Bordering the *terai* on the north was the *duars*, a region of more contiguous forest with taller trees. The *duars* area was not so wet but still provided many streams and ponds. As people drained the *terai* to develop cropland, they also cut the *duars* for wood. The combined effect was habitat loss that probably discouraged the white-bellied heron from inhabiting a peripheral expanse of its range. Similar habitat loss occurred in Nepal, Bangladesh, and Myanmar, and undoubtedly was what caused the heron to dwindle in numbers.

The first step in preserving the white-bellied heron must be an extensive field search to verify its presence or absence in areas where it used to occur. As a species of solitary habits, the heron's population may be thinly scattered over suitable habitat. The next action must be basic natural history research to document the species' nesting habits, dietary preferences, feeding behavior, predators, reaction to habitat modification, and so on.

Only after these projects are completed and interpreted can useful plans be drafted to offer the species some protection. Such research was not a priority among international ornithological groups as of 1990.

Kevin Cook

Clay's Hibiscus
(Hibiscus clayi)

ESA: Endangered

IUCN: Endangered

Order: Magnoliopsida
Family: Malvaceae
Height: 13–26 ft. (4–8 m) tall
Leaves: Dark green and shiny, oval or elliptical, leathery
Flowers: Bright scarlet with five oblong petals
Seeds: Fruits are pale brown capsules 10–15 mm long, with 10 brownish black seeds 4–4.5 mm long
Habitat: Lowland dry forests at 755–1,150 ft. (230–350 m)
Range: Eastern Kauai, Hawaiian Islands

IN 1928, ALBERT W. DUVEL discovered several trees of a wild hibiscus that had been damaged by cattle, and he brought the plant into cultivation. Later, Horace F. Clay, a botanist and instructor at Leeward Community College in Hawaii, brought the unidentified species to the attention of Otto and Isa Degener, botanists who were working on the flora of the Hawaiian Islands. The Degeners formally described the hibiscus for science in 1959 and named it after Horace F. Clay.

The plant was listed as endangered by the U.S. Fish and Wildlife Service in 1994, and there is now an officially approved recovery plan for the species. At the present time, a group of four trees on the Nonou mountain of Kauai appears to be the only definite wild population. The damage caused to this plant by cattle was realized when the species was first brought into cultivation in 1928. Fortunately, the threat from cattle has now been removed, but the habitat continues to be degraded steadily. The problem is from the spread of invasive non-native plants and by feral pigs. In fact, there are more plants of Clay's hibiscus today at Horace F. Clay's commemorative site on the Leeward Community College campus than can be found in the wild.

Clay's hibiscus, also known in Hawaiian as *aloalo*, has been found in various scattered locations on private and state-owned land on Kauai. Sister Margaret James Roe, in her study of hibiscus in the Hawaiian Islands, described *Hibiscus newhousei* for science in 1959. This plant, also from Kauai, is now considered to be the same species as Clay's hibiscus. Today, Clay's hibiscus is known with certainty only on Nonou. Such an extremely limited gene pool as four plants could severely reduce the reproductive vigor of any species. In addition, a tiny population like this is prone to being destroyed by a single human-caused or natural environmental catastrophe.

The natural habitat of Clay's hibiscus is dry, lowland forest characterized by an annual rainfall of 20 to 80 inches (50 to 200 centimeters). This rain falls between November and March. The volcanic substrate is well drained, highly weathered, and rich in aluminum.

Before cattle were removed from the area, they greatly damaged the habitat of Clay's hibiscus. Now, feral pigs still pose a threat to the species, but the main problem is stiff competition with aggressive alien plants. These include the strawberry guava (*Psidium cattle- ianum*), a shrub or small tree and the greatest threat. Also present are the following alien species: Brazilian pepper tree (*Schinus terebinthifolius*), an escapee from cultivation; common guava (*Psid-*

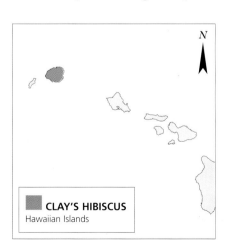

CLAY'S HIBISCUS
Hawaiian Islands

ium guajava), a shrub or small tree that invades disturbed sites and forms dense thickets; Hilo grass (*Paspalum conjugatum*); Java plum (*Syzygium cumini*); kukui (*Aleurites moluccana*); lantana (*Lantana camara*), an aggressive, thicket-forming shrub brought to Hawaii as an ornamental plant; and ti (*Cordyline fruticosa*), a shrub that sometimes forms dense stands, brought by the original Polynesian immigrants. Kukui is the official state tree of Hawaii, although it is not a native plant. Originally native to Southeast Asia, it was brought to Hawaii by the Polynesians and is now part of the vegetation on all the main islands except Kahoolawe. Clay's hibiscus does not grow under a dense canopy, so kukui trees could prevent it regenerating where they dominate the habitat.

Other threats

In addition, the area of the hibiscus population on Nounou mountain has been planted with Cook pine (*Araucaria columnaris*). This is a coniferous tree introduced for reforestation and timber production. It is reseeding itself and may stop regeneration of native plants.

The scarlet flowers of Clay's hibiscus attract many visitors and collectors, who can damage the plant's habitat.

Recreational activities

Another potential threat to Clay's hibiscus is the recreational use of land for hiking, camping, and hunting, as well as excessive visits by individuals interested in seeing rare plants.

Another threat to the plant is tourism. This is an expanding industry in Hawaii, and as more and more people take part in such activities, they are more likely to come into contact with threatened native or endemic plants. People can unintentionally introduce invasive alien plants by carrying seeds on their footwear or clothing, and they can also trample plants, start fires, and cause erosion. Unscrupulous persons can also deliberately damage plants by collecting seeds or stems for commercial or horticultural purposes. The close proximity of most of the plants of Clay's hibiscus to a hiking trail makes them easily accessible to people and puts them at risk of suffering damage or disturbance.

Nick Turland

Pygmy Hippopotamus

(Hexaprotodon liberiensis)

IUCN: Vulnerable

Class: Mammalia
Order: Artiodactyla
Family: Hippopotamidae
Weight: 397–606 lb. (180–275 kg)
Shoulder height: 27½–37 in. (70–95 cm)
Diet: Aquatic plants, leaves, twigs, and grasses
Gestation period: 180–210 days
Longevity: 45 years
Habitat: Lowland forests and swamps
Range: Western Africa

THERE ARE TWO TYPES of hippos found on the continent of Africa—the only place the hippopotamus is found in the world. First there is the great river hippo, or Nile hippo, which is found over most of the water courses south of the Sahara. The second form is the much smaller pygmy hippo, which can be found in pockets in west Africa. The pygmy hippo prefers lowland forest, swamps, and river courses. It tends to be a secretive animal, and it is nocturnal in much of its habits.

It is most often found alone. Occasionally pygmy hippos will be found in pairs, or a twosome consisting of a mother and a calf, but the most common existence for the hippo is solitary.

The diet of this hippo consists of grasses, shoots, fruits—any kind of vegetation that is readily available. As for the animals that feed on hippos, leopards have been known to take young ones near the bank of a river; however, this is rare because the female is very protective of her calves. Some calves may occasionally be taken by crocodiles, but this is also uncommon due to the cautious behavior of the mother.

Water logged

The pygmy hippo tends to resemble a young river hippo in its appearance; however, it retains this appearance through life. It has a proportionately smaller head, its eyes are less

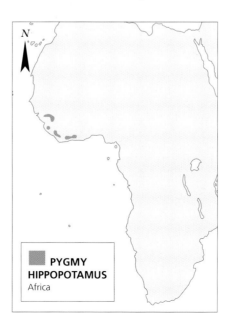

PYGMY HIPPOPOTAMUS
Africa

The hippo is a secretive animal that is nocturnal in habit. Occasionally hippos will be found in pairs, but generally they are quiet creatures and seem to prefer a solitary existence.

prominent than those of the great river hippo, and it also tends to be somewhat less aquatic.

There is a difference in hoof structure between these two hippos—the pygmy hippo's toes are less webbed and more free. The skin of the hippo is extremely tough and thick, but the upper layer, or epidermis, is surprisingly thin. This thinness allows water to be absorbed through the skin and at a much greater rate than in other animals. This feature gives the pygmy hippo considerable cooling ability when it is out of the water. For this reason, pygmy hippos need to be close to an aquatic environment. A hippo fares badly far away from water because it could rapidly become dehydrated.

Hippo skin lacks sweat glands. However, there are glands below the skin that secrete a pinkish fluid that resembles blood. It is a thick, highly alkaline solution that controls temperature and protects the hippo's thin skin from too much ultraviolet radiation—an aid against sunburn.

Sexual maturity happens in the pygmy hippo somewhere between four to five years of age. The birth season occurs during the rainy period in Africa, when the females find a secluded spot to give birth. The pygmy hippo normally produce a single offspring although occasionally twins have been known.

The pygmy hippo is relatively inoffensive to people and it rarely causes any particular problems. Problems arise if a female with a calf is cornered. Then the mother will spring to the defense of her calf and can indeed be quite formidable. Like the great river hippos, the pygmy hippo has immense canine teeth that can deliver a wicked wound.

Habitat problems

The pygmy hippo's downfall has been mainly through the destruction of its forest habitat because it tends to be intolerant of human intrusion. It is also killed for food, but the destruction of the river courses, forests, and areas adjacent to the rivers has been the major factor in its decline. Any pollutants added to their aquatic habitat would make the situation worse.

Easy to rear

This is an animal that has been kept in captivity for some time, and it does well in captivity. The pygmy hippo is relatively easy to care for and manage, is long lived, and is a successful breeder through most of its life. The only current problem with managing the pgymy hippo in captivity is the apparent marked disparity between the numbers of males born compared to females. In more than 130 zoos worldwide, there are only about 131 males

The pygmy hippo is seldom aggressive toward humans, but its size makes it rather intimidating. When frightened, it can deliver a nasty bite.

and 206 females. In nature the balance is probably a little better. In captivity, however, some animals that might not have survived in the wild can now survive because they are in a less demanding environment. Thus, there always seems to be an overabundance of females. The captive population is large and healthy enough to act as a future stock for the wild population.

Tolerant creatures

Pygmy hippos in captivity are quite tolerant of other animals. They have been kept with a number of different kinds of water fowl, for example. They were kept with a family of otters, and the two groups actually seemed to enjoy each other's company.

Although this species occurs widely through Sierra Leone, Liberia, and the Ivory Coast it is only legally protected in Sierra Leone, so the existing wild population is vulnerable.

Warren D. Thomas

Pygmy Hog

(Sus salvanius)

ESA: Endangered

IUCN: Critically endangered

Class: Mammalia
Order: Artiodactyla
Family: Suidae
Weight: 13–26 lb. (6–12 kg)
Shoulder height: 8–12 in. (20–30 cm)
Diet: Omnivorous
Gestation period: About 100 days
Longevity: 10–12 years
Habitat: Thick bush and grassy uplands
Range: India, Nepal, Sikkim, Bhutan

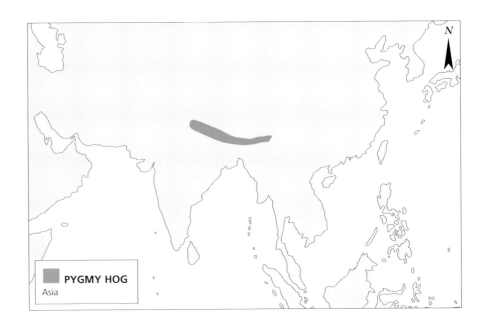

PYGMY HOG
Asia

THE PYGMY HOG is, as its name implies, a small animal. It comes primarily from the area of Assam in India, but its range spills over into portions of Nepal, Sikkim, and Bhutan. Not a lot is known about this species in the wild because it is a secretive animal. The pygmy hog is often mistaken as the young of the common Asiatic wild boar, and their habits are very similar to those of the wild boar. The adult hog tends to be solitary, especially the male which is almost always solitary. It will seek out a sow only during the mating season.

The female with her piglets generally stays in a given area, and the young are born some-

where between April and the middle to latter part of May. Litter sizes can be from two to six. The pygmy hog has only three pairs of teats as opposed to the wild boars, who have six pairs. Because of this some researchers believe it should be placed in a separate genus from other pigs. When the young are born, they have light stripes over their body that change and become darker with age. Pygmy hogs reach maturity at about 18 months, and their life span in captivity is probably around 10 to 12 years.

Burrowing hog

The pygmy hog digs burrows and spends some of its time in the burrow. However, it is a diurnal animal, being most active from dawn to about mid-morning, retreating to the burrow until the mid-afternoon, when it will venture out again until dusk. The pygmy hog tends to live in broken terrain with a heavy grass cover and heavy vegetation; thus, it is easily missed.

Primarily a grazing animal, the pygmy hog forages by eating grasses and digging out roots and

The word *pygmy* is Greek and describes a race of dwarfs that was written about by authors in ancient times. The small pygmy hog gets its name from this ancient lore.

tubers. Like most pigs, it is omnivorous and will eat anything it can catch, including small birds, lizards, and insects. The other remarkable thing about its feeding habits is that it appears to consume a lot of earth along with the food it eats. Some experts believe that almost half of what the pygmy hog ingests is earth.

Once fairly widespread, the pygmy hog has fallen on hard times. After World War II the forest and grasslands were cleared for agricultural purposes, and it appears that this species does not adapt well to any other habitat. The pygmy hog was simply destroyed along with its surroundings. By the 1950s it was thought to be extinct.

However, in 1971 the animal was discovered again after a brush fire caused some animals to flee their impenetrable elephant grass habitat in Assam.

The pygmy hog has been kept in captivity a number of times. The earliest of these attempts to raise the pygmy hog date all the way back to a male and three females that were purchased by the Zoological Society of London in 1882. These hogs lived in captivity a few years and then died off. This species has not done well in captivity. A small group was obtained by a zoo in Zurich in the 1970s, and they were bred for a short time, but mostly males were born. When the female died the group simply died out.

There have been many attempts to keep pygmy hogs in captivity in Assam, but zoo managers have met with only limited success until recently. A successful captive program exists in India. One of the primary reasons for the pygmy hog's demise is simply destruction of its habitat. Native people use the elephant grass for roofing and find that setting the grass afire aids them in harvesting it. The hogs are also trapped and eaten by the locals.

There is much about this animal's habits that still needs to be determined. With proper management it probably could be kept in captivity successfully but, unfortunately, knowledge about the pygmy hog is not extensive enough to instigate this step.

Confined mostly to the Manas Tiger Reserve in Assam, India, the pygmy hog is considered by some experts to be one of the most endangered of all hoofed mammals.

Warren D. Thomas

Crested Honeycreeper

(Palmeria dolei)

ESA: Endangered

IUCN: Vulnerable

Class: Aves
Order: Passeriformes
Family: Drepenididae
Subfamily: Drepanidinae
Length: 6½–7 in. (16.5–17.8 cm)
Weight: Unknown
Incubation: Unknown
Diet: Nectar
Habitat: Wet forests
Range: Maui, Hawaiian Islands

THE CRESTED honeycreeper looks like a bird that cannot get its hair combed quite right. Its black plumage gives it a dark overall appearance, but it is more colorful than a first impression would convey. The crested honeycreeper has a striking, unusual tuft of stringy, white feathers that puff up from the forehead and forecrown and curve forward.

Constantly chattering, the crested honeycreeper whistles, chirps, buzzes, and wheezes as it works the blossoms of ohia (*Metrosideros collina*) to extract the nectar. In its tropical homeland, enough flowers bloom year-round to keep these birds fed.

Once common on Molokai and Maui, it has fallen silent on Molokai and now lives only in eastern Maui. The last crested honeycreeper was seen on Molokai in 1907. Though once abundant, these birds were not reported from Maui during the first three decades of the 1900s. Since the bird is known to be surviving in fair numbers today, the period of obscurity is explained by a lack of observers who published records. In 1980 a forest bird survey was cooperatively conducted by federal and state wildlife officials. Participants recorded 415 crested honeycreepers between 4,200 and 7,100 feet (1,280 and 2,165 meters) above sea level. One group was found on about 4,000 acres (1,600 hectares) of private land west of Koolau Gap. Another group was found east of the gap in a mile-wide corridor of forest about 6 miles (9.6 kilometers) long. The total population estimate in 1980 was 3,800 crested honeycreepers and at the end of the 1990s there was no indication that the population was declining. This species experienced population declines following the human settlement of the Hawaiian Islands. Polynesians were the first humans in Hawaii. They cleared the lower forests for building materials and to open up land for planting crops. They also brought Polynesian rats (*Rattus exulans*), pigs (*Sus scrofa*), and dogs (*Canis familiaris*) to the islands.

When the first Christian missionaries arrived in Hawaii in 1820, they unwittingly brought mosquitoes that carried avian malaria. Subsequent waves of settlers and visitors introduced a host of other plants and animals, none of which the Hawaiian honeycreepers had ever had to confront before.

Today pigs, goats (*Capra* sp.), cattle (*Bos* sp.), and axis deer (*Cervus axis*) graze the native plant communities, but no such plant-eating mammals are native to the Hawaiian Islands.

As these exotic mammals feed, they scatter seeds of exotic plants. The exotic plants outcompete the native plants and change the character of the habitat.

Other exotics include Indian mongooses (*Herpestes auropunctatus*), which are known to eat birds' eggs, as do the Polynesian rats. Later settlers also cut more

CRESTED HONEYCREEPER
Hawaiian Islands, Pacific Ocean

forests to higher elevations so that they could expand their land for agriculture on the islands. The crested honeycreeper, in only one century, had to adapt to less forest habitat, exotic plants, exotic mammals, exotic diseases, and possibly competition from exotic birds. The wonder is not that the bird has merely declined but that it is not already extinct.

The State of Hawaii, through its State Forest Reserve system, manages about one third of the native forests remaining on the islands. The National Park Service manages some native forest, including Haleakala National Park on Maui. Officials have prioritized exotic plant control and they have fenced a large portion of the Haleakala Crater area to exclude feral pigs, goats, and cattle. The Nature Conservancy also manages some tracts of native forests. Together, these agencies work to maintain native habitat for Hawaii's native birds. The

The crested honeycreeper is now found only on the Hawaiian island of Maui. Years ago it was common on Molokai and prevalent on Maui.

U.S. Fish and Wildlife Service has been researching a captive-breeding program so that a captive flock can be used to breed birds that can be released to bolster wild populations.

Mysterious bird

Unfortunately, the noisy little crested honeycreeper does not help its own cause. Very little is known about its natural history. No nests have ever been found so no one knows where, when, or how it breeds.

The number of eggs it lays, where it builds its nests, and many other questions need answers, but the dense, wet forests where the crested honeycreeper lives are difficult places to research. The answers to these questions will come slowly.

Kevin Cook

Dusky Hopping Mouse

(Notomys fuscus)

IUCN: Vulnerable

Class: Mammalia
Order: Rodentia
Family: Muridae
Weight: ¾–1¾ oz. (20–50 g)
Body length: 3½–7 in. (9–18 centimeters)
Diet: Plants, fruits, and seeds
Gestation period: 32–38 days
Longevity: 26–38 months
Habitat: Sand dunes, grasslands, and sparse woodlands
Range: South-central Australia

IN THE ARID INTERIOR portions of Australia there is a genus of small mammals that at first glance, seems in appearance and behavior like their distant relatives, the kangaroos. Closer inspection, however, reveals that these small hopping mammals are not marsupials like the kangaroo, but rodents. They are members of the genus *Notomys*, and are much like other small rodents found in similar habitats elsewhere in the world. These other rodents include familiar forms such as gerbils (*Gerbillus* sp.), jerboas (*Jaculus* sp.), and kangaroo rats (*Dipodomys* sp.).

Many of these other rodents have another thing in common with one member of the species,

The large hind feet of the hopping mouse are a valuable asset when this tiny rodent is threatened. It can move swiftly to safety when faced with a dangerous situation.

the dusky hopping mouse. Their populations have been diminished, and they appear to be moving toward extinction.

The dusky hopping mouse is a small, pale brown mammal with white underparts. The most striking external features of the hopping mouse are its large ears and hind feet, as well as its long tail. The tail is much longer than the body, and both are covered with soft fine hair. The long hairs at the tip of the tail give it the appearance of a brush.

Are they clumsy?

Due to its large hind feet, the hopping mouse is somewhat clumsy when it slowly moves about to feed or to inspect its surroundings. It is only when a dusky hopping mouse is threatened in the open that we see the value of the large hind limbs. When danger appears, this mouse is able to bound rapidly to the safety of its burrow system.

Sometimes hopping mice are found in close association with

their marsupial equivalent, the kultarr (*Antechinomys laniger*), and have even been known to share tunnel systems with them. Hopping mice also use their burrows to avoid the heat and dryness of their habitat, often remaining underground all day.

Female dusky hopping mice come into estrus several times a year, with no apparent seasonal pattern existing for breeding times. Each estrus cycle lasts about one week.

If impregnated, a female gives birth a little over one month later to two to four young. The young are tiny, weighing only 2 to 4 grams, and are born blind. They immediately attach to a teat and remain clinging there, dragged about by the mother wherever she goes. The young open their eyes during their third or fourth week, and are weaned at approximately one month of age.

When adult the dusky hopping mouse may reach up to about 7 inches (18 centimeters) in length.

Both sexes of the dusky hopping mouse become sexually mature at a little over two months of age. Males are then able to breed until at least three years of age, and females can bear as many as nine litters during their lifetime. Due to this ability to breed several times a year, this species is able to take advantage of the increased food available after a substantial rainfall. However, the unpredictable weather of Australia's interior can result in widely fluctuating population numbers. High rainfalls lead to swarms of hopping mice, while droughts result in the apparent disappearance of the species.

A lifestyle on the edge

Hopping mice maintain themselves on a diet of leafy vegetation, berries, and seeds. Although they will drink water when it is available, they can go for prolonged periods without any water other than that contained in their food. They are able to accomplish this because they have efficient kidneys that reclaim most of their waste water, producing some of the most highly concentrated urine found in mammals.

Precarious existence

The dusky hopping mouse is one of the few at-risk species whose situation is due as much to its evolved style of life as to the behavior of human beings. Living in a habitat with such limited rainfall and the possibility of extended drought, the dusky mouse has probably long experienced a shaky existence. While no studies have been done regarding

DUSKY HOPPING MOUSE
Australia

the effects of ranching on this species, it is likely that during dry periods the vegetation is more highly stressed by grazing today than was the case before the arrival of Europeans. It is very important that studies are undertaken to determine what effect grazing by domestic sheep and cattle has on the population of this fascinating little rodent.

Terry Tompkins

Sumba Hornbill

(Aceros everetti)

IUCN: Vulnerable

Class: Aves
Order: Coraciiformes
Family: Bucerotidae
Length: Unknown
Weight: Unknown
Clutch size: Probably 2–4 eggs
Incubation: Unknown
Diet: Figs, possibly insects and other small animals
Habitat: Forests and woodlands
Range: Sumba in the Lesser Sunda Islands of Indonesia

HORNBILLS LIKE TO make themselves conspicuous, like rowdy guests at a party. Life for the hornbills on Sumba Island, however, is no party. The human presence on Sumba has nearly ruined the island for several unique birds, the Sumba hornbill among them.

Birds of the hornbill family make various loud noises including grunts and whistles. They often congregate in flocks, either for feeding during the day or for roosting during the night. Long, skinny necks plus long, narrow tails and sometimes awkward flight give them a gangly look. Despite appearances, however, these are not clumsy or awkward birds. They can deftly peel a fruit, neatly discarding the skin before swallowing the pulp.

Large protuberances, known as "casques," appear on the upper half of the beak, clearly indicating the origin of the name *hornbill*. All hornbills have the casques, although some species grow larger casques than others. Casques are sponge-like structures encased by the same horny sheathing that covers a bird's beak. The helmeted hornbill (*Rhinoplax vigil*) offers the single exception. It sports a solid casque that Asian artisans once coveted as much as ivory and jade. The casques and beaks of hornbills are often brightly colored—red, orange, or yellow, sometimes accented by brightly colored bare skin around the face. Hornbills are also noted for their well-defined eyelashes, which are really veinless feathers.

Undoubtedly the most remarkable characteristic of hornbills is their unique breeding behavior. All 44 or 45 species nest in tree cavities, and some

693

Large protuberances known as "casques" on the upper half of the beak give this bird the name *hornbill*. All hornbills have casques, and the Sumba species is no exception.

will even use burrows in embankments. Before laying her clutch, the female uses her own body wastes to plaster the entrance hole closed. In some species the male assists by bringing mud. She leaves a small slit through which the male passes food, first to the female but eventually to the chicks as well. The female remains enclosed for two months and keeps the nest cavity clean of body waste. Hornbills have a powerfully muscular cloaca, the single organ that passes all body wastes from the kidneys and the digestive tract as well as sperm and eggs. To expel her wastes, the female hornbill backs up to the small hole and forcefully ejects them to the outside. Young hornbills learn the procedure long before leaving the nest.

As a distinct species, the Sumba hornbill has adapted to the environmental conditions unique to Sumba. What those adaptations might be is not clearly understood, because the sumba hornbill has not been thoroughly studied. In fact, little is known about its natural history. Sumba is a remote island, and its birds are not as easily studied as those species in more accessible locations. Ornithologists do know that surveys taken in 1989 and in 1992 showed that there were approximately 6,100 individuals, and by the closing decades of the 1900s, conditions on Sumba threatened the survival of its hornbill.

One of thousands of Indonesian islands, Sumba lies south of the strait between Sumbawa and Flores. Together with Bali, Lombok, Timor, and many smaller islets, these islands comprise the Lesser Sunda Islands that separate the Java and Flores Seas from the Indian Ocean. Sumba stretches about 140 miles (224 kilometers) northwest to southeast, never exceeding 50 miles (80 kilometers) in width. It covers 4,306 square miles (11,196 square kilometers) and reaches up to 2,913 feet (888 meters) at its highest. A narrow coastal plain has been converted mostly to agriculture. The island's native forests and woodlands were cut and recut for sandalwood. Sandalwood (*Santalum* sp.) grows as a small tree throughout much of the tropics. The freshly cut green wood dries to develop a fine aroma that is prized in the crafting of small jewelry boxes and chests.

Agricultural clearing and sandalwood cutting, plus other human demands on the land, all combined to eliminate much of the native forests and woodlands on Sumba, the preferred habitat of the Sumba hornbill. Beyond habitat loss, the hornbill suffers some collection pressure. Its body parts and feathers have no value on the Oriental folk-medicine market, and it does not have the broad appeal of colorful parrots, but local citizens trap the birds and offer them for sale as novelties, particularly to tourists.

Specific research on the Sumba hornbill has shown that it is a threatened species, and ornithologists believe that habitat destruction on Sumba threatens the species' survival. Although many hornbill species have been kept in captivity and successfully bred, records do not show that the Sumba hornbill has ever been held by a reputable zoo or aviary. Captive breeding could take many years to build a viable captive population. From these circumstances, preserving the Sumba hornbill would seem to depend almost entirely on protecting what remains of Sumba's native forests and woodlands.

Kevin Cook

Przewalski's Horse

(Equus przewalskii)

ESA: Endangered

IUCN: Extinct in the wild

Class: Mammalia
Order: Perissodactyla
Family: Equidae
Subfamily: Equinae
Sub-genus: Equus
Weight: Up to 770 lb. (350 kg)
Shoulder height: 39–55 in.
(100–140 cm)
Diet: Grasses, leaves, and twigs
Gestation period: 330–360 days
Longevity: 30 or more years
Habitat: Open grasslands
(steppe)
Range: Formerly Mongolia and
China

THIS HORSE IS THE only true wild horse left in modern times. At one time there was a variety of wild horses found in Eurasia, but the European forms, such as the tarpan, were driven to extinction.

The only surviving wild horse today is Przewalski's horse, named in honor of a Polish explorer who brought the species to the attention of animal experts in the West.

Also called the Mongolian wild horse, it was found in the wild in great open grasslands. Although it can go for long periods of time without drinking, it was always found near water sources. While it is smaller than a domestic horse, Przewalski's horse has a much larger head in proportion to its body size. Unlike the domestic horse, it has a dark stripe that runs down its back from the mane to the tail. This horse has a uniform reddish brown coat. Its coat is short in summer and shaggy in winter, helping it survive the severe central Asian winters. Its maximum life span in captivity is not much more than 30 years, meaning that it has a slightly shorter life span than the average domestic horse.

This horse has not been seen in the wild since 1968. There are two reintroduced populations, one at Hustain Nuruu close to Ulaanbaatar and one in the Gobi Desert. Przewalski's horse was reintroduced to these areas because this is where the last wild horses were captured. However, this desert and semidesert environment is not the ideal habitat for Przewalski's horse and both of these populations require assistance with supplementary food and water. For this reason they are not classified as wild.

Once Przewalski's horse lived in small family groups—usually with a stallion, five or six mares, and their offspring. A stallion fiercely controls other males and its own territory, and is extremely protective of its family.

One foal is born at a time to a Przewalski's mare; foals have a light-colored coat that is replaced by a darker coat in about four or five weeks. The foal is usually precocious, following its mother within an hour after birth.

Wild populations of Przewalski's horse have not been observed since 1968. When it roamed its range freely, it was generally seen in small family groups made up of a stallion and five or six mares, together with their offspring.

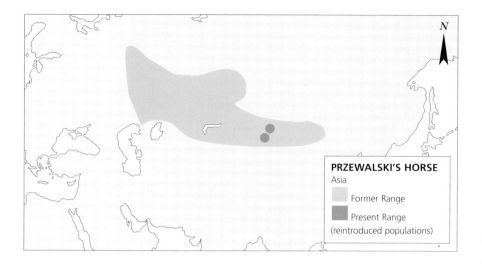

PRZEWALSKI'S HORSE
Asia

Former Range

Present Range
(reintroduced populations)

The demise in the wild of Przewalski's horse is primarily due to hunting pressures and competition from domestic animals. Another threat to this horse has been interbreeding with domestic Mongolian ponies.

Long captive history

Fortunately, however, this horse has a long history in captivity. The first living examples were exhibited in Europe around 1900, when a Russian landowner took some live specimens to his estate at a place called Askania Nova. They are still kept there today, but the most important effort to preserve this animal was made by a famous animal collector from Hamburg, Germany, named Carl Hagenbeck.

Around the turn of the 20th century, Hagenbeck sent his agents to Mongolia, where they hired a large group of local people to start rounding up and capturing Przewalski's horses.

Unfortunately, the first horses caught were young adults that did not adjust well to captivity, so the collectors changed their tactics and started capturing young foals that were still nursing. They captured 17 colts and 15 fillies, then matched them with domestic Mongolian mares that were lactating (able to give milk). These young animals were then reared and moved back to Europe, where they were held in zoological collections. It is from this captive group that the vast majority of existing Przewalski's horses have descended.

This animal is preserved today because of the efforts of animal conservationists. In addition to the reintroduced populations there are now at least 1,000 specimens in captivity in both Europe and North America.

Warren D. Thomas

Houting
(Coregonus oxyrinchus)

IUCN: Data deficient

Class: Actinopterygii
Order: Salmoniformes
Family: Salmonidae
Length: 12 in. (30 cm)
Reproduction: Egg layer
Habitat: Estuaries, lakes, and rivers
Range: Coastal and inland waters of northern Europe

THE HOUTING AND other members of the genus *Coregonus* have long been sought after as food fish in Europe, Asia, and North America. The houting, which is a European variety—and other coregonids—are closely related to salmon and trout and they are all members of the family Salmonidae.

Like many salmon and trout, the houting is an anadromous species. This term refers to its ability to hatch in fresh water, move from fresh water to salt water as a juvenile, live its adulthood in saltwater, and return to fresh water to spawn. This capability is relatively rare among fishes and requires a physiological transformation to adapt to two very different environments.

Like the salmon and trout, this transformation and migration is not mandatory for the fish's survival, and some populations of houting manage to live their entire lives within freshwater river and lake systems.

Once roaming inshore areas and estuaries of the North Sea and Baltic Sea and their associated coastal waterways in northern Europe, the migratory seawater houting populations are today most likely extinct. Some vestiges of these populations may still exist, however. There is insufficient information to determine the status of any remaining houting populations.

Decline

There are several primary reasons for the severe decline in houting numbers. They are overfishing,

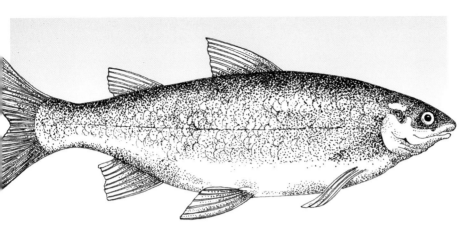

As for many fish, pollution of water habitats has played a primary role in the disappearance of the houting. Habitat destruction has also had its effects on the fish's population.

pollution, migratory barriers, and destruction and degradation of reproductive habitat.

Dams that produce hydroelectric power or control seasonal flooding on rivers are particularly destructive to migratory fish like the houting that depend on free passage to spawning areas. Without the ability to reach spawning grounds, the reproductive potential of such a population is quickly and dramatically undermined. Equally devastating are the effects of silt and other waterborne debris that cover clean river gravel (a necessity for nest building) and smother eggs that have been laid. For houting that remain within freshwater lakes, the results of nearby deforestation and subsequent soil erosion and siltation into rivers that the houting uses for spawning are just as disastrous.

If the houting is to survive within its historic range, priority must be given to maintaining and restoring coastal lakes and streams. Other migratory salmonids, as well as the houting,

would benefit from this. Additionally, while fishermen may not agree with laws or regulations restricting or prohibiting commerical fishing, the days of abundant supplies of houting are long gone. Clearly, restrictions on fishing remain appropriate until the habitat is restored and the houting has recovered from its current brush with extinction.

Modest appearance

The houting is an unassuming fish both in size and coloration. Common adult size is about 12 inches (30 centimeters), but some can grow much larger.

Skin coloration is a fairly even silver, underlain by some light green coloration on the back; the body has few or no markings. The torpedo-like body is tipped with a pointed snout and upper jaw. The lower jaw reaches only halfway from the eye to the tip of the snout, and it has clear, soft-rayed fins. The dorsal fin on the back and the anal fin just behind the anus are square at the ends and are swept back, while the pectoral fins behind the gills and the pelvic fins on the belly are pointed. The tail fin is deeply forked to give maximum control in strong currents.

Like all salmonids, the houting has a fleshy adipose fin on the back, located between the dorsal fin and the tail fin.

Houting consume smaller fish and plankton as adults. They begin to eat microscopic plankton during their post-hatch and juvenile stages.

William E. Manci

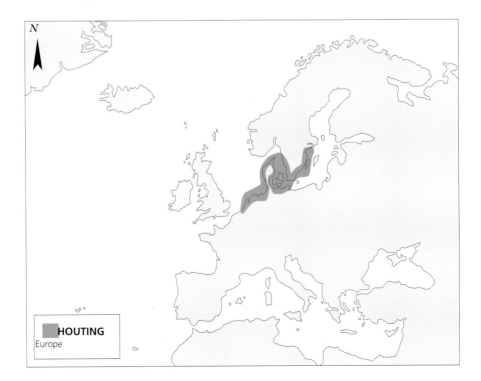

HOUTING
Europe

North Andean Huemul

(Hippocamelus antisensis)

ESA: Endangered

IUCN: Data deficient

South Andean Huemul

(Hippocamelus bisculcus)

ESA: Endangered

IUCN: Endangered

Class: Mammalia
Order: Artiodactyla
Family: Cervidae
Subfamily: Odocoilinae
Weight: 99–154 lb. (45–70 kg)
Shoulder height: 29½–35½ in. (75-90 cm)
Diet: Grasses, leaves, lichens, and mosses
Gestation period: About 240 days
Longevity: 10-plus years
Habitat: Mountain grasslands
Range: South America

THE HUEMUL IS A DEER found in the Andes mountains of Peru, Bolivia, Chile, and Argentina. There are two forms of this deer: the northern Andean form, *Hippocamelus antisensis*, and the southern Andean form, *Hippocamelus bisculcus*.

These two huemul species are found in similar environments, both preferring elevations from about 4,600 to 5,575 feet (1,400 to 1,700 meters). Both species stick to the northern and western exposures of the rocky terrain where they are found.

In winter, huemuls move to lower elevations—about 3,600 to 4,900 feet (1,100 to 1,500 meters). If there is heavy snow, they may be forced to even lower altitudes. In the summer months they ascend to higher altitudes, including some forested areas.

Huemels are browsers, eating whatever vegetation they can find. Males are often solitary but can be found in pairs or small family groups. Larger groups often consist of females with their most recent offspring and immature males.

Stocky build

Huemuls are one of the largest deer found in South America. They are also found at the highest altitudes of all deer. At first glance, they resemble heavily built, stocky mule deer. However, their color is markedly different, as are the markings around the head and face. Their compact body provides protection against the severe Andean cold weather. Males are larger and heavier than females and are further distin-guished by a dark band that runs along the top of the muzzle. Their antlers are fairly insignificant when compared to the North American mule and white-tailed deer. The most common number of tines on the antlers is four—two on each side.

Huemuls have a gestation period of about 240 days. Mating most commonly occurs in June and the young are born from February to April.

The males shed their antlers in September and October, at the beginning of the rainy season. The young are born unspotted and there is usually only one. The most commonly observed group size is three, consisting of one male and two females.

Easy prey

Early accounts of this deer suggest that it was easy prey because it showed little fear of humans.

The unobtrusive coloring of the northern Andean huemul allows it to blend into its environment, sometimes going unnoticed by would-be predators. It is known to freeze in place when it sees danger coming. Unfortunately, this is not enough to save the deer all the time.

Now it is much more common for this animal to flee when it is approached by humans. However, if it notices something threatening approaching, the huemul characteristically freezes

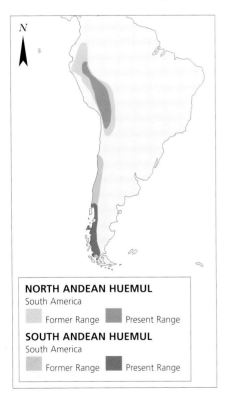

NORTH ANDEAN HUEMUL
South America

Former Range   Present Range

SOUTH ANDEAN HUEMUL
South America

Former Range   Present Range

in place. This is apparently effective when it is preyed upon by the puma, because the huemul is difficult to distinguish against its rocky habitat.

The biggest problems causing the decline of these animals are that they have been severely hunted and their habitat has been cut and burned. The hunting is primarily done by the locals, but not for commercial value. Still, huemuls have been severely reduced in number as locals often use dogs to hunt them. The southern Andean or Chilean huemul has been more severely reduced than the northern Andean or Peruvian huemul.

It is believed that there are only about 1,500 Chilean huemuls left, while the Peruvian huemul fortunately appears to have fared rather better. Huemels have been kept in captivity only rarely. A number of years ago occasional specimens were kept

The southern Andean huemul, or Chilean huemul, is in greater danger of extinction than its relative of the north. Estimates suggest that only 1,500 of the Chilean species still survive. Both species have suffered from overhunting by humans and the uncontrolled destruction of their habitat.

in the zoo in Lima, Peru, and some were kept in private collections in Chile. However, breeding was either not encouraged or was unsuccessful. Thus there is no captive population to support the wild population. The northern Andean huemuls were successfully bred in Berlin in the 1930s, but today the animals living in the wild are a vulnerable population. Unless the huemul is strictly protected, their numbers may be easily decimated.

The southern population is already severely endangered and, even though it is now protected, it is declining in numbers.

Warren D. Thomas

HUTIAS

Class: Mammalia

Order: Rodentia

Family: Capromyidae

Although found today only on a few scattered islands, fossil evidence indicates that hutias are members of a family that was once widespread in the Caribbean and northern South America. At the time of the arrival of Europeans in the New World, this family was composed of eight genera and about 30 species. Even though half the genera and over half the species are believed to be extinct, hutias continue to be the most diverse and widely distributed native terrestrial mammals in the Caribbean. Today there is one species each on Jamaica and Little Swan Island, one in the Bahamas,

two species on Hispaniola, and nine species found either on Cuba or on small islands near Cuba.

All hutias, endangered hutias in particular, are among the least studied groups in the rodent order, so reasons for their decline involve guesswork. One theory is based on their vulnerability as an island species. Because of the limited predation and competition that occurs on islands, such species are not prepared for sudden increases in competition, predation, or both.

Some of the traits common to these island species are low population sizes, low reproductive rates, a lack of fear of potential predators, and a limited ability to avoid new predators. In addition, island species often have specific environmental needs that can only be met in limited areas on any given island. All of the endangered hutias appear to

have most, if not all, of these traits. This means that even slight changes in the hutia's environment can be lethal.

It appears that people have had a profound effect on these small mammals. Human cooking artifacts and hutia fossils are often found together. This suggests that hutias were a common food for the newly arrived humans in the Caribbean. Both pre-Columbian and European peoples brought other predators to these islands. Even today hutias are highly prized as a source of food and are illegally hunted. However, deforestation for agriculture does more harm.

All species of endangered Cuban hutias—in fact all hutias in general—are in dire need of field studies to learn more about their distribution, natural history, and population sizes. Their ability to survive and breed in captivity should be investigated as well.

Cabrera's Hutia

(Meso angelcabrerai)

| **ESA:** Endangered |
| **IUCN:** Critically endangered |

Weight: Unknown

Head-body length: Unknown

Diet: Herbivorous

Gestation period: Unknown

Longevity: Unknown

Habitat: Mangrove thickets

Range: Anna Maria Keys

FIRST DISCOVERED in 1974, this species of hutia is believed to exist only on a few small islets off

Fossils indicate that the family to which the hutia belongs was once widespread in the Caribbean and across northern South America.

the south coast of Cuba. Feared extinct in the early 1980s, it was later reported to be abundant in very localized areas in 1990. The red mangrove forest habitat in which Cabrera's hutia occurs is remote, and no plans exist for development of the area.

Cabrera's hutias band together and build communal nests in the red mangroves. These nests are composed of mangrove twigs covered with leaves, with four or five openings. Although no in-depth ecological studies have been done on this species, it

is believed that, like other hutias, its diet is herbivorous.

Females produce litters of one-to-three well-developed young. It appears that hutias in general have long gestation periods and low reproductive rates.

Even though the habitat of this species appears safe from development for now, it is still at risk from fishermen and other locals who hunt this animal for its meat. Its reported method of escape—by leaving the nest and jumping into the water (where it swims clumsily)—makes it an easy target. The apparent increase in population size of this hutia, following the passage of a law forbidding all hunting in areas critical to wildlife, may mean that legal penalties are having the desired effect.

Dwarf Hutia

(Meso nanus)

ESA: Endangered

IUCN: Critically endangered

Weight: Unknown
Body length: About 8½ in. (22 cm)
Diet: Herbivorous
Gestation period: Unknown
Longevity: Unknown
Habitat: Mangrove thickets
Range: Zapata Peninsula, central Cuba

ONCE WIDESPREAD IN CUBA, this is the only endangered Cuban hutia that occurs on the main island. Now greatly reduced in

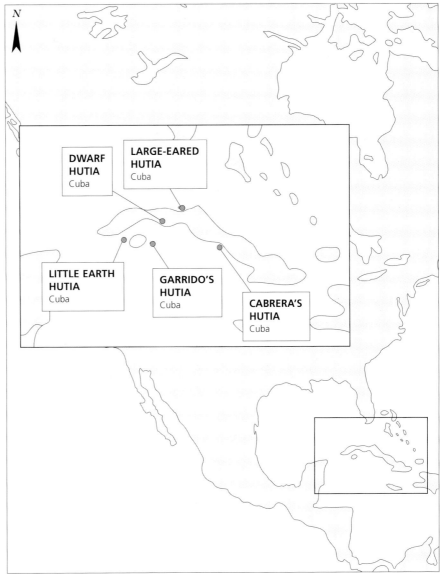

both number and range, there have been no verified sightings of this species since 1937. On the basis of recent tracks and fecal droppings, however, it is believed to survive in limited numbers in the Zapata swamp. In addition to the tracks and droppings, a survey of the swamp in 1978 resulted in both the discovery of nests and the chasing of a hutia by tracking dogs.

Brushy islands

The dwarf hutia is known to inhabit small brushy islands scattered about the Zapata swamp, and mangrove thickets that bor-

der the swamp. Other than this limited information about habitat preferences, very little information is known of this hutia's ecology or life history.

This species has been threatened by a number of different factors. Agricultural development has dramatically reduced the available habitat. Predation by both exotic rats and mongooses (introduced to control the rats) has also drastically reduced hutia numbers. Hunting hutias for human consumption also takes its toll.

Local fishermen are known to have conducted raids into the

swamp where they killed large numbers of hutias and other wildlife. Fortunately, active enforcement of a nationwide ban on all hunting in areas critical to wildlife appears to have curtailed these raids to a great extent. Elimination or reduction of the rat and mongoose populations would also greatly improve the outlook for the dwarf hutia. Continued protection, coupled with surveys and studies of its natural history, would help ensure the survival of this, the smallest Cuban hutia.

Garrido's Hutia

IUCN: Critically endangered

Weight: Unknown
Body length: Unknown
Diet: Unknown
Gestation period: Unknown
Longevity: Unknown
Habitat: Mangrove thickets
Range: Majaes and Largo Keys, south of central Cuba

THIS SPECIES WAS FIRST described in 1967 on the basis of a single specimen. Between 1967 and the late 1980s no other individuals were seen, and the species was feared to be extinct. Hope for the species increased in 1989 when two individuals were trapped alive on small islets near Majaes and Largo Keys.

Garrido's hutia is another of the many hutia species about which almost nothing is known. The population size is unknown, as are its breeding behavior and

diet. Hunting by fishermen is currently the major threat to its survival. Another threat is environmental events, such as hurricanes, that can have devastating effects on animals that live on tiny islands.

Little protection

Its only protection comes in the form of a nationwide resolution that prohibits hunting year-round in all areas of importance to Cuban wildlife. At the present time, continued active enforcement of this law, as well as investigations into the natural history of this hutia, is absolutely vital to saving this species.

Large-eared Hutia

(Meso auritus)

ESA: Endangered

IUCN: Critically endangered

Weight: Unknown
Body length: 10½–11½ in. (27–30 cm)
Diet: Fruit, bark, and vegetation
Gestation period: Unknown
Longevity: Unknown
Habitat: Red mangrove swamps
Range: Fregoso Key, north of central Cuba

APPARENTLY RESTRICTED to a single island, the large-eared hutia is the only member of Cuba's endangered hutias found north of the main island. First discovered in 1970, the large-eared hutia is the most arboreal

of these endangered mammals. Its population is estimated to be extremely small, limited to a single red mangrove swamp near the middle of Fregoso Key—an island only 23⅔ miles (38 kilometers) long, and 2½ to 3 miles (4 to 5 kilometers) wide.

Roomy nests

This hutia is particular about the location of its large, communally built nests. They are found only in areas where no dry land emerges from the standing water. The nests are over 4 square yards (3.5 square meters) in area, located between the mangrove roots about 1 foot (0.3 meter) above the high water level. They are constructed with small sticks, and contain several chambers or rooms and many entrances.

Conspicuous creatures

These large, easily spotted nests attract the fishermen who visit many of the small islands around Cuba. Illegal hunting of this animal is surprisingly easy. When nests are discovered, sacks are placed over the exits. Then the nest is disturbed to expel and capture the unwitting prey. Any individuals escaping the sacks are easily picked out of the shallow swamp water.

Research needed

Continued enforcement of the current laws that protect wildlife habitat appears to be the measure most needed at this time. However, it is important that studies be undertaken to increase our understanding of the needs of this small creature. Unfortunately, the smallest species are all too often overlooked in the rising tide of endangered species.

Little Earth Hutia

(Meso sanfelipensis)

ESA: Endangered

IUCN: Critically endangered

Weight: Unknown
Body length: Around 10 in. (25 cm)
Diet: Herbivorous
Gestation period: Unknown
Longevity: Unknown
Habitat: Vegetation bordering mangrove swamps
Range: South of western Cuba

AS OF 1990 this species (described from four specimens captured in 1970) was feared to be extinct. It was only known to exist on a single island, Juan Garcia Key, and appears to have succumbed because of damage caused by people. All sightings of this species occurred amid samphire (*Salicornia perennis*), a plant found on beaches bordering mangrove thickets.

Unknown habits

Footprints and fecal droppings indicate that this nocturnal animal ranged a considerable distance from the samphire clumps. Anecdotal reports tell of little earth hutias eating samphire when in captivity. Since no evidence was ever found of samphire grazing in the wild, it is not known whether the clumps were the species' feeding habitat, nesting habitat, or both (or perhaps neither). Nests or burrows were never discovered, and nothing is known of the breeding biology of this species.

As with other Cuban hutias, this species was sought after as a source of food. The little earth hutia also suffered either competition, predation, or both, from rats. These rats were introduced onto the island, and dispersed when the human dwellings were abandoned. Since the island is tiny (about 340 acres, or 137.5 hectares), interactions between hutias and rats must have been intense. The final blow was an increase in human activity on the island in the late 1980s. Several fires, set to deter mosquitoes, probably burned critical habitat. Although species sometimes disappear then reappear, there is little hope that this hutia still exists.

Terry Tompkins

HYENAS

Class: Mammalia

Order: Carnivora

Family: Hyaenidae

The hyena is an unfortunate scapegoat for all that human beings most revile about carnivores and predation. To humans, a hyena looks like a domestic dog, yet behaves in a savage manner. It whoops as it hunts and sometimes appears to laugh at death.

The hyena eats carrion, hunts and scavenges in groups, preys upon the weak and defenseless, and often displays behavior that suggests cowardice. And yet this complicated animal has an important role to play in nature.

It is true that the hyena is a carrion feeder—it does, indeed, eat dead animals that other carnivores have left or found unfit to consume. With its massive head, powerful jaws, and teeth strong enough to crack even the toughest bones, the hyena can chew up and digest what other predators and scavengers with weaker teeth and jaws are unable to manage.

That the hyena is scorned as an eater of carrion seems unfair given that most carnivores, including domestic dogs, are not above eating some carrion now and then. Despite its fondness for carrion, the hyena is also a proficient hunter in its own right.

Groups of hyenas regularly bring down prey that other carnivores avoid. In this way, hyenas help to maintain a control over other animal populations. By preying on the weak and defenseless, the hyena makes it possible for the strongest and healthiest members of the species that it preys upon to survive—and even flourish.

Despite its undeserved reputation for cowardly behavior, the hyena is tough. Fights for dominance begin early in life and, particularly among females, such contests can be fatal.

However, although the females dominate hyena clans, they also have their maternal side. Lactating females share in the nursing of young, and both females and males bring food to the den to offer to the offspring.

There are three different species of hyena, each with a distinctive, easily identifiable coat. The largest of the three, the spotted hyena, is the most plentiful and is found in many African countries. It is classified as lower risk, although this is dependent on conservation.

The populations of the brown hyena discussed here are being closely monitored by conservation groups. This hyena is now lower risk and of least concern.

Brown Hyena
(Hyaena brunnea)

ESA: Endangered

Weight: 82–105 lb. (37–47½ kg)
Shoulder height: 25–35 in. (64–89 cm)
Diet: Birds, rodents, livestock, reptiles, carrion, fish, fruit
Gestation period: About 90 days
Longevity: 17 years in captivity
Habitat: Dry savannah, plains, semidesert, sea coast
Range: Botswana, Namibia, South Africa

WITH ITS DARK BROWN coat and mane, and grayish neck and lower legs, the brown hyena is smaller than the spotted hyena and larger than the striped hyena. Its dark brown coat sometimes bears indistinct stripes and always produces dark bands or rings around its legs.

Experts believe that the brown hyena is able to smell the stomach contents of many prey animals killed by lions and leopards from as far away as 2 miles (3.4 kilometers).

Hyenas also have keen hearing and good night vision. Sometimes the brown hyena will succeed in driving lions from their own kills.

Although hyenas are sometimes scattered by either lions or packs of hunting dogs, the hyena generally dominates competing carnivores in their habitats, forcing leopards, cheetahs, jackals, and other would-be competitors to retreat, or—as the leopard does—carry its quarry into trees where hyenas cannot follow.

Voracious eater

The hyena will eat rodents, birds, and other small mammals, as well as insects, bird eggs, and fruits. The latter are particularly prized by hyenas for their high water content. Ostrich eggs are sometimes stolen from nests and hidden away to be eaten later.

The brown hyena often lives near the shore. It eats whatever is washed ashore, including dead crabs, fish, or even beached whales. The brown hyena is sometimes called the strand wolf because of its liking for shoreline habitation.

Like the striped hyena, the brown hyena has a long-haired mane which stands erect in situations of stress and conflict. Such threat displays are intended to frighten attackers into thinking they are facing a larger animal.

Typically, brown hyenas form small clans to defend their dens and hunting territories. Their behavior, including dominance, helps keep harmony within the clan. A typical clan has a dominant female and male, three or four subordinate males, four to six adult females, and offspring. Ranking and order are maintained through ritualized displays of aggression and subservience.

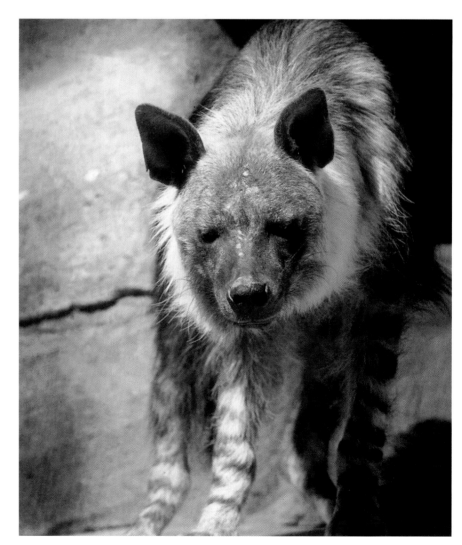

The brown hyena is an aggressive animal that travels in clans. These fierce animals are capable of scaring away competitors like leopards, cheetahs, and jackals.

Nocturnal hunters

Hyenas are nocturnal. In hotter climates, during warmer times of the year they sleep during the day in lairs abandoned by other animals. Sometimes they dig their own dens. Often, they enlarge existing spaces, emerging from them each evening to hunt. When no young are present, hyenas sleep in the open among rocks or in tall grass.

Killed as pests

Although protected in game preserves, brown hyenas are regarded as pests because of their tendency to attack livestock. Large numbers of them have been killed by farmers. The brown hyena is a victim of habitat encroachment, and its natural prey is also diminishing.

Renardo Barden

BARBARY HYENA
Africa

BROWN HYENA
Africa

IBEXES

Class: Mammalia

Order: Artiodactyla

Family: Bovidae

Subfamily: Caprinae

Tribe: Caprini

Ibexes are a type of mountain goat, that occurs in Africa, Asia, and the Middle East.

Goats are part of the larger bovine family of hoofed animals that includes gazelles, wildebeests, and sheep.

Equipped with horns and hooves, goats are ideally suited for climbing rugged mountain paths that people find difficult.

The ibexes belong to the genus *Capra*. All of the males in this genus have a beard and are usually noticeably larger than the females.

Pyrenean Ibex

(Capra pyrenaica pyrenaica)

ESA: Endangered

IUCN: Critically endangered

Weight: 55–176 lb. (25–80 kg)
Shoulder height: 24–30 in. (60–75 cm)
Diet: Grass, leaves, and shoots
Gestation period: 165 days
Longevity: 15–20 years
Habitat: Mountain terrain
Range: Pyrenees Mountains, Spain

THE SPANISH IBEX is found only on the Iberian Peninsula in Spain. Where once it covered almost all the mountainous portions of that region, now it has been reduced to small pockets. At least four subspecies of the Spanish ibex have been described by scientists. The southwest and western forms of this ibex still exist. In the case of the western ibex, probably more than 10,000 animals are in existence, and the population seems stable. However, the Pyrenean form from the mountains of the north is critically endangered, with as few as 50 animals left.

The preferred habitat of this goat are rocky regions between 1,640 and 11,400 feet (500 and 3,500 meters) in elevation. This ibex is sociable and can usually be seen grouped in substantial numbers—in some cases up to 50 in a group. The ibex is active off and on during the day, but it

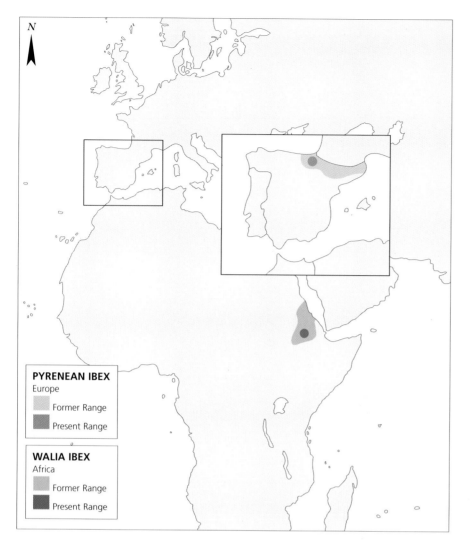

PYRENEAN IBEX
Europe
- Former Range
- Present Range

WALIA IBEX
Africa
- Former Range
- Present Range

easily be established. Because they are relatively productive breeders, it is hoped that they can bounce back if given adequate protection.

Walia Ibex
(Capra walie)

ESA: Endangered

IUCN: Critically endangered

Weight: 176–275 lb. (80–125 kg)
Shoulder height: 35½–43 in. (90–110 cm)
Diet: Grasses, leaves, shoots, and twigs
Gestation period: 150–165 days
Longevity: 15-plus years
Habitat: Mountain terrain
Range: Simyen and Gojjam Mountains, Ethiopia

is mostly active at dusk. The ibex is a grazer and browser, meaning it will eat vegetation on the ground or on bushes. Its diet consists of grasses, leaves, shoots, twigs, and—like most of the goat family—whatever is available.

Reduced predators
The ibex in this part of Europe used to be preyed upon by wolves and lynxes, but the number of predators has been so severely reduced that its biggest threat now comes from people.

Although the horn pattern varies, in general the Pyrenean ibex has horns that are widely spread and heavier at the base compared to some other ibexes (which tend to have longer,

straighter curves to their horns). The Pyrenean ibex population has been harassed by severe hunting for the last 150 years. In addition, many areas in the Iberian Peninsula are popular with ranchers whose domestic sheep and goats are competing with the wild ibex. Furthermore, the Spanish ibex is very susceptible to diseases transmitted by these domestic animals.

The Pyrenean ibex is currently found only in a national park in the Ordesa Valley of the Pyrenees Mountains. There are small captive populations of this animal in China, North America, and Spain. It is known that this animal lends itself well to captivity, so captive populations can

ALTHOUGH WILD GOATS apparently originated in Europe and Asia, two forms spread to the continent of Africa. They are the Nubian ibex in the Middle East, and the walia ibex, which is restricted to Ethiopia. The walia ibex makes its home in the Simyen Mountains, where the extremely rugged terrain with its many sheer cliffs provides some of the most spectacular scenery in all of Africa.

The walia ibex has probably never been numerous and,

This Alpine, or European ibex, is a mountain goat, and therefore, is part of the large bovine family of hoofed animals. This group includes such diverse animals as gazelles, wildebeests, and sheep.

because of severe hunting, its numbers have been further reduced. In physique, this ibex is considerably larger than the Nubian ibex, but its habits are similar. The walia inhabits much higher altitudes in the Simyen Mountains than the Nubian ibex.

The walia ibex does most of its feeding in the morning on whatever is available (meaning it is an opportunistic feeder): it eats grasses, shoots, twigs, and sometimes will even dig up roots. During the drier seasons the walia ibex will descend into the neighboring valley regions to browse, but as soon as there is a hint of rain, it migrates back up to the higher elevations.

Old males tend to be solitary. Females, on the other hand, move and feed together. When they rest, it is common to have a single animal, usually an older female, act as a sentinel.

In the Simyen Mountains the walia ibex has few predators because of the treacherous landscape and the high altitude. However, when the ibex moves down into the valleys, it comes in contact with domestic sheep and goats that compete for the available vegetation. The walia is also susceptible to the diseases that these domestic animals contract.

The primary cause for the walia's endangerment is hunting by people. In addition, for decades there has been considerable fighting over their range because of civil war in Ethiopia.

The walia and the Nubian ibex are the two species of ibex that exist on the continent of Africa. The Nubian species, shown here, still exists in healthy populations, but the walia ibex faces possible extinction if protective measures are not taken.

These conflicts, combined with disease and prolonged drought, have severely reduced their numbers. It is thought that there are probably no more than 100 to 150 individuals left in the wild.

Captivity

The walia ibex has been kept in captivity only rarely, primarily only in ones and twos. Captive animals were kept in the Royal Menagerie of the late Ethiopian emperor Haile Selassie, but no significant reproduction ever took place.

If properly managed in captivity the walia ibex—like the Nubian ibex—could in a short time produce a healthy captive reservoir. Its present status in the wild is hard to gauge, but because of the ongoing political unrest in Ethiopia, the situation does not look promising.

Warren D. Thomas

IBISES

Class: Aves
Order: Ciconiiformes
Family: Threskiornithidae
Subfamily: Threskiornithinae

The ibis has an unusual appearance. It sports a long, stout beak that curves slightly downward. The beak is used to probe shallow water and dense grasses in search of food. The spoonbill, also in the ibis family, has a flat beak that does not curve but is broad and sometimes enlarged at the tip. Rather than probing, a spoonbill will sift water for its food.

The ibises and spoonbills make up a distinct family that is related to herons and storks, but also to pelicans and flamingoes. Ibises lack the kink in the neck that characterizes herons. When they fly, they extend the neck fully, unlike herons, which pull the neck back to their shoulders. Of the family's thirty-plus species, at least six ibises and one spoonbill are considered threatened to some degree. One ibis is considered endangered, while three are critically endangered.

Crested Ibis

(Nipponia nippon)

ESA: Endangered

IUCN: Critically endangered

Length: 30 in. (76.2 cm)
Weight: Probably 2–3½ lb. (0.95–1.6 kg)
Clutch size: Unknown
Incubation: Unknown
Diet: Unknown
Habitat: Hilly woodlands, especially wetlands such as lakes, rice paddies, swamps
Range: Siberia, China, Japan

FOR MANY YEARS the crested ibis has been thought the rarest bird in the world. That status is an improvement; ornithologists once believed the bird extinct.

A medium-sized bird, the crested ibis wears an overall white plumage that is faintly tinted pink. The underwings are a darker salmon-pink hue, giving the bird its Japanese name, *toki*. The bird's English name is derived from its shaggy crest that lays back over the crown. The skin around the eye and lore is red, as are the leg, foot, and toe. The stout, decurved, black beak has a red tip. In summer it has a gray head, neck, and back.

At home in wetlands, the crested ibis became a common sight in rice paddies as agriculture replaced native marshes. Because it consumed so many insects and other creatures objectionable to farmers, the ibis was welcome. No one has yet found an explanation for its demise.

Deadly pesticides

Habitat loss and pesticide contamination are suspected, however, because the evidence is strong. The crested ibis was common one hundred years ago, before the dawn of heavy pesticide use. These deadly poisons took their toll on various forms of wildlife, and it is likely that the crested ibis is among them.

An Asian bird

The crested ibis historically ranged from extreme southeastern Siberia into two Chinese provinces, southward into Shaanxi and westward into Xizang. It also inhabited portions of Japan, and migratory birds were known to winter in Taiwan and the Ryukyu Islands, which lie just south of the Japanese archipelago. By the mid-1960s this bird had disappeared from Siberia, and it was feared the same situation was true in China.

The Japanese began a captive breeding program in 1969 with assistance from the World Wildlife Fund. The captive population grew to 14 birds in 1973. By 1981 only five wild crested ibises were found on Sado Island, the last stronghold of the species in Japan. Those five birds were trapped and added to the captive flock. That same year seven birds were discovered in China. The population was guarded, and it grew to 17 birds by 1984. Additional discoveries and careful guardianship probably account for the 1987 estimate of 40 crested ibises, but the Japanese breeding program did not succeed and was discontinued. At the close of the 1990s only one wild breeding program existed. It contains an estimated 22 individuals. Several crested ibises are reproducing in captivity in China and there are two in Japan.

The future

The recovery of the crested ibis, however slight or small it may be, kindles some optimism for its future. Its survival depends on learning what caused the decline and reversing the process.

Giant Ibis
(Pseudibis gigantea)

> **IUCN:** Critically endangered

Length: 41 in. (104 cm)
Weight: Unknown
Clutch size: Probably 2–3 eggs
Incubation: Unknown
Diet: Probably various invertebrates and vertebrates
Habitat: Swamps, wet woodlands, lakes
Range: Southeast Asia

PEOPLE ARE GENERALLY the only ones counted as casualties of war, but wildlife and the environment also suffer devastation. Quite probably, the giant ibis has been such a casualty.

The people in Southeast Asia have endured wars for centuries, but the ancient battles were limited and the extent of damage to the landscape was comparatively minimal. The twentieth century ushered in a new era, however, in which technology improved military firepower. With napalm and chemical defoliants, automatic rifles and high explosives, people in Southeast Asia fought against each other and against European and American forces.

Destruction of habitat
Solid proof that warfare has harmed the giant ibis is lacking. However, given the drastic extent of warfare in Southeast Asia and the visible destruction of the land, there is little room for doubt that war has taken its toll on the giant ibis. People have cut forests, drained marshes and swamps, planted crops, and built cities. The use of chemical pesti-cides has also changed the environment. All of these activities create vast changes in the landscape, which nearly always translate into habitat loss. If the giant ibis has not suffered from human warfare in Southeast Asia, it has certainly suffered from the loss of habitat.

Subtle coloring
Generally a drab dark brown bird, the giant ibis shows a little color with a greenish shine to the back. Its bare head and neck are dull brown with black bars on the nape of the neck. The flight feathers are black, but the smaller wing feathers have narrow white edges. The giant ibis walks on red feet and toes, and has a long, narrow, decurved brown beak.

The giant ibis once ranged through Cambodia, Laos, and Vietnam. A few sightings have been recorded in Thailand, but not recently. The last sighting was two individuals in a protected area in southern Laos in 1993. Current population estimates for this species are not available, but in the 1970s the count was a few hundred birds. Wars and land conversion have contributed to their decline.

Northern Bald Ibis
(Geronticus eremita)

> **ESA:** Endangered

> **IUCN:** Critically endangered

Length: 27½–31½ in. (70–80 cm)
Weight: Unknown
Clutch size: 2–4 eggs
Incubation: 24–25 days
Diet: Invertebrates, amphibians, reptiles, fish, rodents, birds; some berries and plant shoots
Habitat: More arid lands, less wetlands than other ibises
Range: Breeds in Morocco and Turkey; the Turkey population winters in Africa and the Arabian peninsula

ON THE LEDGE OF a cliff overlooking the dry shrub land of northwestern Africa, a dark bird sits on a flat pile of sticks. The bird's feathers glint in the midday sun. A ruff of long, pointed feathers stands out around its neck like a shaggy collar. The bird's head and throat are bare. The

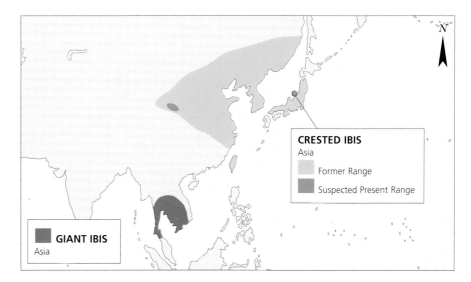

CRESTED IBIS
Asia

Former Range

Suspected Present Range

GIANT IBIS
Asia

bird looks like a vulture except that it has a long, dull-colored, decurved beak. It is a northern bald ibis nesting on this cliff.

Just a few feet away, a couple of other bald ibises also nest. Many miles of desert and desert-like country with scattered rocky outcroppings lie between these ibises and the next closest colony of their kin. This once common bird has declined, and it has completely disappeared from some of its historic range.

In centuries past, the northern bald ibis nested on the battlements and ledges of castles and on other town buildings. Historically, the species bred along the Danube and Rhone rivers of Europe. It was also known in the mountains of northern Italy, Switzerland, Germany, and Austria. By the 1600s the ibis was disappearing from many of its traditional European haunts.

There is no exact record of when the last ibis was seen in Europe, but the bird vanished from that continent sometime during the last three centuries.

An ancient bird

Hieroglyphics indicate that the northern bald ibis was familiar to the ancient Egyptians. It once bred in Syria but has not been found there since 1916. Today, the northern bald ibis breeds only in one site in Turkey and in a dozen places in Morocco. In 1911 the Turkish population numbered 1,000 pairs, then declined to less than 800 in 1954. Only 25 pairs were counted in 1975, and by the mid-1980s the ibis population near Birecik, Turkey, held only 35 birds. Discounting nonbreeding birds, this represents only a dozen, or fewer, breeding pairs. A captive breeding program in

Turkey has succeeded in raising many additional birds, some of which have been released to bolster the wild population.

Breeding groups

Some breeding northern bald ibises are protected within Morocco's Oued Massa National Park. Whereas some Turkish bald ibises migrate to Ethiopia, the Sudan, and northern Yemen for the winter, the Moroccan ibises do not migrate. Most of them breed in groups of three or four pairs. When not breeding, they frequent the Atlantic coast in fields and croplands, pastures, and even swamps, although they do not use wetlands to the same extent many other ibises do. They look for crickets, grasshoppers,

The long, stout beak common to all ibis species is a useful tool. These birds use it to search for food in shallow water and dense grasses.

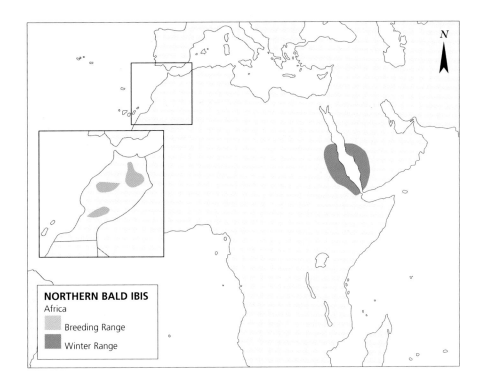

NORTHERN BALD IBIS
Africa

▨ Breeding Range

■ Winter Range

spiders, and scorpions, but also catch frogs, lizards, fish, mice, and occasionally young birds.

Some observers have blamed pesticides for the northern bald ibis's decline. They cite the vast increase in agricultural poisons as a source of contamination of food supplies. The research is not extensive, however, and it does not account for the bird's disappearance from Europe centuries before pesticide use.

Despite the ibis's rarity, many people still hunt it for food. They probably do not hunt the northern bald ibis specifically, but they shoot one when they find it. Small populations are extremely vulnerable to any hunting pressure. Although both Turkey and Morocco have banned hunting of this ibis, enforcing that ban is very difficult if not impossible.

There are scattered populations and it is hoped that captive breeding can keep the northern ibis alive as a species indefinitely. Several captive breeding groups exist in zoos from which individ-

uals may be selected for reintroduction. If the reasons for the species' decline cannot be learned and corrected, however, the northern bald ibis will soon cease to exist as a wild bird.

White-shouldered Ibis

(Pseudibis davisoni)

IUCN: Endangered

Length: 30 in. (76 cm)
Weight: Probably 2–3½ lb. (0.95–1.6 kg)
Clutch size: Unknown
Incubation: Unknown
Diet: Unknown
Habitat: Wetlands lakes, marshes, and rice paddies
Range: Southern China, Southeast Asia, Borneo

A RICE PADDY WELL populated with crayfish and frogs and aquatic insects would seem to be

a great place for a bird such as the white-shouldered ibis. Under ordinary circumstances rice paddies did attract the bird. Decades of war, however, have changed the circumstances. Where people once welcomed the ibis for its habit of controlling insects and vermin, they began to consider the ibis as a potential meal. People left destitute by war will eat whatever they can catch.

Chestnut colored

The white-shouldered ibis is a dark, chestnut brown bird with sheen to its plumage. Its wings and tail are black and shiny. Large white patches on the fleshy part of the wing give the bird its name. Growing to 30 inches (76 centimeters) in length, this bird of lake shores, river flats, and marshes declined as these wetlands were altered.

Yunnan Province in southern China and the island of Borneo in Indonesia once marked the northern and southern limits of this ibis's range. Yunnan borders Vietnam, and the ibis inhabited

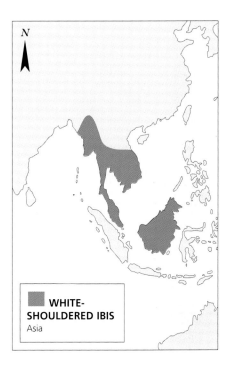

■ **WHITE-SHOULDERED IBIS**
Asia

much of the appropriate habitat in intervening Burma, Thailand, Cambodia, Laos, and Vietnam. The extent of its range has diminished, but it is not known by how much. Although there are

The northern bald ibis is an ancient bird that was depicted in the hieroglyphics of the ancient Egyptians. Today populations are found only in Turkey and Morocco, with migrations into eastern Africa and the Arabian peninsula during the winter months.

no recent records from much of its former range, it has been observed in other parts in late 1989 and the early 1990s.

The cost of war

The political conditions of many Southeast Asian countries do not favor visits by ornithologists from the United States or Europe. Reports are therefore sketchy and inconclusive. No specific popula-

tion estimates have been published for this species. Like the crested and giant ibises, the white-shouldered ibis will suffer and perish because of devastating clashes between warring nations. The cost of warfare is rarely measured in environmental terms, although the Persian Gulf War caused concern over the effects of oil spills and burning oil wells.

Kevin Cook

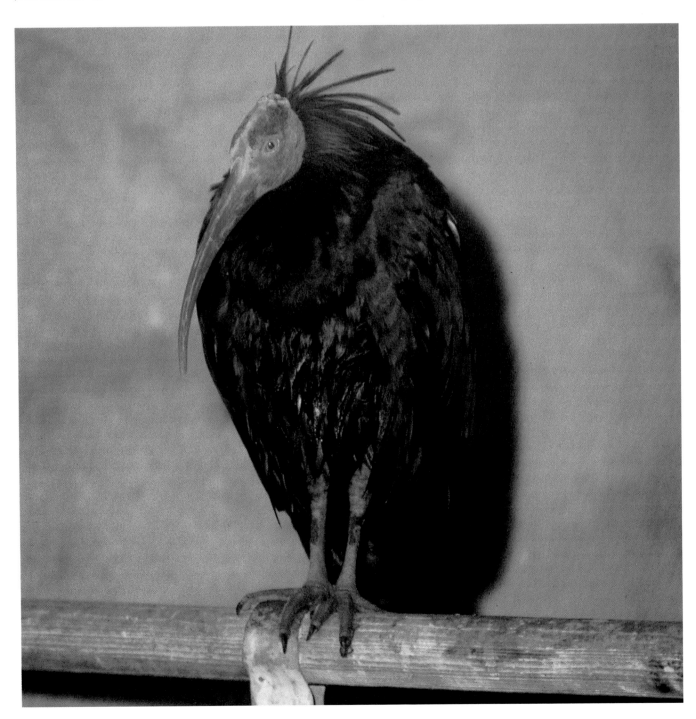

IGUANAS

Class: Reptilia

Order: Squamata

Family: Iguanidae

Iguana is the common name given to several related lizards of the family Iguanidae. They are all fairly large lizards, and they are herbivorous, meaning that they feed on plants. These lizards also lay eggs.

Lizards of the family Iguanidae are known as Iguanids. The family was once distributed throughout the world but is now found primarily in the New World. The remaining Old World genera can be found on the Fiji and Tonga islands and on the island of Madagascar. These are rough-scaled lizards with the ability to change color at will. While most lizards can change their color slightly to reflect heat and light, the iguana can achieve a more obvious color change, so it is inconspicuous to predators. Only true chameleons can change their color in response to mood or environment. They abound in rain forests and desert regions of the Old World and in tropics and subtropics.

Like all lizards, iguanas are ectotherms—that is, they are animals whose temperatures are controlled by their environment, and behavioral mechanisms are used to maintain body temperatures.

These diurnal animals derive heat from exposure to the sun. They regulate heat by sunning themselves; when they have reached the correct temperature, they move to a shaded area.

Their skin is used for bags, wallets, and shoes. They are taken as pets and, in rural areas, used for insect control. They are caught for food by poor people.

In addition to the iguanas mentioned here, several other species are in trouble: the Barrington Island iguana (*Conolophus pallidus*) is considered rare; two other species are threatened, the Cuban ground iguana (*Cyclura nubila*) and the Fiji crested iguana (*Brachylopuus vitiensis*). Two species of iguana are endangered, the Anegada ground iguana (*Cyclura pinguis*) and the Jamaican ground iguana (*Cyclura collei*).

Fiji (South Pacific) Banded Iguana

(Brachylophus fasciatus)

ESA: Endangered

IUCN: Endangered

Clutch size: Unknown

Diet: Probably herbivorous

Habitat: Secondary forest and coconut plantations along the coast

Range: Fiji and Tonga islands, South Pacific

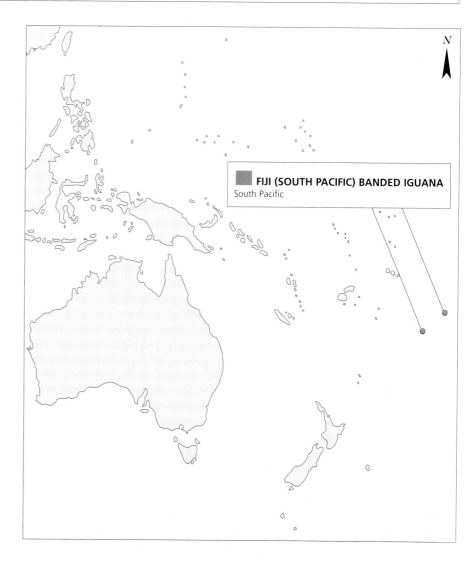

FIJI (SOUTH PACIFIC) BANDED IGUANA
South Pacific

THE SOUTH PACIFIC banded iguana was apparently not uncommon at the beginning of the 20th century. Studies conducted as recently as 1915 indicated relatively sizable populations, but it must now be considered exceptionally rare. There is some concern that the

The South Pacific banded iguana is also known as the Fiji crested iguana. It is one of the few remaining iguanas that can be found in the Old World. Unfortunately, it is endangered because exotic species, such as mongooses, have devastated the iguana population. If care is not taken, the South Pacific islands may one day lack members of the Iguanidae family.

Galápagos Land Iguana
(Conolophus subcristatus)

IUCN: Vulnerable

Clutch size: Up to 9 eggs
Diet: Herbivorous
Habitat: Arid or transitional zones with sparse or moderate vegetation and soil for burrowing
Range: Galápagos Islands

species may, in fact, be extinct on many of the islands in the chain and very scarce on Fiji.

As has been the case with many other species in regions around the world, exotic animals presented an immediate threat to the South Pacific banded iguana.

The mongoose devoured both eggs and young of the banded iguana for many years. Other introduced animals, including poisonous toads and mynah birds, greatly reduced the potential habitat of this iguana.

Humans have also done their share to hurt the species. Iguanas are often persecuted by native Fijians. Deforestation and development have greatly reduced the potential habitat of an already vulnerable species.

Recovery and conservation
In order to protect the banded iguana, protection from introduced predators and food competitors must be a priority. Individuals could be transferred to islands where there are no exotic species, allowing the populations to increase.

Public education alerting people to the scarcity of the lizard and the creation of national parks, which include suitable habitats and no predators, are viable options in creating a recovery plan for the South Pacific banded iguana.

THE GALÁPAGOS LAND IGUANA is placed in its own genus. It is a big-headed, stout-bodied lizard with yellowish coloration on the head and a rusty-brown colored body. It was originally found on six islands of the archipelago: Fernandina, Isabela, Santiago, Santa Cruz, Baltra, and South Plaza. Apparently it is now extinct on Santiago. Charles Darwin found the reptile very common on this island in his exploration in 1835, but it may have been extinct there by 1905, when only bones were found by a California Academy of Science expedition. On this island, it was probably destroyed by pigs. On Baltra, it was destroyed by United States military personnel who were stationed there during World War II. There is now a small population on Seymour Island, which was introduced in the 1930s from Baltra.

There are no accurate estimates made for most populations, but the South Plaza group is thought to be made up of between 200 and 300 lizards. Since the discovery of the islands in 1535, large numbers of the land iguanas have been slaughtered. The tail became a food source for various visitors to the islands, including whalers, hunters and colonists, but this was not the major cause of the iguana population's decline.

Cats and dogs

The land iguanas have suffered much the same fate as the giant tortoises found on the islands. They have been reduced by humans hunting for their skins, predation by introduced cats, and habitat reduction by farmers who are destroying natural nesting areas. Young lizards on Isabela are being killed in large numbers by feral cats; young and perhaps even adult lizards are being destroyed by feral dogs and pigs. Rats are a major predator of

The Galápagos Islands are an archipelago rich in flora and fauna, as biologist Charles Darwin discovered in the 19th century. As humans put greater and greater stress on the island wildlife, species like the Galápagos land iguana suffered greatly.

both tortoise and iguana eggs and hatchlings. Predation of this nature is also a problem on Santa Cruz. Another significant problem has been the goats that graze on the islands. They clear the vegetative cover of the iguana, exposing the vulnerable young to birds of prey and other predators. Scientists have not made casual observations when studying the Galápagos land iguana because the animal, particularly the juveniles, are elusive and rarely seen.

Conservation

Since 1959 all uninhabited areas of the Galápagos have been a national park, and it is now illegal to hunt, capture, or remove any species of plant or animal, as well as rocks and minerals, from the islands. This includes the land iguanas. Fernandina is the largest uncolonized and least penetrable island, and a stable but unmeasured population apparently persists there. Isabela was once thought to have few iguanas, but

GALÁPAGOS LAND IGUANA
South America

the island was difficult to explore. Now it seems that this largest island of the Galápagos archipelago may have the largest surviving population. A detailed study of the distribution, population dynamics, reproductive potential, general ecology, and threats caused by predators needs to be conducted to establish a feasible recovery plan for the Galápagos land iguana.

Elizabeth Sirimarco

GLOSSARY

actinopterygii: the scientific name for bony fish

amphibia: the Latin scientific name for amphibians

apically: relating to, or situated at the apex

aves: the Latin scientific name for birds

barbels: a slender growth on the mouths or nostrils of certain fishes, used as a sensory organ for touch

bipedal: any organism that walks on two feet

bract: a leaf at the base of a flower stalk in plants

buff: in bird species, a yellow-white color used to describe the plumage

calyx: the green outer whorl of a flower made up of sepals

captive breeding: any method of bringing several animals of the same species into a zoo or other closed environment for the purpose of mating; if successful, these methods can increase the population of that species

carnivore: any flesh-eating animal

carnivorous: flesh eating

carrion: the decaying flesh of a dead organism

clear cutting: a method of harvesting lumber that eliminates all the trees in a specific area rather than just selected trees

clutch, clutch size: the number of eggs laid during one nesting cycle

corolla: the separate petals, or the fused petals of a flower

cotyledon: the first leaf developed by the embryo of a seed plant

decurved: curving downward; a bird's beak is decurved if it points toward the ground

defoliate: to strip trees and bushes of their leaves

deforestation: the process of removing trees from a particular area

diurnal: active during the day; some animals are diurnal, while others are active at night (see nocturnal)

dominance: the ability to overpower the behavior of other individuals; an animal is dominant if it affects others of its own species in a way that benefits itself; also, the trait of abundance that determines the character of a plant community: grasses dominate a prairie, and trees dominate a forest

dorsal: pertaining to or situated on the back of an organism; a dorsal fin is on the back of a fish

ecology: the study of the interrelationship between a living organism and its environment

ecosystem: a community of animals, plants, and bacteria and its interrelated physical and chemical environment

elliptic: egg-shaped or oval

endemic: native to a particular geographic region

estrous: the time period when female mammals can become pregnant

exotic species: a plant or animal species that is not native to its habitat

feral: a wild animal that is descended from tame or domesticated species

fishery, fisheries: any system, body of water, or portion of a body of water that supports finfish or shellfish; can also be used as an adjective describing a person or thing (for example, a fisheries biologist)

fry: young fish

gestation: the period of active embryonic growth inside a mammal's body between the time the embryo attaches to the uterus and the time of birth; some mammals carry dormant embryos for several weeks or months before the embryo attaches to the uterus and begins to develop actively, and this dormancy period is not part of the gestation period; gestation period is the time length of a pregnancy

granivore: any seed-feeding animal

granivorous: seed feeding

guano: manure, especially of sea birds and bats

habitat: the environment where a species is normally found; habitat degradation is the decline in quality of a species' home until it can no longer survive there

halophyte: salt lover

herbivore: any plant-eating animal

herbivorous: plant eating

hibernate: to spend the winter season in a dormant or inactive state; some species hibernate to save energy during months when food is scarce

hierarchy: the relationships among individuals of the same species or among species that determine in what order animals may have access to food, water, mates, nesting or denning sites, and other vital resources

home range: the area normally traveled by an individual species during its lifespan

hybrid: the offspring of two different species who mate; see interbreed

hybridization: the gradual decline of a species through continued breeding with another species; see interbreed

immature(s): a young bird that has not yet reached breeding maturity; it usually has plumage differing from an adult bird of the same species

in captivity: a species that exists in zoos, captive breeding programs, or in private collections, perhaps because the species can no longer be found in the wild

incubation: the period when an egg is kept warm until the embryo develops and hatches

indigenous species: any species native to its habitat

inflorescence: a group of flowers that grow from one point

insecta: the Latin scientific name for insects

insular species: a species isolated on an island or islands

interbreed: when two separate species mate and produce offspring; see hybrid

invertebrate(s): any organism without a backbone (spinal column)

juvenal: a bird with an intermediate set of feathers after its young downy plumage molts and before growing hard, adult feathers

juvenile(s): a young bird or other animal not yet mature

litter: the animals born to a species that normally produces several young at birth

lore(s): the irregularly shaped facial area of a bird between the eye and the base of the beak

mammalia: the Latin scientific name for mammals

migrate, migratory: to move from one range to another, with the change of seasons, or for feeding or

breeding; many species are migratory

milt: the reproductive glands of male fishes; also, the breeding behavior of male fishes

mollusca: the Latin scientific name for mussels, clams, and snails

montane forest: a forest found in mountainous regions

nocturnal: active at night; some animals are nocturnal, while others are active by day (see diurnal)

nomadic species: a species with no permanent range or territory; nomadic species wander for food and water

offal: waste products or leftovers; usually the internal organs of a slain animal

old growth forest: forest that has not experienced extensive deforestation

omnivore: any species that eats both plants and animals

order: a biological ranking of species sharing characteristics, below the rank of class, and above family

ornithologist(s): a scientist who studies birds

pelage: the hairy covering of a mammal

pelagic: related to the oceans or open sea; pelagic birds rarely roost on land

perennial: persisting for several years

plumage: the feathers that cover a bird

prairie: a plant community without trees and dominated by grasses; a grassland; often incorrectly used synonymously with plain or plains, which is a landform feature and not a plant community

predation: the act of one species hunting another

predator: a species that preys upon other species

primary forest: a forest of native trees that results from natural processes, often called virgin forest

primate(s): a biological ranking of species in the same order, including gorillas, chimpanzees, monkeys, and human beings (*Homo sapiens*)

range: the geographic area where a species roams

recovery plan(s): any document that outlines a public or private program for assisting an endangered or threatened species

relict: an isolated habitat or population that was once widespread

reptilia: the Latin scientific name for reptiles

riffle(s): a shallow rapid stretch of water caused by a rocky outcropping or obstruction in a stream

riparian: relating to plants and animals close to and influenced by rivers

roe: fish eggs

rosulate: in a rosette formation

rufous: in bird species, plumage that is orange-brown and pink

secondary forest: a forest that has grown back after cutting, forest fire, or other deforestation; secondary forests may or may not contain exotic tree species, but they almost always differ in character from primary forests

sedentary species: one that does not migrate

serrate: the leaf margin has tiny jagged teeth

siltation: the process of sediment clouding and obstructing a body of water

tubercle: a prominent bump on a fish's body connected to a spine

tussock: a thick bunch of twigs and grass, often found in swamps

veldt: a grassland region with some scattered bushes and virtually no trees; other terms are *steppe*, *pampas*, and *prairie*

ventral: on or near the belly; the ventral fin is located on the underside of a fish and corresponds with the hind limbs of other vertebrates

vertebrates: any organism that has a backbone (spinal column)

zygomorphic: symmetrical in one plane only

INDEX

The scientific name of a plant or animal is entered in *italics*; its common name is in roman type. Page numbers in *italics* refer to picture captions.